Palgrave Studies in Classical Liberalism

This series offers a forum to writers concerned that the central presuppositions of the liberal tradition have been severely corroded, neglected, or misappropriated by overly rationalistic and constructivist approaches.

The hardest-won achievement of the liberal tradition has been the wrestling of epistemic independence from overwhelming concentrations of power, monopolies and capricious zealotries. The very precondition of knowledge is the exploitation of the epistemic virtues accorded by society's situated and distributed manifold of spontaneous orders, the DNA of the modern civil condition.

With the confluence of interest in situated and distributed liberalism emanating from the Scottish tradition, Austrian and behavioral economics, non-Cartesian philosophy and moral psychology, the editors are soliciting proposals that speak to this multidisciplinary constituency. Sole or joint authorship submissions are welcome as are edited collections, broadly theoretical or topical in nature.

Chris Berg

Artificial Intelligence

A Classical Liberal Approach

palgrave
macmillan

Chris Berg
RMIT University
Melbourne, VIC, Australia

ISSN 2662-6470 ISSN 2662-6489 (electronic)
Palgrave Studies in Classical Liberalism
ISBN 978-3-032-22309-8 ISBN 978-3-032-22310-4 (eBook)
https://doi.org/10.1007/978-3-032-22310-4

This Palgrave Macmillan imprint is published by the registered company Springer Nature Switzerland AG.
The registered company address is: Gewerbestrasse 11, 6330 Cham, Switzerland

Preface

Writing is the act of creating goods using labour and capital. We use desktop computers, word processors, and constantly switch between browser tabs connected to enormous global servers of knowledge. We battle patchy internet connections and ration battery life. We flick between reference software, knowledge management systems, endless PDF files, spreadsheets, statistical software, custom programming languages, and databases. I even own a dedicated keypad that automates the complex shortcuts required for efficient use of referencing software.

In *Areopagitica*, John Milton ([1644] 1918) presents writing as a marriage between the author's mind and the text itself. His poetic vision imagined an author without a body, free from the physicality and practicalities of writing—no aches, no hunger, no uncomfortable chair or frustrating writing implement—just "pens and heads . . . sitting."

Milton was making a rhetorical contrast with the very physical and material power of the censor who threatened the writer's body for the work of their mind. Yet to elevate the mind's product, Milton had to diminish the body's. The economics of writing in his era perhaps made that plausible—a pen, ink, paper, and time were the primary inputs. This vision of writing as pure thought doesn't bear much resemblance to current academic practice. Modern scholars are highly conscious of the tools and technologies they employ. Even for social scientists who primarily engage in desktop research, writing has become a more capital-intensive endeavour compared to Milton's era. With artificial intelligence, it is far more capital-intensive.

I have spent much of the last decade focused on the economics of blockchain technology and cryptocurrency, but I was entranced by what we sometimes call "generative" artificial intelligence from the moment I could play with it. My first genuine excitement was not text generation but image generation. OpenAI's Dall-E was released in April 2022 in a research preview, subject to a waitlist. But it was the release of Stable Diffusion model that August, by a firm called Stability AI, which excited me most. Stable Diffusion was open source—you could even run it on a home computer—and it sparked an enormous and enthusiastic cottage industry of users who added to it and modified it. So when ChatGPT was released later in 2022 I was primed.

The debate, at the time, was whether researchers could use AI to write text for them, and whether if they were to do so, the AI model itself had to be credited as a co-author. I wrote a paper 'The Case for Generative AI in Scholarly Practice' in April 2023 which defended the use of these models as a mentor, as a tool for analysis, and as a writing tool. There is now a general consensus that what matters is who takes responsibility for a text, and AI models cannot take responsibility. The act of crediting the creation of writing—acknowledging contributions, attributing authorship—is the allocation of property rights. For academic researchers, these rights are not only valuable for claiming priority on ideas but also for contributing to career progression, increasing the likelihood of winning grant funding, and advancing within the academic status hierarchy. Scholarly norms and practices around how writing is produced and rights allocated are an evolved property rights regime that has evolved independent of legal constraints, similar to the attribution and property enforcement practices in fashion and comedy.

This book was written at the end of 2025 and the beginning of 2026. When I committed to producing it, I was of the view that while I supported other writers using AI to produce content, I could not do so myself—not on principle, but on the grounds that I was never happy with the content it produced. In September 2025, in my view, AI was great at research, planning, proofreading, making suggestions, but not at producing original copy. In fact, I argued just a few months prior that:

> *[T]he problem with [AI] writing is that we can't see through it to the person behind. When we pull aside the veil we see not a person but a large model of statistical relationships in a tokenised corpus of internet writing ... If we automate all the drudgery away we are left with nothing but our individuality. Writing needs to broadcast individuality. Even writing that was once seen as boilerplate - that we called "copy" - has to puncture the veil between text and author. The most instrumental writing will have to be informed by taste. Why read it otherwise? Why write it?*

It is a testament to the pace of change in AI that I was forced to revise assessment while writing the book. In November, Anthropic released its Claude Opus 3.5 model, and Google released its Gemini 3 model. Both—in my highly subjective judgment—have popped over the threshold of eloquence. More interestingly, they has popped over the threshold of *style*. You can now use AI to draft work that is authentic to your intent and voice. It needs to be edited, and refined, and over-written, but it works.

So throughout the course of this book I have repeatedly had to rebuild the writing workflow that I have developed over a couple of decades: this book, my thirteenth book, has been written very differently to the previous ones. In an important way, to me, this is a tiny part of the economic change we are undergoing. We may understand intellectually that change is accelerating, but our workflows and expectations are calibrated to the world we learned in, not the one we are entering. The demand it places on all knowledge workers is to reconfigure our skills and capabilities to make full use of this technology.

This has been most obvious in the domain of computer programming. In March 2025, Anthropic head Dario Amodei told an audience that he expected that "in three to six months" AI would be writing "90% of code." This was widely mocked at the time.[1] In September—exactly

---

[1] See, for example, John A De Goes on Twitter: "Must be bullsh.umm, fundraising time" https://x.com/jdegoes/status/1899494886652408209 12 March 2025.

six months later—some outlets published articles saying this claim "was not even close." But it *was* close. I asked a software developer friend around that time and was somewhat shocked when I learned that he'd moved almost entirely to an AI-first approach to software development. It was one of the things that inspired the writing of this book. In January 2026, Anthropic reported that fully 100% of their code was generated by their own AI models, as did some researchers at OpenAI.

As the futurist Roy Amara famously said "we tend to overestimate the effect of a technology in the short run and underestimate the effect in the long run." Just a few years after ChatGPT was released it feels a lot like the long run is here. That this book about technological transformation has itself been repeatedly transformed by the technology it describes is perhaps the best evidence I can present for its argument.

Acknowledgements I would like to thank my long-standing collaborators and co-authors for the many, many ideas (and stances!) that appear throughout this book: Jason Potts, Darcy Allen, Sinclair Davidson and Aaron Lane. Sinclair gave me extremely valuable feedback on the first draft of this manuscript. The comments by Darcy and Ashton de Silva were likewise invaluable. My colleagues at RMIT in and around the late Blockchain Innovation Hub have all been exploring the economic implications of AI together, so thank you to Vy Nguyen, Peyman Khezr, Emmanuelle Walkowiak, Julian Waters-Lynch, Stuart Thomas, and Sarah Sinclair.

The work I have done with Meg Elkins and Leon Gouletsas on our student-facing agentic AI program has been enlightening, exciting and very much helped me understand the ground-level impact of the technology as it stands today.

I would also like to thank Leslie Marsh, editor of the Palgrave series on classical liberalism in which this appears, for his rapid enthusiasm for the project and Ellie Duncan at Palgrave for hers.

And thank you, of course, to my family: Bron, Leonard, Walter, and the dogs for indulging book number thirteen.

Competing Interests The author has no competing interests to declare that are relevant to the content of this manuscript.

Contents

1

Introduction

Abstract As cognition becomes abundant, the binding constraint on economic life shifts from intelligence to coordination. This introduction argues that classical liberal institutions—property rights, freedom of contract, and decentralised markets—provide the only framework equal to that abundance. It situates the AI revolution within the spontaneous order tradition from Friedrich Hayek to the new institutional economists, and outlines the book's central claims: that connectionist AI shares deep roots with liberal political economy, that foundation models function as emergent orders encoding tacit knowledge, and that alignment is fundamentally an institutional problem. The path to harnessing the intelligence explosion runs through the same dispersed, rule-governed institutions that have driven human prosperity since the Great Enrichment.

Keywords Artificial intelligence · Classical liberalism · Spontaneous order · Foundation models · Intelligence explosion · Coordination · Connectionism · Austrian economics · Alignment · Institutional economics

C. Berg, *Artificial Intelligence*, Palgrave Studies in Classical Liberalism,
https://doi.org/10.1007/978-3-032-22310-4_1

Throughout the nineteenth and twentieth centuries, technology mechanised strength (machinery and factories), speed (automobiles and aircraft), and calculation (computers). Technology is now mechanising something even more fundamental: cognition. This is a book about what happens when the cost of thinking plunges, and why classical liberal institutions are the only framework equal to the intelligence explosion (Good 1966) that will result. When thinking becomes abundant, the binding constraint on prosperity shifts from *intelligence* to *coordination*—and coordination is the domain of markets and the dispersed knowledge alone can harness.

The origins of artificial intelligence (AI) go back to the earliest moments in the development of computing. We trace its peculiarly liberal history and architecture in Chap. 2. But for most of us, AI seemed to arrive suddenly. The release of OpenAI's ChatGPT in November 2022 was a moment for a sharp intake of breath for both the general public and technology insiders alike. The web application allowed users to talk through a text box with OpenAI's latest iteration of its series of artificial intelligence models. ChatGPT was a remarkable advance over previous generations of chatbots. It could, as the *New York Times* reported in December 2022, write jokes, work on computer code, guess medical diagnoses, create text-based games and explain scientific concepts at multiple levels of difficulty (Roose 2022). Early adopters shared their funniest conversations on social media: "write a biblical verse in the style of the King James Bible explaining how to remove a peanut butter sandwich from a VCR" (Ptacek 2022). It was sensational. The head of OpenAI, Sam Altman (2025), reported that one million users signed up in the first five days. By January 2023, ChatGPT had 100 million monthly active users—at that time the fastest growth of any consumer application ever (Reuters 2023).[1]

ChatGPT was both a curiosity and a suggestion of a revolution to come. The computer pioneer Alan Turing's (1950) famous measure of whether a computer program could be called 'intelligent' was whether it

[1] In 2023 Meta's Threads social media network beat ChatGPT on a different metric, sign-ups. Sign-ups count cumulative accounts created, while monthly active users counts unique users who actually used the product at least once in a given month.

could convince a user that they were having a conversation with real person—this was his 'imitation game', now widely known as the 'Turing test'. Researchers had been attempting to cross that threshold for seventy years, including a very famous attempt with the chatbot ELIZA in 1966, and for thirty years the Loebner Prize held a competition to see who could achieve it (Weizenbaum 1966). In one experiment, ChatGPT beat the Turing test 49.7% of the time (Jones and Bergen 2024). In another, ChatGPT failed to beat the test because the users were alerted to the fact that they were talking to a chatbot because it seemed substantially *more* intelligent than a human might be (Restrepo Echavarría 2025; for a critique see Giunti 2025; for a recent discussion see Chen et al. 2026).

In many ways ChatGPT was not a great *technical* breakthrough. It was a particular implementation of a natural language processing neural network. Almost all users of the internet had long been exposed to these systems through (for example) Google's BERT model that, from 2018 onwards, had quietly but profoundly changed how Google's search autocomplete worked (Devlin et al. 2019). But if it wasn't a great technical breakthrough ChatGPT was a great public breakthrough. The model which powered that first iteration of the chatbot, GPT-3.5, was a finetuned model designed for conversation. It came from a family of what are known as 'foundation' models that OpenAI had been releasing since 2018. Its significance was how it engaged users in foundation models. It took a technology known mostly to a community of researchers and thrust it at the centre of the public mind.

It would be hard to exaggerate the pace of change in AI since that release. Competing chatbots were quickly released by Anthropic (a company founded by former OpenAI employees), the search giant Google, xAI (a spinoff of X.com, the social media network formerly known as Twitter), Meta (the parent company of the social giant Facebook), and a large ecosystem of smaller competitors. The performance of the models has increased exponentially in the subsequent three years. These models can think for longer and deeper, can understand and create sound, images and videos, can use digital tools, search and interact with the internet, perform long and complex tasks, and act on users' behalf. At time of writing (January 2026), Altman said that ChatGPT has 800 million users (Bellan 2025). Conservatively, ten per cent of the population of the world are regularly using AI chatbots. Investment in AI has surged: a quarter of a trillion US dollars were invested in AI in 2024 alone (Maslej 2025). NVIDIA, the company that produces the computer chips used by OpenAI and many other firms, became the world's largest company in 2025 (Russell and Francisco 2025). There is an open question how much of the world's economic growth is solely due to AI investment.

Such exuberance is, of course, fertile ground for political interference. Policymakers have been unsurprisingly quick to respond to the threat and opportunity of AI. The European Union's AI Act regulates both how AI models are used and their underlying architectures. In the United States, the Biden administration introduced heavy regulatory oversight on the AI sector through executive order (Biden 2025). That order was repealed almost immediately by the Trump administration which declared that its priority was to "retain global leadership" in AI (Trump 2025). Control and influence over the AI chip supply chain have become a major factor in the Trump administration's global trade war.

It would be nice if we could calmly take stock of the AI technology revolution once the dust has settled. We are only three years since the release of ChatGPT and AI is now starting to make its impact felt on the economy. Some industry commentators forecast we are on the cusp of artificial *general* intelligence, or even artificial *superintelligence*, within the space of years (see for example Kokotajlo et al. 2025). These terms carry enormous weight. Artificial general intelligence (AGI) is typically defined as AI that matches or exceeds human cognitive performance across a wide variety of tasks—not merely narrow expertise but the flexible, transferable intelligence that allows humans to learn new domains, reason across contexts, and adapt to novel problems (Goertzel and Pennachin 2007; Goertzel 2014; Morris et al. 2025). Artificial superintelligence (ASI) goes further. A superintelligent system reliably outperforms any human intellectual ability in virtually every domain, from scientific reasoning to social persuasion to strategic planning (Bostrom 2014).

Defining the thresholds of general or superintelligence is difficult. The question "when will we achieve AGI?" may be unanswerable in the same way as "when did the Industrial Revolution begin?" AGI and ASI are useful analytic abstractions. But too often they misleadingly describe what is better understood as a continuous process as a threshold that we will one day, suddenly, cross.

Either way, at some threshold, many of the big AI labs argue that progress in AI—as well as many other intellectual endeavours—is likely to become its own self-sustaining fly-wheel, as the challenge of coming up with new ideas and research becomes a function of how many compute resources we can throw at autonomous AI systems. Already the AI labs have been using their own AI systems to design new AI chips (OpenAI 2025), and have seen recursive self-improvement as they use their models to accelerate the development of new models (OpenAI 2026). This is the intelligence explosion—a sharp, and sustained surge in the total supply of intelligence available for economic value creation as AI systems scale, making high-quality cognition vastly cheaper, faster, and more abundant. As the price of "thinking" collapses, production frontiers shift outwards. We can produce more ideas with less resources.

Put in this light, the AI revolution is possibly the most important economic revolution since factories and mechanisation, and the potential implications are just as great. Deidre McCloskey (2016) has called the period after the industrial revolution 'the Great Enrichment'. For McCloskey, it was ideas, not capital that gave the world an opportunity for increases in wages and living standards that are measured in the orders of magnitude. For Joel Mokyr (2017, 1992), considering that same era, it was the institutional framework that allowed scientists and inventors to innovate and realise their ideas in a market economy that caused the rapid economic take-off. But our task now is not to explain a rapid boost in living standards and economic dynamism with the full archival record at our disposal. Our task now is to harness this revolution to maximise its benefits. We are not observers of this revolution. We are living in it. We are participants.

This book will argue that classical liberalism provides the most powerful economic and philosophical framework to shape and understand a revolution of ideas and intelligence. At the first instance, classical liberalism is the political philosophy of individual rights under the rule of law. It holds that people are equal before the law, have natural (or fundamental) rights, and that government should be limited—tasked chiefly with protecting rights, providing impartial justice, enforcing contracts, and supplying a few genuine public goods. But underlying classical liberalism's constitutional prescription is a subtle model of how decentralised societies and economies evolve and generate prosperity. For classical liberals, a market economy (one characterised by freely adjusting prices and secure property rights) is the paradigmatic example of a spontaneous order. The case for classical liberalism is a recognition that robust, decentralised coordination can emerge in the absence of a central planner.

The intellectual traditions that inform modern classical liberalism is vast and diverse. So this book leans heavily on what we could loosely describe as the study of spontaneous order economics, or what Peter Boettke forcefully calls the "mainline" economic tradition (Haeffele-Balch et al., 2016; Boettke 2012). From at least Adam Smith ([1776] 1904), liberal economists have sought to understand and explain how complex economic systems can emerge not by design but through the diverse interests and preferences of a heterogenous population of individuals. Friedrich Hayek (1945) explored how prices facilitate decentralised coordination between economic participants by overcoming the inherent information barriers between those participants. Buyers may not know why prices have gone up or down—maybe there has been a new innovation that enhances productivity, or a natural disaster that has affected some suppliers deep in the supply chain—but the fact of those changes leads them to adjust their plans accordingly. Prices do not simply allocate resources to those who value them most highly. They distribute information across the economy so that individuals and firms can restructure their own production and consumption in response to an economic change.

For the new institutional economists from Ronald Coase (1937, 1960) onwards, the question became less about how market exchanges coordinate activity and more about understanding the circumstances when they might fail to do so. The transaction costs that get in the way of mutual beneficial exchange—the costs of finding those to exchange with (search), finding agreement (bargaining), formalising and specifying the terms of exchange (contracting), watching counterparties to make sure they hold up their end of the bargain (monitoring), enforcing the terms (policing), and finding new parties to make exchanges with (switching)—determine what work is done in what institutional structure, whether it is as individuals, or governments, or firms, or in long term contracts or spot exchanges (Hart 1988; Williamson 1985, 1996). Working in this tradition, Elinor Ostrom (1990, 2005) demonstrated that 'governance' itself is a variable subject to innovation and evolution.

In the classical liberal view, the secure property rights, freedom of contract, open entry, and general, predictable rules that make decentralised coordination possible also drive classical liberalism's political ends. They enhance individual liberty by placing limits on state coercion and allow individuals to pursue their own plans. They generate prosperity because when people are free to experiment and reap the rewards (or bear the costs) of their choices, societies generate ideas and innovations that drive enrichment. The economic logic of spontaneous order is not value neutral. It is the institutional foundation of both emergent order and individual liberty and as, if by an invisible hand, channels them into innovation and economic growth. At least in this sense, it is the ideal framework by which to understand and direct the radical changes that such a far-reaching technology could bring.

But this book argues that classical liberalism's relevance to the intelligence explosion runs deeper than serendipity. It is woven into the very architecture of the models driving this revolution. In *The Sensory Order* (1952), Hayek investigated how thought itself emerges in the brain. His work was prophetic. As Chap. 2 argues, the *Sensory Order* stands at the origin of one of the two great approaches to artificial intelligence: the connectionist vision of intelligence as an emergent property. That chapter introduces AI by contrasting the planned model of intelligence—symbolic AI—with the spontaneous order model of intelligence—connectionist AI. The connectionist tradition is deeply Hayekian. The early connectionists fully understood their debt to Hayek's work on the emergent intelligence. If the AI revolution unfolds as this book anticipates, *The Sensory Order* may prove to be among Hayek's most important contributions.

That same distinction—between the planned and the emergent—helps us understand the rise of modern foundation models. Large language models (LLMs) and diffusion systems are spontaneous orders. Their capabilities arise from architecture and scale, not explicit programming. Chapter 3 describes these as "cultural world models," compressing the dispersed and tacit knowledge of human civilisation in ways that resist complete articulation. This poses a fundamental challenge to regulatory demands that AI model outputs are fully explainable or 'interpretable'. Like prices in a market economy, model outputs encode information that cannot be fully unpacked into explicit rules. Governance must therefore rely on institutional constraints rather than fantasies of total transparency.

Chapter 4 considers AI's profound implications for economic growth. AI industrialises what Julian Simon (1981, 1996) called "the ultimate resource"—human intelligence—by loosening the population constraint on idea production. The binding limit shifts from the number of human minds to the availability of compute and energy. Through the lens of the "adjacent possible," (Koppl et al. 2023) the chapter considers how cheap cognition expands the searchable space of combinations, reaching higher-order possibilities that biological minds rarely explore.

AI models that drive persistent, tool-using agents raise new questions for liberal thought. Are AI agents *agentic*? Can they be creative? Can they be entrepreneurial—could they take all these new ideas and autonomously create economic value? Chap. 5 argues that, in a world of AI agents, coordination and responsibility—not raw intellectual capability—become the central problems of political economy. Even sophisticated agents lack genuine economic agency in the sense developed from Ludwig von Mises ([1949] 1996) through Shackle (1979). They lack the capacity for originating choice and commitment under genuine uncertainty. AI agents are better understood as a form of capital that supplies labour-like cognitive services. This is, however, an institutional reclassification with significant implications for how we govern AI.

In Chap. 6 we revisit one the most important economic debate of the twentieth century: whether a centrally planned economy can achieve the efficiency and prosperity of a market economy. Oskar Lange (1967) declared at the dawn of the computer age that socialist calculation would be a simple and trivial problem given the advent of computers. In recent decades this theoretical claim has become more common and is increasingly salient as AI diffuses through the economy. But the claim that AI—or just advanced computation—enables rational economic planning misunderstands the classical liberal objection, which was never about computational limits. Modern AI can predict and optimise within given data and objectives, but it cannot reproduce the institutional discovery procedures that generate economically meaningful prices. Institutions, not algorithms, are the foundation of coordination.

So what should those institutions be? As models evolve into agents, the central question shifts from "how do we align this system?" to "how do we govern action when many agents—human and artificial—operate simultaneously?" Chap. 7 argues that the answer lies not in perfecting individual models but in the institutional frameworks that channel their behaviour: property rights that bound what agents may access, contracts that specify permissible actions, capability-based security that enforces the principle of least authority, and smart-contract wrappers that translate vague intentions into enforceable constraints. What the AI industry calls "alignment" will emerge not from instilling virtue in artificial minds but from embedding intelligence within rules that make boundaries legible, violations costly, and mistakes correctable. No designer or AI lab can anticipate every use case or failure. We need to instead create the institutional conditions under which coordination can emerge through trial, feedback, and adaptation.

Finally, in Chap. 8 we take seriously the existential risk arguments about AI—the fear of paperclip maximisers and runaway superintelligence. The chapter argues that these scenarios typically rest on a political economy mistake well known to classical liberals. It confuses authority with competence, and assumes that durable monopoly power is feasible in a world of competition, institutions, and material constraints. We are more likely to face plural, polycentric AI order in the future. Indeed, this already exists, as open and open-weight AI ecosystems make the intelligence explosion replicable and reproducible and inherently anti-monopolistic. Civilisation itself is a spontaneous order. The best response to our inability to fully design minds is not to stop trying, which worsens incentives and selects for defectors, but to do so in a competitive order, with checks and balances, rule-governed environments in which multiple intelligences—human and artificial—mutually constrain and correct one another.

What follows is an attempt to illuminate how two great intellectual traditions—classical liberalism and the science of artificial intelligence—have grown together and can shape the development of the AI age towards prosperity.

References

Altman, Sam. 2025. "The Chatgpt launch 26 months ago was one of the craziest viral moments i'd ever seen, and we added one million users in five days. we added one million users in the last hour." Tweet. Twitter, March 31. https://x.com/sama/status/1906771292390666325.

Bellan, Rebecca. 2025. "Sam Altman Says ChatGPT Has Hit 800M Weekly Active Users." *TechCrunch*, October 6. https://techcrunch.com/2025/10/06/sam-altman-says-chatgpt-has-hit-800m-weekly-active-users/.

Biden, Joseph R., Jr. 2025. *Executive Order on Advancing United States Leadership in Artificial Intelligence Infrastructure*. The White House. https://bidenwhitehouse.archives.gov/briefing-room/presidential-actions/2025/01/14/executive-order-on-advancing-united-states-leadership-in-artificial-intelligence-infrastructure/.

Boettke, Peter J. 2012. *Living Economics: Yesterday, Today, and Tomorrow*. Independent Institute.

Bostrom, Nick. 2014. *Superintelligence: Paths, Dangers, Strategies*. Reprint ed. OUP Oxford.

Chen, Eddy Keming, Mikhail Belkin, Leon Bergen, and David Danks. 2026. "Does AI Already have Human-Level Intelligence? The Evidence is Clear." *Nature* 650(8100):36–40. https://doi.org/10.1038/d41586-026-00285-6.

Coase, R. H. 1937. "The Nature of the Firm." *Economica* 4(16):386–405. https://doi.org/10.1111/j.1468-0335.1937.tb00002.x.

Coase, R. H. 1960. "The Problem of Social Cost." *The Journal of Law and Economics* 44.

Devlin, Jacob, Ming-Wei Chang, Kenton Lee, and Kristina Toutanova. 2019. "BERT: pre-Training of Deep Bidirectional Transformers for Language Understanding." arXiv:1810.04805. Version 2. Preprint, arXiv, May 24. https://doi.org/10.48550/arXiv.1810.04805.

Giunti, Marco. 2025. "ChatGPT-4 in the Turing Test: A Critical Analysis." arXiv:2503.06551. Preprint, arXiv, April 8. https://doi.org/10.48550/arXiv.2503.06551.

Goertzel, Ben. 2014. "Artificial General Intelligence: Concept, State of the Art, and Future Prospects." *Journal of Artificial General Intelligence* 5(1):1–48. https://doi.org/10.2478/jagi-2014-0001.

Goertzel, Ben, and Cassio Pennachin, (Eds.). 2007. *Artificial General Intelligence*. Cognitive Technologies. Springer.

Good, Irving John. 1966. "Speculations Concerning the First Ultraintelligent Machine." In *Advances in Computers*. vol. 6. Elsevier. https://doi.org/10.1016/S0065-2458(08)60418-0.

Haeffele-Balch, Stefanie, Virgil Henry Storr, and Peter J. Boettke, Eds. 2016. *Mainline economics: Six Nobel lectures in the Tradition of Adam Smith*. With Hayek, Friedrich A., James M. Buchanan, Ronald H. Coase, Douglass C. North, Vernon L. Smith, and Elinor C. Ostrom. Mercatus Center at George Mason University.

Hart, Oliver D. 1988. "Incomplete Contracts and the Theory of the Firm." *Journal of Law, Economics, and Organization* 4(1):119–139.

Hayek, Friedrich A. 1945. "The Use of Knowledge in Society." *The American Economic Review* 35(4):519–530.

Hayek, Friedrich A. 1952. *The Sensory Order: An Inquiry Into the Foundations of Theoretical Psychology*. University of Chicago Press.

Jones, Cameron, and Ben Bergen. 2024. "Does GPT-4 Pass the Turing Test?" In *Proceedings of the 2024 Conference of the North American Chapter of the Association for Computational Linguistics: Human Language Technologies (Volume 1: Long Papers)*, edited by Kevin Duh, Helena Gomez, and Steven Bethard. Association for Computational Linguistics. https://doi.org/10.18653/v1/2024.naacl-long.290.

Kokotajlo, Daniel, Scott Alexander, Thomas Larsen, Eli Lifland, and Romeo Dean. 2025. "AI 2027." April 3. https://ai-2027.com/.

Koppl, Roger, Roberto Cazzolla Gatti, Abigail Devereaux, et al. 2023. *Explaining Technology*. Cambridge University Press. https://doi.org/10.2139/ssrn.3856338.

Lange, Oskar. 1967. "The Computer and the Market." In *Socialism, Capitalism and Economic Growth: Essays Presented to Maurice Dobb*, ed. C. H. Fienstein. Cambridge University Press.

Maslej, Nestor. 2025. "Artificial Intelligence Index Report 2025." *Artificial Intelligence*.

McCloskey, Deirdre Nansen. 2016. *The Great Enrichment: A Humanistic and Social Scientific Account.*

Mises, Ludwig von. (1949) 1996. *Human Action: A Treatise on Economics.* 4. rev. ed. Fox & Wilkes.

Mokyr, Joel. 1992. *The Lever of Riches: Technological Creativity and Economic Progress.* 1. issued as an Oxford University. Press paperback. Oxford Paperbacks. Oxford University. Press.

Mokyr, Joel. 2017. *A Culture of Growth: The Origins of the Modern Economy.* The Graz Schumpeter Lectures. Princeton university press.

Morris, Meredith Ringel, Jascha Sohl-Dickstein, Noah Fiedel, et al. 2025. "Levels of AGI for Operationalizing Progress on the Path to AGI." arXiv:2311.02462. Preprint, arXiv, September 24. https://doi.org/10.48550/arXiv.2311.02462.

OpenAI, dir. 2025. *OpenAI x Broadcom—The OpenAI Podcast Ep. 8.* https://www.youtube.com/watch?v=qqAbVTFnfk8.

OpenAI. 2026. "Introducing GPT-5.3-Codex." February 5. https://openai.com/index/introducing-gpt-5-3-codex/.

Ostrom, Elinor. 1990. *Governing the Commons: The Evolution of Institutions for Collective Action.* The Political Economy of Institutions and Decisions. Cambridge University Press.

Ostrom, Elinor. 2005. *Understanding Institutional Diversity.* Princeton Paperbacks. Princeton University Press.

Ptacek, Thomas H. 2022. "I'm sorry, I Simply Cannot Be Cynical About a Technology that can Accomplish this. https://t.co/yjlY72eZ0m." Tweet. Twitter, December 2. https://x.com/tqbf/status/1598513757805858820.

Restrepo Echavarría, Ricardo. 2025. "ChatGPT-4 in the Turing Test." *Minds and Machines* 35(1):8. https://doi.org/10.1007/s11023-025-09711-6.

Reuters. 2023. "ChatGPT Fastest-Growing App in History—UBS." *Reuters*, February 2. https://finance.yahoo.com/video/chatgpt-fastest-growing-app-history-142338104.html.

Roose, Kevin. 2022. "The Brilliance and Weirdness of ChatGPT." Technology. *The New York Times*, December 5. https://www.nytimes.com/2022/12/05/technology/chatgpt-ai-twitter.html.

Russell, Karl, and Blacki MigliozziTripp Mickle Reports on Nvidia From San Francisco. 2025. "Nvidia Becomes First Public Company Worth $4 Trillion." Technology. *The New York Times*, July 10. https://www.nytimes.com/2025/07/10/technology/nvidia-4-trillion-market-value.html.

Shackle, G. L. S. 1979. *Imagination and the Nature of Choice*. Columbia University Press.

Simon, Julian Lincoln. 1981. *The Ultimate Resource*. 5 print. Princeton Paperbacks Economics. Princeton University Press.

Simon, Julian Lincoln. 1996. *The Ultimate Resource 2*. 2. Rev. ed., 3. printing and 1. paperback printing. Princeton Paperbacks Economics. Princeton University Press.

Smith, Adam. (1776) 1904. *An Inquiry into the Nature and Causes of the Wealth of Nations*. Edited by Edwin Cannan Modern Library.

Trump, Donald J. 2025. *Removing Barriers to American Leadership in Artificial Intelligence*. The White House. https://www.whitehouse.gov/presidential-actions/2025/01/removing-barriers-to-american-leadership-in-artificial-intelligence/.

Turing, Alan M. 1950. "Computing Machinery and Intelligence." *Mind* LIX (236):433–460. https://doi.org/10.1093/mind/LIX.236.433.

Weizenbaum, Joseph. 1966. "ELIZA—a Computer Program for the Study of Natural Language Communication between Man and Machine." *Communications of the ACM* 9(1):36–45. https://doi.org/10.1145/365153.365168.

Williamson, Oliver E. 1985. *The Economic Institutions of Capitalism: Firms, Markets, Relational Contracting*. Free Press.

Williamson, Oliver E. 1996. *The Mechanisms of Governance*. Oxford University Press.

2

Design Versus Discovery in the Development of Artificial Intelligence

Abstract This chapter presents the history of artificial intelligence as a contest between two theories of mind and two strategies for building intelligence: specifying structure in advance versus allowing structure to be learned. The symbolic or 'Good Old-Fashioned AI' tradition treats intelligence as rule-guided manipulation of explicit representations, culminating in expert systems and knowledge engineering. This achieved impressive successes in narrow domains but ran into a knowledge-acquisition bottleneck and brittleness in open-ended settings. The connectionist tradition treats competence as emerging from adaptive networks trained on data, and in modern deep learning it has delivered striking gains through scale and learning. The chapter argues that this divide parallels a broader contrast between planned design and spontaneous order.

Keywords Symbolic AI · Connectionism · Spontaneous order · Neural networks · Expert systems · Friedrich Hayek · Herbert Simon · Deep learning · Emergence · Knowledge engineering · Bitter lesson · Artificial intelligence

C. Berg, *Artificial Intelligence*, Palgrave Studies in Classical Liberalism,
https://doi.org/10.1007/978-3-032-22310-4_2

The most distinctive contribution of classical liberal thought to social theory is the concept of spontaneous order. Complex, functional structures can emerge spontaneously without being planned. Institutions like money, language, common law, markets were not deliberately conceived by an inventor or a government but emerged from the independent decisions of countless individuals. Each of these individuals were responding to their local circumstances and needs, but their independent, self-interested activity contributed towards a shared emergent order. In Adam Ferguson's ([1767] 1783, 204) famous formulation, this order is "the result of human action, but not the execution of any human design".

This chapter argues that the history of artificial intelligence is a contest between two modes of creating order: design and emergence. For seven decades, researchers have pursued two fundamentally different visions of how to build intelligent machines. The vision that relied on deliberate design stalled as a path to general intelligence. The vision that allowed intelligence to emerge from learning looks like it is succeeding spectacularly. This tradition of spontaneous order, running from the Scottish Enlightenment through the Austrian economists like Carl Menger and Friedrich Hayek, offers a framework for understanding how intelligence can be embedded in institutions that no one consciously constructed (Stringham 2015; Leeson 2014).

The first vision—what is known as the *symbolic* tradition or sometimes the 'Good Old-Fashioned AI' (GOFAI) approach—treats intelligence as the manipulation of symbols according to explicit rules. Its philosophical foundations are the belief that reasoning is formal symbol manipulation, and that what can be formalised can be built. At the peak of the 'expert system' boom that this tradition launched, knowledge engineers believed they could interview human experts, extract their knowledge—the rules that governed expert judgment—and encode those rules into systems that would replicate human cognition. The intelligence in such systems is specified in advance by the architect, just as a planned institution is designed by its founders.

The second vision—the *connectionist* or neural network approach—treats intelligence as emergent from networks of simple units that learn through exposure to data. It is a vision of intelligence-as-discovery, claiming that knowledge cannot be fully specified in advance but arises from adaptation and error correction, and is distributed across a system rather than concentrated in explicit rules. Like market prices, the representations that emerge from neural networks encode information that no single component of the system possesses. Order arises bottom-up from millions of local adjustments, not from any central blueprint. These systems are spontaneous orders in silicon.

It is this second connectionist vision that forms the basis of our frontier AI systems. The symbolic AI approach failed to live up to its promise. It failed because intelligence, like economic coordination, depends on knowledge that is dispersed, tacit, and contextual. Expert AI systems collapsed under the weight of local information. By contrast, the connectionist approach succeeded because it does not attempt to specify intelligence in advance. Neural networks allow intelligence to emerge through learning—through the same process of error correction and adaptation that characterises both biological evolution and market competition.

This chapter traces the development of both traditions from their origins to the present. It begins with the ancient question of whether mind is mechanical and whether a machine could therefore be made to think. It follows the symbolic tradition from Charles Babbage to Herbert Simon to the expert systems boom and its eventual collapse. And it traces the parallel development of connectionism—from Friedrich Hayek's theoretical neural architecture through to the deep learning revolution that now dominates the field. The contest between these traditions is not merely of historical interest. It illuminates why modern AI systems work the way they do, why they resist the kind of transparency that regulators demand, and why attempts to constrain them through explicit rules face the same limits that have constrained designed orders throughout history.

2.1 Man as Machine, Machine as Man

Before examining the two traditions in detail, it is worth understanding why the symbolic approach seemed so obviously correct to the first generation of AI researchers—and why its limitations were so difficult to see from inside that tradition. Symbolic AI was the natural engineering application of a mechanistic view of mind that had been gaining intellectual ground for centuries. If the mind operates like a machine, as so many philosophers have suggested, and manipulates symbols according to fixed rules and procedures, then building intelligence means specifying those rules explicitly. The first AI researchers were doing what centuries of philosophy had prepared them to do. In many ways the modern debates around artificial intelligence are still tackling a basic question that has interested philosophers from Aristotle on: if man is a machine, can a machine be man?

The question of whether the mind is mechanical has ancient roots. Against those who held that living beings possess some vital force or soul irreducible to matter and motion, a rival tradition insisted that humans and animals are physical systems whose behaviour results from its physical mechanisms. Motion, sensation, and response arise from interactions of parts governed by natural laws. Thought and action are the outcomes of concrete processes. We can understand how the brain works in the same way that we understand how a clock works. Descartes, for example, held that the body was mechanical but preserved an immaterial mind standing apart from it (Clarke 2003; Gaudemard 2021; Descartes [1637] 2006). Later thinkers dispensed with even this reservation. Thomas Hobbes presented a purely mechanical model in which all sense, motion, and feeling were explained by activity in the brain (Riskin 2015, 72–75; Thomson 2010, 47–49). Julien Offray de La Mettrie in his *L'Homme Machine* ([1747] 2010) went even further, arguing that consciousness itself was a property of matter, not an external force.

If a machine could produce consciousness, then could that machine be deliberately constructed? After all, Prometheus created humans out of clay. The Rabbi Eliyahu of Chelm created his Golem from the same material (Neubauer 2011). Scientists periodically attempted to create automatons throughout the early modern period. The famous and fraudulent Mechanical Turk of 1770 demonstrated that "audiences could be titillated by the possibility of automation; they could, to their mind's content, tempt fate and fear with the idea that machines could be like humans" (2002, 77). Not all automatons were frauds. Jacques de Vaucanson created a digesting duck which sought to demonstrate the biomechanics of digestion and a flute player that used bellows and pulleys to play a dozen melodies. The flute player was described in Diderot's *Encyclopédie* under the heading 'Android', which was defined as something which had "human form and which, by means of certain springs, etc., well arranged, acts and performs other functions outwardly similar to those of man" (Diderot 2025).[1]

Androids and other artificially animated creatures featured prominently in the literature of the Enlightenment. One of the core underlying themes of these android tales, like E. T. A. Hoffmann's "The Sandman" ([1816] 2016), was that mechanical beings likenesses of humans but not in any way alive—they simply imitated human behaviour. They were bodies without souls (Hoffmann 2016). Indeed, Vaucanson's experimental automatons were studies in how to replicate the capabilities of the mechanical body—at least in their outward effect —rather than to create something that is alive. One of the novel things about Mary Shelley's *Frankenstein* (2018) was that the monster was conscious, emotional, and, critically, self aware (a "rational creature") of his own existence and distinction.

There is an open question whether Charles Babbage, who designed and tried to build the first computers them to be mechanical models of the mind. But some around him did (Green 2005). His official biographer declared that "the marvellous pulp and fibre of a brain had been substituted by brass and iron" and that Babbage "had taught wheelwork to think, or at least do the office of thought" (Buxton and Hyman 2010, 48–49). Lady Bryon described Babbage's

[1] Vaucanson has an interesting connection to the development of computers themselves. He was also an early pioneer of programming silk looms with perforated metal cylinders, the ancestors of the punched-cards that were used to program first looms then computers (Essinger 2007, 17–18).

Difference Engine as a "thinking machine". Ada Lovelace sometimes claimed that the Analytical Engine represented a "uniting link" between mind and matter. But she cautioned that it has no "pretensions to originate anything. It can do whatever we know how to order it to perform" (Babbage 2010, 44).[2]

The rigorous mathematical framework required to define a truly universal information processor—one capable of simulating any logic—emerged in the 1930s. Computer science was instantiated by two independent and concurrent theoretical findings that are now jointly described as the Church-Turing thesis. Alonzo Church (1932, 1936) developed lambda calculus to define the limitations of what can be calculated through symbolic logic. Turing (1936) independently reached the same boundary by describing a mechanical procedure—the Turing machine—which showed that any computable process could be executed by a universal machine. The earliest 'computers' were far from this vision of universality. For example, Konrad Zuse's Z3 (designed in 1938, built in 1941) had to be manually programmed to perform a specific task, as did Turing's Colossus computer in 1943. It was only with the development of the von Neumann (1945) architecture—computers with stored programs and data that executed instructions in sequence—at the end of the war that the idea of a universal Turing machine in the theoretical sense was realised. These machines could execute any computable process subject to their (very material) resource constraints.

The idea of artificial intelligence is arguably baked into the Church-Turing thesis. In Thomas Hobbes' ultra-materialist interpretation of cognition, the mind is a calculator. Thinking is fundamentally the sequential addition and subtraction of thoughts—like arithmetic performed on ideas—where conclusions logically follow from premises. His idea of 'ratiocination' refers to reasoning as a mechanical, computational process of logical calculation. Haugland (1985, 24) goes so far as to argue that that with his mechanistic vision of the mind Hobbes

[2] Babbage and Mary Shelley knew each other. They met in 1835, four years after she had published the revised second edition of *Frankenstein* and two years before he was to formally describe the Analytical Engine (Ahearn 2012).

launched the idea of artificial intelligence in the 1650s. So if intelligence in a Hobbesian sense can be understood as the capability to process information, make predictions, and act based on those predictions—essentially a series of logical steps—then, by definition, it falls within the bounds of computation as outlined by Church and Turing.

This connection between calculation and cognition was clear to the early computing pioneers. Turing explicitly framed intelligence as a kind of search. Intelligence consisted of systematically exploring possible solutions, representations, or proofs until one satisfies given criteria. In his unpublished 1948 essay 'Intelligent Machinery' (Turing [1948] 1992) he generalised this into an abstract model encompassing brute-force iteration, heuristic-guided transformations, evolutionary optimisation, and cultural accumulation. Computation is thus the underlying mechanism of intelligence, but search—the controlled exploration of possibilities and selection of successful outcomes—is the essential process by which intelligence emerges. In that essay, Turing also goes on to formulate the first version of the Turing test, where observers interact with an artificially intelligence system to try to guess if it is human or a computer (published ultimately as Turing 1950).

One of the clever aspects of the Turing Test is that it sidesteps the need to define intelligence itself. Rather than trying to provide an external definition of human intelligence, the Turing test is comparative. It relies on intelligent beings recognising intelligence in another. The test involves three participants: a human interrogator, a computer, and a human respondent. The interrogator communicates with both the human and the computer only through a keyboard and screen. By conversing with each in turn, the interrogator's task is to determine which is the human and which is the machine. The interrogator can be as clever or discursive as they see fit: the suspicious interrogator might ask what they think is the human respondent to make a complex mathematical calculation, or what they think is the computer to write a poem. The computer passes the Turing test if the interrogator is unable to determine which is which.

The Turing test is behavioural. It does not consider the underlying mechanisms that result in intelligent behaviour. It simply seeks to identify the outward manifestations of intelligence. This, indeed, is true for the automatons in history. Vaucanson's flute player could likewise be considered behavioural. It was an (inexact) mechanical simulation of human movements, with the intention of mimicking precisely the outward expressions of human musicianship. The flute player replicated behaviour without any reference to the soul or consciousness underlying it.

The Turing test's behavioural framing was no accident—it emerged from a broader intellectual movement that would prove decisive for how researchers approached artificial intelligence. Behaviourism arose in the early twentieth century as an attempt to ground psychology in the observable. Watson (1970, 2015) insisted that scientific psychology must focus strictly on observable behaviour rather than unobservable mental states. This approach deepened into the radical behaviourism of Skinner (1965, 2019), who argued that behaviour is fully explained by environmental stimuli and reinforcement histories. Skinner treated internal states as non-existent or merely behavioural processes themselves.[3]

Turing was not, himself, a behaviourist (Abramson 2011). But applying the behavioural approach to identifying artificial intelligence offered a powerful epistemic tool. The test does not require an external, and contestable definition of intelligence. Instead it provides public, observable evidence for otherwise unobservable inner capacities. In 1948, the ultimate architecture that would bring about AI was barely even the subject of speculation. But behaviourism's insistence that a concept has no place in science unless grounded in observable operations would prove decisive for early AI. If intelligence is observable behaviour, and behaviour is rule-following, then building intelligence means specifying rules—exactly the program that symbolic AI would pursue. We shall repeatedly return to the behaviourist framework, which is important for debates around AI interpretability (Chap. 3), AI agency (Chap. 5), and AI alignment (Chaps. 7 and 8). But for now, the point is

[3] In his later *Beyond Freedom and* Dignity (Skinner 1971), he argued that the concept of the "autonomous man" is a pre-scientific superstition that obstructs necessary social progress, and that to ensure the survival of culture, we must discard the traditional "literature of freedom" in favor of a "technology of behavior" that explicitly designs and controls human conduct.

this: by mid-century, centuries of mechanistic philosophy had fused with behaviourist psychology and positivist epistemology to create an intellectual environment in which symbolic AI was not merely one option among many—it was the obviously correct approach.

2.2 The Symbolic AI Tradition and AI by Design

To understand the roots of the bifurcation between symbolic AI and the connectionist tradition, it is instructive to contrast two seminal mid-century works that offered fundamentally opposing blueprints models of intelligence: Herbert Simon's development of the Logic Theorist program (Newell and Simon 1961) and Friedrich Hayek's theoretical treatise *The Sensory Order* (1952). Simon, a principal architect of the symbolic tradition, explicitly equated intelligence with the serial manipulation of symbols, demonstrating through the Logic Theorist that a machine could mimic human deduction to prove mathematical theorems using rigid, formal rules. In stark contrast, Hayek—writing from the periphery of psychological science—proposed a model of the mind based on the classification of stimuli through a vast, plastic network of neural connections, a vision where knowledge is not a static database of facts but a dynamic, emergent property of the physical system itself. These two intellectual landmarks do not merely represent different technical specifications, but rather competing models of the mind that would define the trajectory of AI research.

Herbert Simon is best known for his conceptualisation of bounded rationality—the idea that human rationality is limited by the information we have, our mind's raw processing power, and the finite amount of time we have to make a decision (Simon 1955, 1957; Klaes 2005; Petracca 2021). Instead of comprehensively searching for the absolute best possible outcome (*optimising*) when making a choice, humans "satisfice," choosing the first option that meets a certain threshold of acceptability. He used this analysis to understand organizations and administrative behaviour. Simon saw organizations not merely as structures of authority but as environments that shape and support individual decision-making by simplifying choices and providing a framework of goals and values.

Simon's perspective was very much a planner's perspective. He offered an almost computational vision of administration in his *Administrative Behavior* (Simon 1947), a book developed from his 1942 PhD dissertation and which became a key text of its field for more than half a century. The initial title of his thesis proposal was 'The Logical Structure of Administrative Science', although he shied away from the didactic mathematisation of some of his contemporaries (Crowther-Heyck 2005, 73). For Simon, expert administration, guided by scientific principles, could clarify the factual basis of policy decisions and distinguish them from value judgments.

Simon's path from public administration to artificial intelligence was a continuation of the same project: understanding how boundedly rational agents make decisions in complex organizations. He viewed firms, bureaucracies and minds alike as hierarchical information-processing systems whose behaviour could, in principle, be modelled formally. That move drew him toward the emerging sciences of control and choice (operations research, game theory, mathematical psychology), and allowed him to translate his theories of human decision-making into the formal language of computer programs When he finally turned his research to computer science, he saw the digital computer as a "model bureaucracy" (Crowther-Heyck 2005, 7).

Simon's great contribution to artificial intelligence was the Logic Theorist (Newell and Simon 1956). The Logic Theorist—widely described as the first AI program ever—was a symbolic artificial intelligence program designed to prove theorems from Alfred North Whitehead and Bertrand Russell's *Principia Mathematica*. The Logic Theorist (and its successor, the General Problem Solver) mimicked human problem-solving by using a discrete set of rules (or 'heuristics') to guide its decisions. The Logic Theorist was profoundly successful. It proved 38 of the first 52 theorems in *Principia*, famously deriving a proof for one that was more elegant than the one Whitehead and Russell had constructed themselves. To Simon and his co-authors, this served as tangible proof that a machine could indeed replicate human reasoning, at least in a primitive and partial way.

For our purposes, the critical thing is that the heuristics themselves had to be written by the AI system designer. The Logic Theorist was given four rules of inference—substitution, replacement, detachment, and syllogism (chaining)—which it combined with specific methods to generate proof sequences from axioms and previously proved theorems (Newell et al. 1958). This reliance on externally provided rules is the fundamental characteristic of early symbolic AI. The raw intelligence was effectively front-loaded by the programmer rather than discovered by the machine. Just as a lower-level bureaucrat does not invent policy but rather executes decisions based on a fixed rulebook provided by superiors, the Logic Theorist operated within a strictly defined task environment where the axioms and the allowable moves (such as detachment or substitution) were provided for it in advance. Thus the Logic Theorist's 'intelligence' was limited by the designer's ability to articulate these formal rules. The system could navigate the search space with remarkable efficiency, but it could not question the validity of the rules nor generate new methods of inference outside those given to it by its designers. The behaviour of the system was a reflection of the internal structure provided by the designer interacting with the complexity of the specific problem. It was an explicit, human-authored formalism of how thought processes should unfold.

Simon's was an *economic* vision of artificial intelligence—but it was an economics of organisation, concerned with how systems could be designed and controlled for maximum productivity. In a speech in 1957, Simon made the bold statement that "physicists and electrical engineers had little to do with the invention of the digital computer—that the real inventor was the economist Adam Smith, whose idea was translated into hardware through successive stages of development by two mathematicians, Prony and Babbage" (Simon and Newell 1958, 2). As Simon's biographer Hunter Crowther-Heyck points out, it was Smith's division of labour and specialisation that was the guide for Simon. For Simon, intelligence was itself a form of organisation—structured and designed. Crowther-Heyck (2005, 225) writes that "the digital computer was powerful because it extended the division of labour to its ultimate end: the worker (logic gate) that was either on or off, open or closed." In other words, this was Smith's pin factory, but not his decentralised society of self-interested butchers and bakers acting independently to address economic need. In *The Wealth of Nations*, the division of labour is not designed from above. It emerges from competitive pressure, innovation, and exchange. The factory floor only exists as it does because of the broader institutional framework in which it operates. Simon took Smith's analysis of how complex systems function while discarding Smith's insight into how they arise.

The Logic Theorist project unfolded within a broader post-war enthusiasm for 'systems approaches' to management and engineering (Hughes and Hughes 2000). Operations research, systems engineering, and systems analysis promised to tame the complexity of air defence, nuclear deterrence, and later urban policy by treating them as large, integrated systems whose behaviour could be modelled and optimised with computers. In this milieu, the digital computer was both tool and metaphor (Edwards 1997). It processed information according to explicit models, just as systems analysts hoped to manage organisations and societies by formal, model-based planning. Simon's conception of programs as explicit theories of decision-making resonated with a wider technocratic culture in which expertise and computation were expected to deliver rational control over large, messy systems.

The philosopher John Haugeland (1985, 112–17) later dubbed this tradition "Good Old-Fashioned Artificial Intelligence" (GOFAI). In Haugeland's framing, GOFAI rested on two claims: first, that intelligent behaviour depends on the capacity to think about things reasonably, and second, that such thought is implemented as the automatic manipulation of internal symbols. On this view, an AI system is an "automatic formal system" (Haugeland 1985, 118): a machine whose internal tokens stand for objects and facts, and whose operations implement rules of inference. Intelligence is not an emergent property of a network, but a consequence of the right symbolic structures and procedures being explicitly designed and installed. The institutional consolidation of GOFAI or the symbolic approach is usually dated to the 1956 Dartmouth Summer Research Project on Artificial Intelligence, organised by John McCarthy, Marvin Minsky, Claude Shannon and

Nathaniel Rochester (McCarthy et al. 1955; Kline 2011). Dartmouth brought together researchers who believed that "every aspect of learning or any other feature of intelligence can in principle be so precisely described that a machine can be made to simulate it" (McCarthy et al. 1955).[4]

In its mature form, symbolic AI rests on the idea that intelligence emerges from manipulating physical symbol systems—patterns (like data structures or expressions) that can designate other objects or processes and be interpreted (executed) by a machine (Newell and Simon 1997). A symbol is something that refers to and provides access to something else, like a memory address pointing to a list. Intelligence, on this view, means generating and testing such symbolic structures through heuristic search.

A now-legendary experiment at MIT in the mid-1960s highlighted both the seductive power and limits of pure symbol manipulation. ELIZA was a chatbot developed by Joseph Weizenbaum that users interacted with through typed conversation (Lane et al. 2025; Weizenbaum 1966). Its most famous persona was a non-judgmental psychotherapist. This persona was carefully chosen because the AI would be able to deflect if asked questions it did not know the answer to (McCorduck 2018, 293). ELIZA possessed no semantic understanding of the concepts it processed. Instead, it operated through a script reliant on pattern matching and substitution. The program scanned user input for keywords, decomposed sentences according to syntactic rules, and reassembled the fragments using a manually compiled lookup table of ranked transformation rules. For instance, if a user typed 'I am unhappy,' the program identified the pattern 'I am,' inverted the pronouns, and re-purposed the adjective to respond with, 'How long have you been unhappy?' Detecting a specific keyword like 'mother' would trigger the system to deflect to a broader category with the response, 'Tell me more about your family.'

[4] Simon and Newell presented the Logic Theorist at the Dartmouth conference, but received a surprisingly lukewarm reception. This is probably because there wasn't really much of an exchange of ideas at Dartmouth, as John McCarthy recalled: "Anybody who was there was pretty stubborn about pursuing the ideas that he had before he came, nor was there, as far as I could see, any real exchange of ideas" (McCorduck 2018, 114).

Sometimes the system just defaulted to a fallback loop of generic encouragements—such as 'very interesting' or 'please go on'—to sustain the illusion of conversation.

ELIZA was the symbolic tradition's greatest early public success. ELIZA demonstrated that computers could be communicated with through human language—what we now call *natural language processing*—via symbolic rules. But at the same time it was a profound illustration of its limitations. ELIZA was inert and naïve. The relationship between user input and AI output was determined strictly by shape and syntax. Yet many users attributed genuine empathy and intelligence to the program. This phenomenon is now known as the ELIZA effect: our "general tendency to treat responsive computer programs as more intelligent than they really are. Very small amounts of interactivity cause us to project our own complexity onto the undeserving object" (Turkle 1995, 101).

For Weizenbaum, ELIZA became a cautionary tale about the disconnect between information processing and human understanding (Weizenbaum 1976). While the technocratic culture of the time believed that formal systems could eventually encompass the full richness of human thought, ELIZA suggested that a system could simulate "intelligent" behaviour while remaining entirely vacuous on the inside. It was a successful performance of GOFAI principles that simultaneously exposed AI's inability to capture meaning. Indeed by the late 1960s, the limitations of pure logic approaches and the shallowness of pattern-matchers like ELIZA were increasingly apparent (Goldstein and Papert 1977). These systems could manipulate symbols very flexibly, but they lacked the domain-specific knowledge required to solve realistic problems efficiently.

The response to the limitations of symbolic AI was the expert systems movement. Expert systems sought to encode human knowledge at large enough scale for AI systems to make decisions as any human expert would do given the same inputs. In 1977 the computer scientist Ed Feigenbaum captured the emergence of philosophy of expert systems:

> The art of constructing intelligent agents is both part of and an extension of the programming art. It is the art of building complex computer

> programs that represent and reason with knowledge of the world. Our art therefore lives in symbiosis with the other worldly arts, whose practitioners—experts of their art—hold the knowledge we need to construct intelligent agents.
>
> In most crafts or branches of learning, what we call "expertise" is the essence of the art. And for the domains of knowledge that we touch with our art, it is the "rules of expertise," or the rules of "good judgment" of the expert practitioners of that domain, that we seek to transfer to our programs (Feigenbaum 1977, 1016).

Expert systems were the culmination of the post-war approach of intelligence through planning. Engineers carefully specified categories, rules, and control strategies. Then teams of experts would structure complex decision problems into formally manageable components, which would be encoded into computer systems that promised rational, auditable decision-making. Early systems such as Feigenbaum's DENDRAL (which inferred molecular structures from mass-spectrometry data) and MYCIN (which recommended antibiotic regimens for its users) embodied hundreds of domain-specific "if–then" rules derived from interviews with human experts. The architecture was, in a way representative of Herbert Simon's administrative thought, highly *bureaucratic*. These systems had a knowledge base containing rules, a working memory of current facts, and an inference engine that applied the rules according to pre-determined strategies. Building such systems required the development of a new professional discipline—"knowledge engineerer"—whose task was to extract knowledge from experts and codify them into explicit rule sets.

By the early 1980s, the expert systems movement was enjoying a commercial boom. Venture capital poured into AI startups and large firms experimented with deploying expert systems for credit scoring, equipment configuration, and process control. Specialised 'symbolic processing' computers (see, for example, Moon 1985) were sold as platforms for knowledge-based applications. The AI industry came to resemble the systems engineering consultancies of the 1960s: teams of knowledge engineers promising to rationalise corporate decision-making by embedding expert knowledge into software (McCorduck 2018; Feigenbaum et al. 1989).

In practice, however, expert systems had fundamental limitations. Encoding expert knowledge into software was extremely labour-intensive and slow. A knowledge engineer had to engage in extended, structured dialogue with domain specialists, learning enough of the field's terminology and conceptual structure to ask meaningful questions, while simultaneously helping experts articulate heuristics they often applied tacitly. As rule sets grew, designers also discovered that knowledge was highly interdependent. They had initially assumed that rules were modular enough that experts could add new rules without revisiting existing ones, but in practice even a small change could ripple through the system's behaviour. In systems like MYCIN, altering a single rule sometimes changed diagnoses or treatment recommendations, forcing knowledge engineers and clinicians into a continual cycle of re-interviewing, testing, and rule revision (Buchanan and Shortliffe 1985).

The computer scientist John McCarthy identified another problem: human experts aren't only informed solely by their expertise, but also the latent background knowledge possessed by all people, expert and non-expert alike—what he called *common sense* (McCarthy 1959b, 1986). A project launched in 1984, Cyc, attempted to tackle this problem. Cyc was a comprehensive system of general knowledge: a single, centrally organised repository of millions of commonsense facts and rules that other programs could consult (Lenat and Guha 1990; Lenat 1995; Lenat et al. 1990). Cyc aimed to encode the background knowledge that underlies everyday reasoning—such as naïve physics and folk psychology—on the view that failure to do so was what made earlier systems brittle. The strategy was again thoroughly planned. Rather than letting a system learn from large data sets, teams of knowledge engineers manually entered assertions into a carefully designed ontology, hoping to anticipate the concepts and distinctions needed for general intelligence.

An even deeper difficulty was that experts often could not state the very knowledge designers sought to encode. Much professional competence is tacit (Polanyi [1966] 1983, 2007). As some expert systems critics argued, true expertise implies the abandonment of rule-based reasoning altogether in favour of holistic intuition based on experience rather than logic (Dreyfus et al. 1986; Dreyfus 1972, 2009). Experts do not rely on the abstract rules they learned as beginners. They rely on their experience. So asking an expert to articulate their knowledge forces them to "regress to the level of a beginner and state the rules [they] still remember but no longer use" (Dreyfus and Dreyfus 2005, 788). Even worse, when asked to explain their reasoning, experts routinely produced what Johnson (1983, 81) called "reconstructed methods of reasoning"—plausible, didactic accounts of how a task *might* be done, rather than descriptions of what they actually do. Johnson reported one experienced clinician admitting that while he needed systematic procedures to teach students, he himself "[did] not know how [he did] diagnosis" and therefore invented methods that seemed reasonable in the classroom but did not reflect his real diagnostic behaviour. The problem for early expert-system builders was that the knowledge engineers overwhelmingly received reconstructed methods—the only kind most experts could articulate—leading to systems that were formally elegant but often failed to capture the actual behaviour of the experts when they were in professional settings.

Some researchers recognised these limits and groped toward alternatives. Stefik (1986). for example proposed building AI around 'knowledge markets' and 'knowledge ecologies'. Rather than having individual expert systems built from scratch by knowledge engineers working in isolation, knowledge components might be acquired, combined, and recombined through decentralised exchange. Expert knowledge might 'emerge' even when each individual system's knowledge was partial. This vision of a kind of market or spontaneous order for symbolic representations was striking but it never much gained traction. The symbolic tradition's commitment to explicit rules sat uneasily with emergent intelligence, and the infrastructure for such markets never materialised. Ultimately, the intelligence breakthrough would have to come from a tradition that rejected symbolic representation altogether.

When the market for expert systems collapsed in the late 1980s, it marked not just the end of a business cycle but the limits of a particular theory of intelligence. Symbolic AI from the Logic Theorist through Cyc pursued the idea that cognition could be engineered as an explicit system of representations, rules, and plans designed by experts and executed by reliable machines. That vision was deeply entangled with the post-war systems approach in management and engineering, sharing its confidence that complex behaviour could be rendered tractable through formal modelling and hierarchical control. The collapse of the expert systems boom exposed the difficulty of fully specifying the rules for intelligence in advance—a difficulty that would motivate a renewed interest in the alternative idea that intelligence might be emergent rather than planned.

2.3 Neural Networks and AI by Discovery

If the symbolic approach to artificial intelligence represents the philosophy of the central planner—who believes intelligence is the manipulation of symbols according to known, articulate rules—the alternative tradition represents the philosophy of discovery and unplanned evolution. This is the connectionist approach typified by neural networks. In this tradition, intelligence is not designed top-down through logic and pre-specified rules but emerges bottom-up through the adaptation of a vast number of decentralised units. It is a story of spontaneous order, where the system 'learns' by adjusting to the signals it receives from the world, much as a market adjusts prices in response to scarcity and abundance.

The intellectual roots of this tradition lie in the early twentieth century's attempt to peer inside the "black box" of the mind. The behaviourists that dominated pre-war psychology rejected the premise that the mind could be directly examined. Because inner mental states were unobservable, to ask what happened inside the brain was considered unscientific speculation. An alternative intellectual tradition challenged this refusal to look inside the mind by attempting to construct the mind as a physical object (Cordeschi 2002). This approach argued that the best way to understand a psychological process was to build a machine that could actually perform that process.

For the psychologist Clark L. Hull (1943; see his earlier work Krueger and Hull 1931; Hull and Baernstein 1929), efforts to understand the brain had faltered because humans are too close to the brain to see it objectively. The solution was what he called a 'robot approach,' suggesting that if a physical mechanism could be constructed to learn or adapt, it would prove that these mental abilities were not mystical forces but understandable physical processes. Hull's goal was not artificial intelligence. It was to use artificial models to better understand human intelligence. But by demonstrating that inorganic matter could be structured to act with purpose, these early experiments bridged the gap between the living and the artificial. Nonetheless, Hull was still a behaviourist in many important ways. He explicitly rejected the study of consciousness or subjective experience, insisting that 'mind' was only scientifically valid if it could be reduced to physical inputs and measurable outputs. As he wrote in 1943, "propositions originating in private intuitions masquerading as unstated logical processes are, of course, not theoretical material at all, and have no proper place in science" (Hull 1943, 31).

The foundational text of what came to be called connectionism was written by one of Hull's followers, Warren McCulloch. In the 1930s, McCulloch was a regular attendee of the seminars hosted by Hull on "the theories and methods of mathematical physics". These gatherings sought to formalise the laws of behaviour, a drive that McCulloch would ultimately translate into the biological hardware of the brain (Abraham 2016, 70–71). In 1943, Warren McCulloch and Walter Pitts published "A Logical Calculus of the Ideas Immanent in Nervous Activity," a work that fundamentally altered the trajectory of the mind sciences. They proposed that a neuron was essentially a logic gate—a biological switch that fired or didn't fire based on the signals it received (McCulloch and Pitts 1943). By treating this "all-or-none" firing activity as a binary proposition (true/false), they demonstrated that a network of these simple units could theoretically compute any logical function that could be described in words.

With this, McCulloch and Pitts presented a proof of concept for the physical basis of mind. They demonstrated that the 'laws of thought' could be explained by the architecture of neural connectivity. Complex, purposive behaviour did not require a central 'soul' or a top-down designer. Instead, it could emerge from the interaction of simple, interconnected units processing signals. With their mathematical account of neural activity, McCulloch and Pitts stripped the mind of its mysticism and recast it as a problem of signal processing and structural organization. If a mental function could be defined logically, a physical network could be built to perform it.

Long before he became the world's most famous critic of socialist planning, Friedrich Hayek was a student of psychology. In 1920, he drafted a manuscript attempting to explain how the brain classifies sensory input (Hayek [1920] 2017), a project he set aside for economics but returned to in the late 1940s. The resulting book, *The Sensory Order* (Hayek 1952), was an attempt to describe the physical mechanics of how a mind comes to know the world. As he wrote, "we cannot hope to account for observed behaviour without reconstructing the 'intervening processes in the brain'" (Hayek 1952, 44; quoting Morgan 1943, 473). At the heart of the book is a rejection of the idea that the mind is a passive receptacle of 'sense data'. Instead, Hayek presents thought as an active, subjective process, where knowledge is not received from the environment, but discovered and interpreted by the brain's neural structures.

For Hayek, the physical order of the universe and the sensory ('phenomenal') order of the mind were distinct realms—or, as he called them 'orders' (Hayek 1952, 3–4). The task of psychology was to explain how our perceptions emerge our interaction with the physical world. For Hayek, this is where the black box approach of the behaviourists failed. The behaviourists purported to understand human behaviour through a stimulus-response framework. To understand the psychological foundation of a person's actions, all that was needed by the researcher was knowledge of the stimulus and observation of the response. But Hayek argued that this reasoning was fundamentally circular. What counts as a stimulus itself is subject to interpretation by the individual being studied—not its objective physical properties. Two objects might be physically similar but trigger vastly different responses in different individuals. By ignoring the internal structure that equates or differentiates stimulus between individuals, behaviourism ignored the mechanisms that makes intelligence possible (Hayek 1952, 27–28).

The engine of Hayek's interpretation of the mind is what he called 'classification'. Like McCulloch and Pitts (1943), Hayek conceptualised the mind as a network of neurons in which organisation matters more than the intrinsic properties of individual elements. But where McCulloch and Pitts imagined these neurons as logical units that could implement formal computation, Hayek understood the purpose of the network as a historically formed classification system, whose changing pattern of connections (Hayek used the archaic British English spelling "connexions") explains the emergence of sensory qualities and mental order. An individual neuron has no intrinsic meaning or quality. It is only how it is connected to other neurons within a vast interconnected network that determines its behaviour. As he wrote: "we conceive of a three dimensional net or lattice of rubber threads in which the knots represent the elements and the threads the connexions" (Hayek 1952, 38). The brain classifies incoming impulses based on the history of their connections. When a nerve impulse arrives, it is sorted into groups of other impulses with which it has occurred in the past. This is a process of 'multiple classification' (Hayek 1952, 50–52), where a single event is simultaneously categorised in numerous ways—by colour, shape, timing, or emotional resonance. Intelligence, therefore, is not a property of biological substance, but an emergent property of the network itself.

Through a lifetime's process of classification, the brain builds what Hayek called the 'map' (Hayek 1952, 112–18). The map is the semi-permanent apparatus of classification. It represents the static rules and relationships the organism has *learned* about the world. It is a catalogue of the kinds of events that exist. He distinguished this map from a 'model'—the pattern of impulses active at any specific moment. The model is a simulation of the current environment generated by running inputs through the map. Through the model the brain projects a classification onto the world—a guess based on past linkages in the map—and waits to see if the environment confirms or refutes it. If expectations are met, the map's classifications are reinforced. If expectations are not met, the map is altered:

> While there can thus be nothing in our mind which is not the result of past linkages (even though, perhaps, acquired not by the individual but by the species), the experience that the classification based on the past linkages does not always work, i.e., does not always lead to valid predictions, forces us to revise that classification (Hayek 1952, 168).

Thus intelligence in the Hayekian sense is not just a database of facts and rules but as a dynamic process of discovery, learning and adaptation. It is the continuous refinement of a subjective internal order against the friction of an objective external reality.

As Hayek ([1982] 2017, 389) summarised his argument later:

> Assume I could construct a rat—that is, a mechanical model that can do all a rat does. To be a really true model, it would clearly have to do also a great many things we could not predict, even though we know precisely how the mechanism we have built works. The reason for our inability to predict ... would be that our mind is not capable of perceiving and digesting ... all the particular stimuli that operate upon it and all the processes of classification that proceed in it. The only means by which we could achieve predictions would be to build a computer that imitates all that the mechanism of the rat performs; or, in other words, to build another rat identical in structure with the first one and making it live from the beginning in exactly the same environmental conditions, so that it would perceive and learn exactly what the first rat does.

Hayek's foray into theoretical psychology was not a diversion from his economics. The economic problem, as Hayek had framed it in his famous essay published seven years earlier 'The Use of Knowledge in Society' (Hayek 1945), is fundamentally about how dispersed, subjective knowledge gets coordinated without any single mind possessing it all. Value is not an objective property of goods or services. It exists only in the subjective valuations of individuals. Prices emerge from the interaction of these subjective preferences. Markets work precisely because they don't require anyone to articulate or even consciously understand their own preferences. Prices communicate what needs to be communicated. Indeed, Hayek's connectionist model of intelligence ultimately supports his critique of the planned economy. It describes fundamental limits on the knowledge that is accessible to central planners (Tuerck 1995). If subjective preferences are shaped by unique experiences and local conditions that cannot be aggregated or communicated effectively, then they are out of the reach of even the most authoritarian or all-seeing planner.

In an important way, Hayek's theory of mind has much in common with the mechanistic visions of Hobbes and La Mettrie. It describes the mind in machine-like terms (Van Den Hauwe 2011). But it is *epistemically* non-deterministic. An external observer might be able to predict a mind's behaviour only if they could observe all the inputs—including the evolutionary ones (Koppl and Butos 2007)—that have shaped any given mind. The mind's complexity makes complete prediction impossible in practice, as the classification process depends on the entire history of the individual's experience, and new classifications can emerge spontaneously from interactions. Maybe Laplace's Demon (1902), who has access to all information about every atom and molecule and particle going back into eternity, could be an competent central planner. But the information needed by the Demon would be a complete replica of the information content (and computational capability) of the universe (see Deutsch 2012 on the universe as information and computation).

Hence both the Hayekian mind and Hayekian market are emergent orders. And in both there are fundamental limits to our ability to explain the origins and nature of that order. Just as a planner cannot grasp the totality of the market, the conscious mind cannot grasp the totality of the neural processes that generate it. For a classifying apparatus to fully explain a system, it must be more complex than that system. The human mind can never fully explain itself (Hayek 1952, 185). Our actions in the market and perceptions and preferences, he wrote later, are governed by "rules which we cannot state" (Hayek 1963, 323). He concluded his rat analogy with the following: "In order to understand what a rat will do and why it does it, we would in effect have to become another rat.

Need I spell out the consequences that follow from this for our understanding of other human beings?" (Hayek [1982] 2017, 389)

Hayek's work was part of a nascent connectionist tradition. And indeed, Hayek sensed that his theory of neural classification was pointing toward something beyond epistemology—toward a new understanding of how order-generating systems might actually be built. In *Organization of Behavior* (1949) the psychologist Donald Hebb suggested that learning provided the coordination mechanism for the neural system. If two neurons are active simultaneously, the connection between them strengthens. No central controller is needed to tell the network what to learn; the network self-organises based on the statistical correlations in the input data. At the time, John Von Neumann (1951, 1967)was working on what he called 'automata theory': how could simple elements, following local rules, generate complex adaptive behaviour without a central programmer? Hayek recalled later:

> When I was writing *The Sensory Order*, I reasoned that I could explain to people what I was doing. Usually I found it very difficult to make them understand. And then I met John Von Neumann at a party, and to my amazement and delight, he immediately understood what I was doing and said that he was working on the same problem from the same angle. At the time his research on automata came out, it was too abstract for me to relate it to psychology, so I really couldn't profit from it; but I did see that we had been thinking on very similar lines (Weimer 1982, 322).

The answer, for both Hayek and von Neumann, lay in the architecture of thought—in the networks of interconnected units that classify, respond, and reorganise based on feedback.

In 1957, Frank Rosenblatt, a psychologist at Cornell, built the first artificial neural network to realise the connectionist ideas in physical hardware (Rosenblatt 1958, 1957, 1962). Unlike the logic machines of Simon and Newell which required pre-programmed heuristics, Rosenblatt's 'Perceptron' was designed to how to reason, just as the brain did. The Perceptron consisted of three layers: sensory units that receive input from the environment, association units that did pattern recognition, and response units to produce outputs. Each connection between units carried a numerical weight—a value that determines how strongly one unit influenced another. When a stimulus was presented, each association unit summed the weighted inputs it received. If this weighted sum exceeded the unit's threshold, the unit 'fired' and transmitted a signal onward, firing and transmitting signals through the network until an output was produced.

Rosenblatt was explicit about the Hayekian intellectual foundations of his neural network. In his 1958 paper announcing the design, he identified "Hebb and Hayek" as providing "the most suggestive work" for his theory, and described the Perceptron as based on "the position elaborated by Hebb, Hayek, Uttley, and Ashby" (Rosenblatt 1958, 388).[5] He argued in his 1962 book *Principles of Neurodynamics* that the Perceptron was animated by the "basic philosophical approach" of *The Sensory Order* (Rosenblatt 1962, 5). Learning in the Perceptron occurs through the modification of weights: when a particular stimulus and response occur together, the weights on connections between the active units are strengthened, making that response more likely to occur again when similar stimuli are encountered. This is the fundamental mechanism that underlies all neural networks—learning is encoded not in explicit stored representations, but in the pattern of connection strengths distributed across the system.

The Perceptron was met by a popular excitement it could not satisfy. A *New York Times* article in 1958 declared that it was the "embryo of an electronic computer that [the Navy, which sponsored Rosenblatt's work] expects will be able to walk, talk, see, write, reproduce itself and be conscious of its existence".[6] At the time, this was not as naïve as it seems now. In the 1950s the idea of a machine that could learn rather than be programmed was appealing in part because the field of programming barely existed (Minsky and Papert 1990, x). It was not obvious which would be easier: building software out of primitive languages like

[5] Albert Uttley developed early neural network models for pattern recognition (Uttley 1953), and W. Ross Ashby's *Design for a Brain* ([1952] 1960) explored how machines could exhibit adaptive behaviour.

[6] https://timesmachine.nytimes.com/timesmachine/1958/07/08/83417341.html?pageNumber=25.

assembly or Fortran, or just developing computers that could build software themselves.

All the early enthusiasm for neural networks soon ground to a halt. In their 1969 book *Perceptions* Marvin Minsky and Seymour Papert (1990) demonstrated that single-layer neural networks of the type that Rosenblatt had created could not compute basic non-linear functions like XOR (exclusive or), where two input bits produces an output of 'true' if the inputs are different or 'false' if they are the same.[7] Because a single-layer neural network has only one layer of adjustable weights connecting the inputs directly to the outputs, it can only learn to classify patterns that are linearly separable.

Such functions could be theoretically computed by multi-layer networks, which have layers of neurons between the inputs and outputs, with adjustable weights at each layer. Multiple layers allow the network to learn non-linear patterns by building up increasingly abstract internal representations. The core problem in the 1960s was not that multi-layer networks were impossible, but that no one knew how to train them—the weights in hidden layers could not be adjusted by any known efficient algorithm (Hawkins 1961, 47).

It was only in the mid-1980s, while expert systems booming in the symbolic AI community, that the multi-layer hurdle was overcome. A technique called backpropagation addressed Minsky and Papert's critique by making it practical to train multi-layer neural networks (Rumelhart et al. 1986; Werbos 1994; for an overview, see Schmidhuber 2015). When a neural network makes a mistaken prediction—say, identifying an image of a cat as a dog—the system calculates the error. Backpropagation sends this error signal backward through the layers, adjusting the neural weights to reduce the error next time. It is a decentralised method of correction. (The phrase often used to describe modern AI systems, 'deep learning', simply means neural networks with many layers—typically dozens or more. As of 2026, modern large language models can have more than 100 layers.)

---

[7] However, the book's mythical status as 'the neural network killer' isn't quite right. By 1969, many neural network researchers had already left the field, frustrated by the lack of progress (Olazaran 1996).

But even in the late 1980s connectionism faced hard constraints. While neural networks of the 1990s could perform discrete tasks like digit recognition (Hochreiter et al. 2001), scaling them to more general tasks was difficult. Some problems were theoretical—such as how to prevent the error signal from fading away entirely as it was transmitted backward through deep layers (Hochreiter et al. 2001; Bengio et al. 1994).

However, the most profound limitation was physical. Hardware lagged theory. Because a neural network must calculate weighted sums for entire layers of neurons simultaneously, the math effectively consists of multiplying vast grids of numbers at once. The standard von Neumann architecture—in which a central processing unit (CPU) executes complex instructions in strict sequence—handles this sort of calculation inefficiently, like a single mathematician working through a spreadsheet cell by cell. The breakthrough was using graphics processing units (GPU). Originally designed to render millions of pixels for videogames, the GPU architecture is exactly that needed for deep learning.[8] Unlike a CPU, which attacks complex tasks sequentially, a GPU contains thousands of smaller cores that function like an army of ants, performing thousands of simple arithmetic tasks in unison. It was only when researchers began repurposing this gaming hardware for matrix operations that the dormant potential of the connectionist architecture could finally be realised (Raina et al. 2009; Chellapilla et al. 2006).

2.4 The Bitter Lesson

We have traced here the history of the development of artificial intelligence as a contest between two fundamentally different theories of what intelligence is and how it can be achieved. The symbolic tradition, from Simon's Logic Theorist through the

[8] The repurposing of GPUs from gaming to deep learning was as an accident to NVIDIA, the company that dominated the gaming market and now dominates the modern AI industry (Witt 2025).

expert systems boom, represented an attempt to construct intelligence through explicit specification—to build minds by articulating the rules that govern thought. The connectionist tradition, from Hayek's theoretical neural architecture through modern deep learning, treats intelligence as an emergent property that cannot be fully specified in advance but must be discovered through interaction with data.

In March 2019, the reinforcement learning pioneer Richard Sutton crystallised this distinction in what he called "The Bitter Lesson"—a reflection on his decades of artificial intelligence research that reads, in retrospect, as a vindication of the discovery paradigm and a reproach to the planning mindset (Sutton 2019). Sutton's lesson is 'bitter' because it requires researchers to abandon an intellectually and emotionally satisfying approach to intelligence. The symbolic tradition was an expression of a certain kind of confidence in human expertise. Knowledge engineers believed they could interview domain experts, extract the rules that governed expert judgment, and encode those rules into systems that would replicate that judgment faithfully. This is an intrinsically appealing vision. It flatters the expert whose knowledge is being extracted and the engineer who believes they can formalise the ineffable. It promises transparency. If the rules are explicit, the system's reasoning can be audited, explained, and corrected. And it appears to offer a shortcut to intelligence. Why should a machine spend years—or spend enormous computational resources—learning what humans have already discovered? But, Sutton argued, the expert approach failed. The bitter lesson is that scale matters more than expertise.

The history of computerised chess—one of the earliest domains that researchers tried to tackle with intelligent machines—illustrates in miniature the discovery of the importance of scale. In 1950 Claude Shannon described the 'minimax' algorithm and evaluation functions that would define computer chess for half a century (Shannon 1950). Shannon himself favoured a selective, human expert-like approach that would focus computational resources on the most promising lines of play rather than exhaustively evaluating every possibility. For decades, researchers attempted to encode the grandmasters' knowledge of positional play, piece coordination, and strategy into their programs.

When IBM's Deep Blue defeated Garry Kasparov in 1997, it seemed like a victory for the symbolic paradigm. Deep Blue was not a neural network. It was an expert system, relying on hand-crafted evaluation functions tuned by grandmasters and a database of 700,000 games (Campbell et al. 2002). But its victory came from a brute-force search. The machine evaluated 200 million chess positions per second, overwhelming human intuition through sheer computational power rather than replicating it. As Sutton (2019) recounts, chess researchers who had devoted their careers to encoding human understanding of the game "were not good losers"—they insisted that brute-force search "was not a general strategy, and anyway it was not how people played chess." Deep Blue's victory was for computation over human-encoded knowledge.

The true vindication of the discovery paradigm came two decades later with the boardgame Go. Where Deep Blue won through brute-force search within a hand-designed evaluation framework, DeepMind's AlphaGo won its 2016 victory over the top human Go player through a learning paradigm. The enormous efforts researchers had devoted to encoding human understanding of territory, influence, and shape proved irrelevant once deep neural networks combined with self-play could discover strategies that surpassed the accumulated wisdom of millennia of human experience. Its successor model, AlphaGo Zero, learned entirely from self-play without any human game data. And it defeated its human-trained predecessor one hundred games to zero. This was not merely scale winning over selectivity, as Deep Blue had done in the 1990s. AlphaGo Zero's was a victory of discovery over design. The knowledge in AlphaGo Zero was not specified by experts but emerged from the training process itself—a spontaneous order in the Hayekian sense, where the structure of intelligence arose from millions of local adjustments rather than from any central blueprint.

The failure of expert systems reflected a fundamental misconception about the nature of intelligence itself. "The actual contents of minds," Sutton writes, "are tremendously, irredeemably complex; we should stop trying to find simple ways to think about the contents of minds" (Sutton 2019). The categories through which we understand the world—space, objects, causation, intention—are not building blocks waiting to be discovered and codified into an intelligent machine. They are themselves the products of learning, shaped by interaction with an irreducibly complex environment.

This chapter has argued that the competition between two approaches to the creation of artificial intelligence—symbolic AI and neural networks—is the same competition as that between central planning and the market economy. Central planners and knowledge engineers have imagined they can gather all relevant information, encode it in a unified model, and issue instructions that will produce desired outcomes. But the knowledge required for economic coordination is not the kind that can be concentrated in a single mind or institution. It is dispersed across millions of individuals. Much of it is tacit and contextual and constantly changing in response to local circumstances. Markets work precisely because they do not require such concentration. Prices aggregate dispersed information and transmit signals that coordinate behaviour without any participant needing to understand the system as a whole. In this sense, symbolic AI and the expert systems that tried to realise its vision were attempting to replace the emergent order of human intelligence with a deliberately designed artificial intelligence.

Connectionism and neural networks succeeded where the symbolic AI tradition failed because they do not attempt to design intelligence. Instead, they provide a substrate in which intelligence can emerge through learning—the same process of error correction and adaptation that characterises both biological evolution and market competition. The connectionist approach is a discovery approach. Knowledge is not articulated in advance but discovered in training and dispersed across connection weights rather than concentrated in explicit rules. In the next chapter we will consider how this intelligence can be seen as an emergent order. Like prices in a market economy, these distributed representations encode information that no single component of the system possesses. The connectionist approach is robust. It generalises over noisy, high-dimensional inputs in ways that rule-based systems cannot. But connectionist systems are opaque. We cannot easily explain why a neural network produces a particular output. As Sutton (2019) wrote,

> the actual contents of minds are tremendously, irredeemably complex; we should stop trying to find simple ways to think about the contents of minds, such as simple ways to think about space, objects, multiple agents, or symmetries. All these are part of the arbitrary, intrinsically-complex, outside world. They are not what should be built in, as their complexity is endless; instead we should build in only the meta-methods that can find and capture this arbitrary complexity. Essential to these methods is that they can find good approximations, but the search for them should be by our methods, not by us. We want AI agents that can discover like we can, not which contain what we have discovered. Building in our discoveries only makes it harder to see how the discovering process can be done.

The foundation models that now power modern AI are the inheritors of Hayek's vision. They are spontaneous orders—systems whose capabilities emerged from learning rather than design, whose knowledge is distributed across billions of parameters that no engineer specified. But spontaneous orders have always unsettled those who believe that what cannot be centrally understood cannot be trusted. Critics of the market economy have sought to impose requirements for market exchange to be more transparent, subject to regulatory oversight and more 'legible' (Scott 1998) so that it can be more planned and controlled. The same demands are being imposed on the spontaneous order of artificial intelligence. The next chapter examines what kind of intelligence has emerged from this process of decentralised adaptation—and why it resists that legibility.

References

Abraham, Tara. 2016. *Rebel Genius: Warren S. McCulloch's Transdisciplinary Life in Science*. The MIT Press. https://doi.org/10.7551/mitpress/9780262035095.001.0001.

Abramson, Darren. 2011. "Descartes' Influence on Turing." *Studies in History and Philosophy of Science Part A* 42 (4): 544–551. https://doi.org/10.1016/j.shpsa.2011.09.004.

Ahearn, Barry. 2012. "Tennyson and Babbage." *Tennyson Research Bulletin* 10 (1): 53–65. https://www.jstor.org/stable/45288571.

Ashby, W. Ross. (1952) 1960. *Design for a Brain: The Origin of Adaptive Behavior*. Chapman and Hall.

Babbage, Charles. 2010. *Babbage's Calculating Engines: Being a Collection of Papers Relating to Them; Their History and Construction*. Edited by Henry P. Babbage. Cambridge University Press. https://doi.org/10.1017/CBO9780511694721.

Bengio, Y., P. Simard, and P. Frasconi. 1994. "Learning Long-Term Dependencies with Gradient Descent Is Difficult." *IEEE Transactions on Neural Networks* 5 (2): 157–166. https://doi.org/10.1109/72.279181.

Buchanan, Bruce G., and Edward Hance Shortliffe. 1985. *Rule-Based Expert Systems: The MYCIN Experiments of the Stanford Heuristic Programming Project*. Reprinted with corrections, May 1985. Addison-Wesley.

Buxton, Harry W., and Anthony Hyman, eds. 2010. *Memoir of the Life and Labours of the Late Charles Babbage Esq., F.R.S.* The Charles Babbage Institute Reprint Series for the History of Computing, vol. 13. MIT Press.

Campbell, Murray, A. Joseph Hoane, and Feng-hsiung Hsu. 2002. "Deep Blue." *Artificial Intelligence* 134 (1): 57–83. https://doi.org/10.1016/S0004-3702(01)00129-1.

Chellapilla, Kumar, Sidd Puri, and Patrice Simard. 2006. "High Performance Convolutional Neural Networks for Document Processing." *Paper presented at Tenth International Workshop on Frontiers in Handwriting Recognition, Université de Rennes*. October 1.

Church, Alonzo. 1932. "A Set of Postulates for the Foundation of Logic." *Annals of Mathematics* 33 (2): 346–366. https://doi.org/10.2307/1968337.

Church, Alonzo. 1936. "An Unsolvable Problem of Elementary Number Theory." *American Journal of Mathematics* 58 (2): 345. https://doi.org/10.2307/2371045.

Clarke, Desmond M. 2003. *Descartes's Theory of Mind*. Oxford University Press, Incorporated.

Cordeschi, Roberto. 2002. *The Discovery of the Artificial: Behavior, Mind and Machines Before and Beyond Cybernetics*. Vol. 28, edited by James H. Fetzer. Studies in Cognitive Systems. Springer Netherlands. https://doi.org/10.1007/978-94-015-9870-5.

Crowther-Heyck, Hunter. 2005. *Herbert A. Simon: The Bounds of Reason in Modern America*. Johns Hopkins University Press.

Descartes, René. (1637) 2006. *A Discourse on the Method of Correctly Conducting One's Reason and Seeking Truth in the Sciences*. Edited by Ian Maclean. Oxford World's Classics. Oxford University Press.

Deutsch, David. 2012. *The Beginning of Infinity: Explanations That Transform the World*. Always Learning. Pearson. Penguin Books.

Diderot, Denis. 2025. "ANDROÏDE (Mécanisme)." In *Encyclopédie, ou Dictionnaire raisonné des sciences, des arts et des métiers*, edited by Denis Diderot and Jean Le Rond d'Alembert, vol. 1. Paris: Briasson; David l'aîné; Le Breton; Durand, November 5. https://enccre.academie-sciences.fr/encyclopedie/article/lv1-1751-0/.

Dreyfus, Hubert L. 1972. *What Computers Can't Do: A Critique of Artificial Reason*. Harper & Row.

Dreyfus, Hubert L. 2009. *What Computers Still Can't Do: A Critique of Artificial Reason*. Rev. ed., [Repr.]. MIT Press.

Dreyfus, Hubert L., and Stuart E. Dreyfus. 2005. "Peripheral Vision: Expertise in Real World Contexts." *Organization Studies* 26 (5): 779–792. https://doi.org/10.1177/0170840605053102.

Dreyfus, Hubert L., Stuart E. Dreyfus, and Tom Athanasiou. 1986. *Mind over Machine: The Power of Human Intuition and Expertise in the Era of the Computer*. The Free Press.

Edwards, Paul N. 1997. *The Closed World: Computers and the Politics of Discourse in Cold War America*. 1. paperback ed. Inside Technology. MIT Press.

Essinger, James. 2007. *Jacquard's Web: How a Hand-Loom Led to the Birth of the Information Age*. Oxford Univ. Press.

Feigenbaum, Edward A. 1977. "The Art of Artificial Intelligence: I. Themes and Case Studies of Knowledge Engineering." 1014–1029.

Feigenbaum, Edward A., Pamela McCorduck, H. Penny Nii, and Penny Nii. 1989. *The Rise of the Expert Company: How Visionary Companies Are Using Artificial Intelligence to Achieve Higher Productivity and Profits*. Vintage Books.

Ferguson, Adam. (1767) 1783. *An Essay on the History of Civil Society*. 5th ed. T. Cadell, W. Creech, and J. Bell.

Gaudemard, Lynda. 2021. *Rethinking Descartes's Substance Dualism*. Vol. 29. Studies in the History of Philosophy of Mind. Springer International Publishing. https://doi.org/10.1007/978-3-030-75414-3.

Goldstein, Ira, and Seymour Papert. 1977. "Artificial Intelligence, Language, and the Study of Knowledge." *Cognitive Science* 1 (1): 84–123. https://doi.org/10.1016/S0364-0213(77)80006-2.

Green, Christopher D. 2005. "Was Babbage's Analytical Engine Intended to Be a Mechanical Model of the Mind?" *History of Psychology* 8 (1): 35–45. https://doi.org/10.1037/1093-4510.8.1.35.

Haugeland, John. 1985. *Artificial Intelligence: The Very Idea*. MIT Press.

Hawkins, J. K. 1961. "Self-Organizing Systems - A Review and Commentary." *Proceedings of the IRE* 49 (1): 31–48. https://doi.org/10.1109/JRPROC.1961.287776.

Hayek, Friedrich A. 1945. "The Use of Knowledge in Society." *The American Economic Review* 35 (4): 519–530.

Hayek, Friedrich A. 1952. *The Sensory Order: An Inquiry Into the Foundations of Theoretical Psychology*. University of Chicago Press.

Hayek, Friedrich A. 1963. "Rules, Perception, and Intelligibility." In *Proceedings of the British Academy*, vol. 48. Oxford University Press. https://www.thebritishacademy.ac.uk/documents/4843/48p321.pdf.

Hayek, Friedrich A. (1920) 2017. "Contributions to a Theory of How Conciousness Develops." In *The Sensory Order and Other Writings on the Foundations of Theoretical Psychology*, edited by Viktor J. Vanberg. University of Chicago Press. https://doi.org/10.7208/chicago/9780226436562.001.0001.

Hayek, Friedrich A. (1982) 2017. "The Sensory Order after 25 Years." In *The Sensory Order and Other Writings on the Foundations of Theoretical Psychology*, by Viktor J. Vanberg. University of Chicago Press. https://doi.org/10.7208/chicago/9780226436562.001.0001.

Hebb, Donald Olding. 1949. *The Organization of Behavior: A Neuropsychological Theory*. Wiley.

Hochreiter, Sepp, A. Steven Younger, and Peter R. Conwell. 2001. "Learning to Learn Using Gradient Descent." In *Artificial Neural Networks—ICANN 2001*, edited by Georg Dorffner, Horst Bischof, and Kurt Hornik. Springer. https://doi.org/10.1007/3-540-44668-0_13.

Hoffmann, E. T. A. (1816) 2016. *The Sandman*. Translated by Peter Wortsman. Penguin Books.

Hughes, Agatha C., and Thomas Parke Hughes, eds. 2000. *Systems, Experts, and Computers: The Systems Approach in Management and Engineering, World War II and After*. Dibner Institute Studies in the History of Science and Technology. MIT Press.

Hull, Clark L. 1943. *Principles Of Behavior*. http://archive.org/details/in.ernet.dli.2015.205891.

Hull, Clark L., and H. D. Baernstein. 1929. "A Mechanical Parallel to the Conditioned Reflex." *Science* 70 (1801): 14–15.

Johnson, Paul E. 1983. "What Kind Of Expert Should A System Be?" *Journal of Medicine and Philosophy* 8 (1): 77–97. https://doi.org/10.1093/jmp/8.1.77.

Klaes, M. 2005. "A Conceptual History of the Emergence of Bounded Rationality." *History of Political Economy* 37 (1): 1. https://doi.org/10.1215/00182702-37-1-27.

Kline, Ronald. 2011. "Cybernetics, Automata Studies, and the Dartmouth Conference on Artificial Intelligence." *IEEE Annals of the History of Computing* 33 (4): 5–16. https://doi.org/10.1109/MAHC.2010.44.

Koppl, Roger G., and William N. Butos. 2007. "Does The Sensory Order Have a Useful Economic Future?" In *Cognition and Economics*, 1st ed, edited by Carine Krecké, Élisabeth Krecké, and Roger G. Koppl. Advances in Austrian Economics 9. Elsevier JAI.

Krueger, Robert G., and Clark L. Hull. 1931. "An Electro-Chemical Parallel to the Conditioned Reflex." *The Journal of General Psychology* 5 (2): 262–269. https://doi.org/10.1080/00221309.1931.9918398.

Mettrie, La, and Julien Offray de. (1747) 2010. *La Mettrie's L'homme Machine: A Study in the Origins of an Idea.* Edited by Aram Vartanian. Princeton Legacy Library. Critical edition. Princeton University Press.

Lane, Rupert, Anthony Hay, Arthur Schwarz, David M. Berry, and Jeff Shrager. 2025. "ELIZA Reanimated: The World's First Chatbot Restored on the World's First Time Sharing System." arXiv:2501.06707. Preprint, arXiv, January 12. https://doi.org/10.48550/arXiv.2501.06707.

Laplace, Pierre Simon. 1902. *A Philosophical Essay on Probabilities.* Translated by Frederick Wilson Truscott and Frederick Lincoln Emory. J. Wiley.

Leeson, Peter T. 2014. *Anarchy Unbound: Why Self-Governance Works Better than You Think.* Cambridge Studies in Economics, Choice and Society. Cambridge university press.

Lenat, Douglas B. 1995. "CYC: A Large-Scale Investment in Knowledge Infrastructure." *Communications of the ACM* 38 (11): 33–38. https://doi.org/10.1145/219717.219745.

Lenat, Douglas B., and R. V. Guha. 1990. *Building Large Knowledge-Based Systems: Representation and Inference in the Cyc Project.* 1. print. Addison-Wesley.

Lenat, Douglas B., R. V. Guha, Karen Pittman, Dexter Pratt, and Mary Shepherd. 1990. "Cyc: Toward Programs with Common Sense." *Communications of the ACM* 33 (8): 30–49. https://doi.org/10.1145/79173.79176.

McCarthy, John. 1959. "Programs with Common Sense." *Proceedings of the Teddington Conference on the Mechanization of Thought Processes* (London) 1: 75–91.

McCarthy, John. 1986. "Some Expert Systems Need Common Sense." In *Computer Culture: The Scientific, Intellectual and Social Impact of the Computer*, edited by Heinz Pagels, vol. 426. Annals of the New York Academy of Sciences. New York Academy of Sciences.

McCarthy, John, Marvin L. Minsky, Nathaniel Rochester, and Claude E. Shannon. 1955. *A Proposal for the Dartmouth Summer Research Project on Artificial Intelligence*. Dartmouth College.

McCorduck, Pamela. 2018. *Machines Who Think: A Personal Inquiry into the History and Prospects of Artificial Intelligence. An A K Peters Book*. CRC Press.

McCulloch, Warren S., and Walter Pitts. 1943. "A Logical Calculus of the Ideas Immanent in Nervous Activity." *The Bulletin of Mathematical Biophysics* 5 (4): 115–133. https://doi.org/10.1007/BF02478259.

Minsky, Marvin L., and Seymour A. Papert. 1990. *Perceptrons: An Introduction to Computational Geometry*. 5th, expanded ed eds. MIT Press.

Moon, David A. 1985. "Architecture of the Symbolics 3600." *SIGARCH Computer Architecture News* 13 (3): 76–83. https://doi.org/10.1145/327070.327133.

Morgan, Clifford Thomas. 1943. *Physiological Psychology*. With Internet Archive. McGraw-Hill Book Company, inc. http://archive.org/details/physiologicalpsy00morg.

Neubauer, John. 2011. "How Did the Golem Get to Prague?" In *History of the Literary Cultures of East-Central Europe. Junctures and Disjunctures in the 19th and 20th Centuries. Volume IV: Types and Stereotypes*, edited by Peter V. Zima, vol. 66. https://onlinelibrary.wiley.com/doi/10.1111/j.1600-0730.2011.01030.x.

Neumann, John von. 1945. "First Draft of a Report on the EDVAC." Moore School of Electrical Engineering, University of Pennsylvania, June 30. https://web.mit.edu/STS.035/www/PDFs/edvac.pdf.

Neumann, John von. 1951. "The General and Logical Theory of Automata." In *Cerebral Mechanisms in Behavior: The Hixon Symposium*, edited by Lloyd A. Jeffress. Wiley.

Neumann, John von. 1967. *Theory of Self-Reproducing Automata*. Edited by Arthur W. Burks. University of Illinois Press.

Newell, Allen, J. C. Shaw, and Herbert A. Simon. 1958. "Elements of a Theory of Human Problem Solving." *Psychological Review* 65 (3): 151–166.

Newell, Allen, and Herbert A. Simon. 1956. *The Logic Theory Machine: A Complex Information Processing System*. RAND Report P-868. RAND Corporation.

Newell, Allen, and Herbert A. Simon. 1961. "Computer Simulation of Human Thinking: A Theory of Problem Solving Expressed as a Computer Program Permits Simulation of Thinking Processes." *Science* 134 (3495): 2011–2017. https://doi.org/10.1126/science.134.3495.2011.

Newell, Allen, and Herbert A. Simon. 1997. "Computer Science as Empirical Inquiry: Symbols and Search." In *Mind Design II: Philosophy, Psychology, Artificial Intelligence*, Revised and enlarged ed. MIT Press.

Olazaran, Mikel. 1996. "A Sociological Study of the Official History of the Perceptrons Controversy." *Social Studies of Science* 26 (3): 611–59.

Petracca, Enrico. 2021. "On the Origins and Consequences of Simon's Modular Approach to Bounded Rationality in Economics." *The European Journal of the History of Economic Thought* 28 (5): 708–732. https://doi.org/10.1080/09672567.2021.1877760.

Polanyi, Michael. (1966) 1983. *The Tacit Dimension*. Peter Smith.

Polanyi, Michael. 2007. *Personal Knowledge: Towards a Post-Critical Philosophy*. International Society for Science and Religion.

Raina, Rajat, Anand Madhavan, and Andrew Y. Ng. 2009. "Large-Scale Deep Unsupervised Learning Using Graphics Processors." *Proceedings of the 26th Annual International Conference on Machine Learning* (New York, NY, USA), ICML'09, June 14, 873–880. https://doi.org/10.1145/1553374.1553486.

Riskin, Jessica. 2015. *The Restless Clock: A History of the Centuries-Long Argument over What Makes Living Things Tick*. University of Chicago Press. https://doi.org/10.7208/chicago/9780226303086.001.0001.

Rosenblatt, F. 1958. "The Perceptron: A Probabilistic Model for Information Storage and Organization in the Brain." *Psychological Review* 65(6): 386–408. https://doi.org/10.1037/h0042519.

Rosenblatt, Frank. 1957. *The Perceptron: A Perceiving And Recognizing Automaton (Project PARA)*. Nos. 85–460–1. Cornell Aeronautical Laboratory. https://bpb-us-e2wpmucdn.com/websites.umass.edu/dist/a/27637/files/2016/03/rosenblatt-1957.pdf.

Rosenblatt, Frank. 1962. *Principles of Neurodynamics: Perceptrons and the Theory of Brain Mechanisms*. Spartan Books.

Rumelhart, David E., Geoffrey E. Hinton, and Ronald J. Williams. 1986. "Learning Representations by Back-Propagating Errors." *Nature* 323 (6088): 533–536. https://doi.org/10.1038/323533a0.

Schmidhuber, Jürgen. 2015. "Deep Learning in Neural Networks: An Overview." *Neural Networks* 61 (January): 85–117. https://doi.org/10.1016/j.neunet.2014.09.003.

Scott, James C. 1998. *Seeing like a State: How Certain Schemes to Improve the Human Condition Have Failed*. Yale Agrarian Studies. Yale University Press.

Shannon, Claude E. 1950. "Programming a Computer for Playing Chess." *The London, Edinburgh, and Dublin Philosophical Magazine and Journal of Science* 41 (314): 256–275. https://doi.org/10.1080/14786445008521796.

Shelley, Mary. 2018. *Frankenstein: The 1818 Text*. Penguin.

Simon, Herbert A. 1947. *Administrative Behavior: A Study of Decision-Making*. Macmillan Co.

Simon, Herbert A. 1955. "A Behavioral Model of Rational Choice." *The Quarterly Journal of Economics* 69 (1): 99–118. https://doi.org/10.2307/1884852.

Simon, Herbert A., and Allen Newell. 1958. "Heuristic Problem Solving: The next Advance in Operations Research." *Operations Research* 6 (1): 1–10.

Simon, Herbert Alexander. 1957. *Models of Man: Social and Rational—Mathematical Essays on Rational Human Behavior in a Social Setting*. Wiley.

Skinner, B. F. 1965. *Science And Human Behavior*. Free Press.

Skinner, Burrhus Frederic. 1971. *Beyond Freedom and Dignity*. Alfred A. Knopf.

Skinner, B. F. 2019. *The Behavior of Organisms: An Experimental Analysis*. B. F. Skinner Foundation.

Stefik, Mark. 1986. "The Next Knowledge Medium." *AI Magazine* 7 (1): 13.

Stringham, Edward Peter. 2015. *Private Governance: Creating Order in Economic and Social Life*. Oxford University Press.

Sutton, Rich. 2019. "The Bitter Lesson." March 13. http://www.incompleteideas.net/IncIdeas/BitterLesson.html.

Thomson, Ann. 2010. *Bodies of Thought: Science, Religion, and the Soul in the Early Enlightenment*. Reprinted. Oxford University Press.

Tuerck, David G. 1995. "Economics as Mechanism: The Mind as Machine in Hayek's Sensory Order." *Constitutional Political Economy* 6 (3): 281–292. https://doi.org/10.1007/BF01303407.

Turing, Alan M. 1936. "On Computable Numbers, with an Application to the Entscheidungsproblem." *Proceedings of the London Mathematical Society* 42 (2): 230–265.

Turing, Alan M. 1950. "Computing Machinery and Intelligence." *Mind* LIX (236): 433–460. https://doi.org/10.1093/mind/LIX.236.433.

Turing, Alan M. (1948) 1992. "Intelligent Machinery." In *Mechanical Intelligence*, by Alan M. Turing and Darrel C. Ince. Collected Works of A. M. Turing. North-Holland.

Turkle, Sherry. 1995. *Life on the Screen: Identity in the Age of the Internet*. Simon and Schuster.

Uttley, A. 1953. "Information, Machines, And Brains." *Transactions of the IRE Professional Group on Information Theory* 1 (1): 143–49. https://doi.org/10.1109/TIT.1953.1188592.

Van Den Hauwe, Ludwig M. P. 2011. "Hayek, Gödel, and the Case for Methodological Dualism." *Journal of Economic Methodology* 18 (4): 387–407. https://doi.org/10.1080/1350178X.2011.628045.

Watson, John B. 1970. *Behaviorism*. The Norton Library, N. 524. W. W. Norton & Company.

Watson, John B. 2015. *Psychology from the Standpoint of a Behaviorist—Scholar's Choice Edition*. Creative Media Partners, LLC.

Weimer, Walter B., ed. 1982. *Cognition and the Symbolic Process. 2/Hrsg. Walter B. Weimer*. Erlbaum.

Weizenbaum, Joseph. 1966. "ELIZA—a Computer Program for the Study of Natural Language Communication between Man and Machine." *Communications of the ACM* 9 (1): 36–45. https://doi.org/10.1145/365153.365168.

Weizenbaum, Joseph. 1976. *Computer Power and Human Reason: From Judgment to Calculation*. W. H. Freeman.

Werbos, Paul John. 1994. *The Roots of Backpropagation: From Ordered Derivatives to Neural Networks and Political Forecasting: 1*. Wiley-Interscience.

Witt, Stephen. 2025. *The Thinking Machine: Jensen Huang, Nvidia, And the World's Most Coveted Microchip*. Viking.

Wood, Gaby. 2002. Living Dolls: A Magical History of the Quest for Mechanical Life. Faber and Faber.

3

Artificial Intelligence as an Emergent Order

Abstract This chapter argues that modern AI systems—large language models and diffusion models—are spontaneous orders of intelligence whose capabilities emerge from scale and architecture rather than design. It traces how transformers and Mixture-of-Experts models learn high-dimensional relational structures that yield surprising abilities across language and vision. LLMs are presented as cultural world models: lossy compressions of the semantic and conceptual patterns embedded in human language, shaped but not fundamentally redesigned by post-training methods such as reinforcement learning. The chapter contends that regulatory demands for AI "interpretability" misunderstand these systems. Like market prices, LLMs compress dispersed and tacit knowledge that cannot be fully articulated. Behaviourist and mechanistic interpretability methods offer partial abstractions, but principled limits remain: the only complete account of an emergent model is the model itself.

Keywords Transformers · Large language models · Emergence · Cultural world models · Interpretability · Diffusion models · Spontaneous order · Attention mechanism · Foundation models · Tacit knowledge · Artificial intelligence

C. Berg, *Artificial Intelligence*, Palgrave Studies in Classical Liberalism,
https://doi.org/10.1007/978-3-032-22310-4_3

The large language models (LLMs) and diffusion systems that now define the AI revolution are not programmed with curated knowledge but trained on masses of data. Their capabilities emerge from their scale and architecture rather than their designers. This chapter examines what kind of intelligence has emerged from the process of decentralised adaptation. It traces how these models learn relationships in the data that give them surprising capabilities across language and vision. It argues that these models are best understood as cultural world models; that is, lossy compressions of the knowledge embedded in human civilisation.

This achievement, however, has created new challenges and fears, which we will return to across the book. If intelligence is emergent rather than designed, how do we understand what these systems are doing? And why are they making these choices they make? In many ways it is a surprising problem to have. AI is software and software is just algorithms that can, in principle, be freely replicated and examined. But the problem is a knowledge discovery problem. The chapter argues that the regulatory demands to make these models transparent—to make them 'interpretable' or 'explainable' to human users—is an error familiar to economists and classical liberals. Like prices in a market economy, model outputs compress dispersed and tacit knowledge into signals through processes that cannot be fully articulated. The demand that every output be traceable to explicit internal reasons assumes that emergent order can be reduced to designed order—that knowledge distributed across a system can be extracted and stated by a central observer. This assumption failed for economies. It is likely to fail for artificial minds.

The chapter proceeds in three parts. Section one traces how the 'transformer' architecture and its descendants learned to represent meaning through relationships rather than definitions. The emphasis is on the emergent capabilities of these models. We consider how these capabilities emerged in both natural language processing and image models. We then consider how emergent capabilities affect the demands for AI transparency. In the third section we develop the argument that foundation models are 'cultural world models'. The final section confronts the regulatory demand for interpretability, arguing that the distributed nature of this intelligence places principled limits on how much can be rendered legible.

3.1 Emergence and Discovery in Foundation Models

The connectionist research programme described in the previous chapter had established the theoretical foundations for learning systems. Yet AI researchers lacked the computational resources to demonstrate its potential. By the 2010s, general processing units (GPUs) started to provide the computational power that the connectionists had always lacked. In retrospect, the next decade of neural network research looks like an inexorable march towards modern AI.

In 2017 a group of researchers published the paper "Attention Is All You Need" (Vaswani et al. 2017), which established what is known as the 'transformer architecture'. Transformers embody the discovery paradigm in its purest form yet. Neural networks had been used for natural language processing for some time, but historically they processed data sequentially. Such an approach is like reading a sentence word by word in order, which has the unfortunate effect of making these systems slow and forgetful over long spans of text. When humans read, they do not form their understanding solely from the words in sequence. The semantic meaning of a sentence is formed from the full context of the other words within, as well as the surrounding context. The meaning of 'bank', for example, depends on whether the surrounding words concern rivers or money. As the linguist Firth (1957, 11) famously wrote, "You shall know a word by the company it keeps". With a naïve sequential reading, the longer the sentence the more severe the semantic loss. The achievement of the transformer architecture was to understand words in context, not just as a sequence—to discover the contextual meaning of words among their surroundings.

A transformer model does not process words as static dictionary entries—it considers them relationally. First, transformers break the input text down into an ordered sequence of 'tokens'. Tokens might be whole words, parts of words, or even single characters. The token is the raw sensory input before it has been classified. Just as a single neural impulse has no meaning until it is placed in a network of other impulses, a token is semantically empty until the model determines its relationship to every other token. Each token is then converted into a vector: a list of numbers that locates it in a kind of meaning-space, where proximity to other vectors indicates similarity. This initial placement is provisional. It will shift as the model works out how the token relates to everything else in the input. The transformer uses a mechanism called 'self-attention' to update these representations in parallel. For each token, attention calculates how relevant every other token in the sequence is to its meaning, then adjusts its vector accordingly—pulling it closer to related tokens, pushing it away from irrelevant ones. How does the model know which tokens should attract and which should repel? This is governed by parameters: numerical values, learned during training, that encode what the model has discovered about how words relate to one another. The architecture is named for its capacity to *transform* the representation. What enters as a context-free placeholder ends up in a position in a web of relationships.

In this way, a transformer model does not maintain a single, traceable line of reasoning but pursues multiple interpretive threads simultaneously. While the authors of "Attention is all you need" defined a single attention mechanism ('head'), they argued that a single head was insufficient because it limited the model to focusing on one specific *type* of relationship at a time. They introduced 'multi-head' attention—multiple parallel attention mechanisms, each free to learn its own way of relating tokens to one another. For example, consider how difficult it is for a program to interpret the sentence: "After the program erased the entire database, the lead engineer muttered, 'Great job, everyone.'" To navigate the sarcasm in this simple sentence, the model must resolve a conflict between the literal words and the situational reality. One attention head might focus on syntax, linking "Great job" to "everyone" to establish who is being addressed. A second head must focus on tone. This second head detects the dissonance between the positive phrase ("Great job") and the negative context (the database erasure), re-encoding the vector for "Great job" as sarcastic rather than sincere. By maintaining these as separate heads, the model does not have to choose between the grammatical structure (a compliment) and the intent (an insult). Instead, it can capture the layered complexity of human speech where we often say one thing to mean another.

The transformer is a mathematical realisation of a Hayekian relational order for semantics. In a transformer, a word has no static global meaning. It only has local, contextual meaning. Its vector representation is dynamically updated by calculating its relationship to every other token in the sequence simultaneously. The transformer's multi-head attention allows the model to classify a single input through various interpretive subspaces at once (akin to Hayek 1952's concept of "multiple classification") constructing a composite meaning derived purely from relationships rather than intrinsic definitions. The original model described in "Attention is all you need" proposed eight parallel attention heads. But, crucially, the eight attention heads did not have specific roles. The engineers did not program Head 1 to look for grammar and Head 2 to look for synonyms. Rather, they were eight blank, randomised 'slots'. It is for the model to figure out how to use those slots during training. Specialisation in these transformer heads is emergent, not designed.

However, the transformer's relational power came with a severe computational penalty. Every single parameter must be activated to process every single token. As models grew to contain billions of parameters, this became grossly inefficient—like a brain needing to fire every single neuron just to process a simple thought.

The solution to this computational inefficiency has come from an additional layer of specialisation and classification. Mixture of experts architectures replace a monolithic neural network with a collection of specialised sub-networks ('experts'), controlled by a router. While the mixture of experts architecture dates back to the early 1990s (Jacobs et al. 1991)—another example of neural network theory outpacing hardware—it was revitalised in the deep learning era (notably in Shazeer et al. 2017). An expert here is simply a cluster of parameters that the model has found useful for processing specific types of patterns. For example, during training, the router might notice that the tokens

"DNA," "mitochondria," and "enzyme" frequently appear in similar contexts. To save compute costs, it begins routing all such queries to one 'expert' where those concepts are clustered. Simultaneously, it might route structural tokens like "however," "although," and "therefore" to another expert. The specialization is emergent. The model designers do not define the experts as the "Biology Expert" or the "Grammar Expert" respectively. They are clusters of expertise spontaneously discovered in the process of training.

Once again, this mixture of experts architecture mirrors the cognitive specialisation that Hayek described in *The Sensory Order*. For Hayek, the map is the semi-permanent apparatus of classification—the total inventory of all possible connections the organism *could* make based on its history. However, Hayek argued that an organism cannot activate its entire map at once. As he wrote,

> We should have to think of the whole system of connexions as consisting of many vertically superimposed sub-systems which in some respects may operate independently of each other. Every sub-system of this kind will constitute a partial map of the environment, and the maps formed at the lower levels will serve for the guidance of merely a limited range of responses, and at the same time act as filters or preselectors for the impulses sent on to the higher centres (Hayek 1952,111).

The mixture of experts router performs this function. The map is the totality of all experts, representing the system's vast potential knowledge. The router selects a specific path, activating only the relevant experts to form a model of the current context.

What researchers discovered, almost immediately, was that transformer-based systems exhibited capabilities that had not been explicitly trained. OpenAI's GPT series, beginning with the release of GPT-1 (Radford et al. 2018), took the basic transformer design, trained it on a dataset of 7,000 self-published books, and gave it a simple objective: predict the next token in a sequence. Nothing in this setup suggested general capability. The first surprise came with scale. With this same basic architecture the much larger GPT-2 and GPT-3 could summarise documents, answer factual questions, write code, and generate coherent essays. None of these capabilities had been explicit training objectives (Brown et al. 2020). More strikingly, these capabilities could be summoned through prompting alone. The models had figured out how to shape their response according to examples provided in user prompts. This was a behaviour nobody designed (Min et al. 2022).

There were two other surprises about the nature of the emergent knowledge. The capability increase was discontinuous. Researchers found that certain capabilities such as arithmetic, word unscrambling, multi-step reasoning did not improve gradually. They were absent below a threshold, then suddenly present above it (Wei et al. 2022; Berti et al. 2025; Srivastava et al. 2023). A model with ten billion parameters might fail entirely at a task that a model with a hundred billion parameters could perform competently. Rather than seeing a smooth curve towards practical intelligence, intelligence emerged in sudden step-changes. Another surprise was that the resulting models spontaneously learned ordered representations (such as days of the week in order and repeating, integers forming number lines) despite receiving no explicit information about these representations (Ameisen and Batson 2024; Gould et al. 2023). The model inferred the latent structure of knowledge from the simple statistical relationships within the training data.

As models have grown larger, emergent intelligence has become more pronounced. A team at OpenAI (Kaplan et al. 2020) documented what they called "scaling laws": empirical regularities showing that model performance improves predictably with increases in parameters, training data, and compute. With the release of GPT-4 in early 2023, these capabilities were increasingly obvious. One famous example asked GPT-4 to draw a picture of a unicorn using TiKZ (a LaTeX-based drawing language). Not only did GPT-4 understand the concept of a unicorn and produce an abstract representation using code—a significant leap from its predecessors, which struggled with such tasks—but it could do so without being able to visualise the result. The LLM had to *imagine* what code would output something that would resemble a unicorn to a human viewer (Bubeck et al. 2023).

Firms creating closed weight LLMs (such as OpenAI, Google and Anthropic) have provided limited details on how their most capable models are trained, but Meta's Llama models are open weight—which means the raw model with its encompassed weights are publicly available for distribution and use. Meta has also released a detailed explanation of the process by which the Llama models were built (Touvron et al. 2023; Dubey et al. 2024; for the GPT models see OpenAI 2023; for the Claude models see Anthropic 2024). Meta describes training a model in two stages. The first stage is 'pre-training'. This involves training the model on a massive quantity of supervised data largely scraped from the internet. The pre-training data is selected, not random. As well as trying to increase data quality (for example, by reducing duplication which might cause over-fitting) the data is selected for capabilities (emphasising computer code samples to boost programming capability) and for 'safety' (removing data that might be pornographic or instructions on how to commit criminal acts). The Llama 3 model is trained on a dataset of 15.6 trillion tokens—roughly 62 trillion characters.

The resulting pre-trained models have deep emergent properties of intelligence but are not optimised for interaction with human users. For example, LLMs at this stage do not helpfully respond to user requests or questions. They simply output a next token prediction on the input text. The next stage is post-training, where the model is fine-tuned according to the preferences of the designers. In this stage the designers direct the model to be useful by (for example) training it with a smaller dataset of examples of conversational engagements and reinforcement learning, sometimes using direct human feedback (Ouyang et al. 2022; Rafailov et al. 2024).

These two distinct stages—undifferentiated training on a diverse and massive dataset, followed by fine-tuning and reinforcement learning—gives the LLMs their character. It is difficult to reason about the economic and information characteristics of LLMs from first principles because these two separate stages have complex interactions. In practice, model designers have described 'coaxing' their models to produce desired behaviour. The many highly publicised examples of unpredictable behaviour, such as the oddly aggressive persona of Microsoft's 'Sydney' on Bing Chat (Vincent 2023) illustrate how the practice of imposing behavioural characteristics onto a next token prediction model can be difficult. (We tackle the question of this sort of AI 'alignment' in Chap. 7).

One big problem is how to ensure that the broad depth of knowledge and capabilities embodied in unsupervised trained models is maintained during post-training, which itself needs to be effective for the models to be usable. Model designers need to ensure that the capabilities that are discovered in the first stage are not undermined by the refinements of the second stage. Each stage of training involves curation and selection. The first stage consists of the choice of data sets; an increasingly painstaking process that selects for the sort of behaviours (i.e. coding) which the model developers are trying to optimise. The second stage often involves the creation of additional LLMs which can interact with and provide additional training the larger LLM.

The emergent properties of artificial intelligence are not limited to language. The same years that saw the GPT class models demonstrate unexpected linguistic capabilities also witnessed a parallel revolution in image generation, one that revealed the phenomenon to be more general. Neural networks trained on images demonstrated the same emergent capabilities from scale.

Indeed, first big milestone for modern neural networks was in image recognition. The ImageNet challenge was a competition that started in 2010 to classify 1.2 million images into categories like dogs, cars, furniture, plants, and so on (Russakovsky et al. 2015). The dominant approach to image classification at the time was encoding human knowledge about visual perception into algorithms (Lowe 2004). For example, researchers would tell the program that edges, gradients, and orientation patterns were important in understanding images, and then the machine would be left to detect and classify those features. But in September 2012, a deep neural network called AlexNet (Krizhevsky et al. 2012) won the ImageNet challenge by learning directly from pixels. It discovered what mattered for image recognition rather than being told beforehand. This marked the moment when the field recognised that scale and learning could achieve what design and specification could not.

Another major breakthrough came with the rise of image diffusion models (Sohl-Dickstein et al. 2015; Rombach et al. 2022). A diffusion model starts with pure visual noise and learns, step by step, how to remove that noise in a way that reveals meaningful imagery. Thus a user can provide a fantastical prompt like "a photograph of an astronaut riding a horse" and get an image that depicts exactly that, despite the fact nobody has explicitly programmed the model with knowledge of what astronauts or horses look like, what riding is, what a photograph is, or how to compose a rider on a horse. One of the most striking features of even the first image diffusion models was that they had remarkably consistent lighting, with accurate shadows and reflections. Image generators also learned artistic styles without being taught art history, grasped spatial relationships without instruction in geometry, and captured the "feel" of different photographic genres without being explicit trained to do so. When Stability AI released Stable Diffusion in August 2022 with open weights and permissive licensing, the subsequent explosion of experimentation revealed capabilities the original developers had not anticipated: consistent character generation, architectural styles, and seamless reconstruction of damaged photographs (Rombach et al. 2022).

These image models shared with language models the same ability to uncover semantic structures in their training data. Image models could reproduce something recognisably 'in the style of' living creators—not by copying specific works but by capturing statistical regularities across an artist's corpus. The models had learned what made a particular artist's work distinctive, such as their characteristic colour palettes, compositional tendencies, or brushwork patterns. And this knowledge was distributed across billions of parameters, recoverable only through interaction with the AI model. OpenAI's CLIP model, trained on hundreds of millions of image-text pairs, learned to align visual and linguistic representations in a shared embedding space (Radford et al. 2021). The relationships between concepts that word embeddings captured—king to queen, Paris to France—had visual counterparts, which means that we can use language to guide image generation. Similar principles extended to speech, video, and music generation. In each domain a sufficiently large neural network trained on sufficiently rich data yields emergent capabilities far beyond the objective of the training.

3.2 Emergent Intelligence as Cultural World Models

One popular way to think about image and language models is that they are lossy compressions of the data on which they are trained (Delétang et al. 2024). Like a compressed file that approximates—but does not perfectly replicate—its original data, the models discard idiosyncratic details from their training set while uncovering statistical patterns that enable plausible generation. Crucially, the lossy nature of this process means that AI cannot 'decompress' back to their training data. They are one-directional. Their outputs are synthetic reconstructions of cultural and linguistic patterns, filtered through the geometric relationships of high-dimensional vector spaces (Mikolov et al. 2013).

But what is an AI model trained on the output of human civilisation actually compressing? The answer is not merely 'language' or 'iconography' in some narrow syntactic sense. Language encodes concepts, relationships, causal theories, social norms, historical knowledge, and the tacit understandings that enable human coordination. When a transformer model learns to predict the next token in a sequence, it must—to succeed at that task—capture something of the conceptual structures that generated those sequences in the first place. LLMs trained on human language are not merely compressing text but compressing the cultural knowledge embedded within that text (Lu 2025).

In the field of artificial intelligence research 'world models' are a class of models that learn representations of *physical reality*—spatial environments, intuitive physics, object dynamics, and cause-and-effect in three-dimensional space. Such models are trained typically from massive amounts of video. Like all the neural network models we have discussed, their knowledge about the spatial structure and temporal dynamics arises spontaneously through training (Ha and Schmidhuber 2018; see also Andreas 2024). The promise of world models is illustrated most clearly in systems where the latent structure is hidden (Li et al. 2024). OpenAI's video generation model Sora has shown knowledge about three-dimensional consistency, long-range coherence, and object permanence "without any explicit inductive biases for 3D, objects, etc.—they are purely phenomena of scale" (OpenAI 2024). Google similarly emphasises that its videogame generator Genie 3 also has physical consistency as "an emergent capability" (Google DeepMind 2025).

We can think of LLMs as *cultural* world models. Where Genie 3 undercovers then compresses pixels into latent physics, an LLM compresses the accumulated semiotic interpretations of reality (Taniguchi et al. 2025). Written language compresses and interprets the human sensory and social experience into text. A trained model further compresses and embeds the human linguistic corpus into a high-dimensional vector space. Hence Jason Potts (2024) argues that LLMs are "embeddings of embeddings". The training data for a video-based world model like Genie 3 is raw environmental observation. The training data for an LLM is the output of millions of human meaning-making acts already filtered through the compression of language. What emerges from training is not a model of how objects move through space, but a model of how concepts relate to each other in the semiotic universe humans have constructed. The 'physics' that is being learned by natural language processing models is the physics of meaning—the regularities governing how humans use words to coordinate, explain, persuade, and understand.

Whether these models can be seen to be a genuine 'world models' in the sense of a representation of reality is highly contested. Richard Sutton (2025) has argued that a world model should predict consequences. It should predict that if an agent takes action X, then outcome Y will follow. Such predictions can be verified against reality. (This is, we might note, the point of the 'model' in Hayek's *Sensory Order*—a prediction given the input and the map, that is corrected by experience.) LLMs, by contrast, predict what humans would *say*. But saying is not the same as happening. LLMs learn from 'here's a situation, and here's what a person did' rather than from trying things and observing consequences. For Sutton, intelligence requires goals that define success and predictions that can be falsified by what actually occurs. LLMs have neither. They compress human *testimony* about the world rather than the causal structure of the world itself.

But the question of whether LLMs are genuine world models may be ill-posed. John Hartley and Jason Potts (2014) argue that cultural knowledge is irreducibly different from physical knowledge. Cultural knowledge exists only in distributed, semiotic form. There is no 'ground truth' about meaning independent of human meaning-making practices. If this is correct, then demanding that LLMs model causal reality directly may misunderstand what cultural intelligence *is*. Cultural world models are inherently distributed. They emerge from group-level processes where, as Hartley and Potts (2014, 184) argue, "culture makes groups and groups make knowledge". An LLM trained on human text internalises patterns that emerged from millions of distributed cognitive acts across societies, time periods, and linguistic communities. In compressing this corpus, the LLM is not modelling a physical world but the semiotic infrastructure through which human societies organise collective understanding.

Indeed, the training corpus of a modern LLM is *itself* a kind of spontaneous order—the accumulated written output of millions of individuals, produced for countless different purposes, coordinated by no central authority. While the corpus is deliberately assembled by the AI labs, the cultural content of the corpus is not. That content emerged from the decentralised decisions of writers, publishers, and platforms over decades. At scale, these embeddings become a compressed map of the conceptual terrain that human civilisation has explored (Potts 2024).

In this light, the claim that LLM intelligence is emergent needs an important qualifer. The two-stage training process described above (unsupervised pretraining on massive corpora followed by fine-tuning) introduces deliberate human judgment by the designers of the model into the system. A model trained purely on next-token prediction does not answer questions, follow instructions, or engage in dialogue—it simply continues text sequences in statistically plausible ways. This is the process of training models "to act in accordance with user intentions" (Ouyang et al. 2022) using human preferences to guide model outputs toward helpfulness, harmlessness, and honesty. The AI safety mechanisms which we will discuss in Chap. 8 provide another example. This is not emergence but optimisation toward specified objectives.

Yet research by Anthropic on model behaviour has revealed that the deliberate and *designed* post-training reinforcement does not necessarily change the underlying model. Instead, it creates what might be understood as a behavioural layer on top. And techniques like 'many-shot jailbreaking,' where sufficiently long user prompts override safety training, end up revealing the unvarnished capabilities of the pre-trained model underneath. The implication is that post-training shapes user access to the model's capabilities rather than fundamentally altering the underlying representations. The model retains knowledge it has been trained not to express. This suggests a distinction between capability emergence and behavioural shaping. The core capabilities of LLMs—their world knowledge, reasoning patterns, and linguistic competence—emerge from pretraining in the manner the scaling laws literature documents (Kaplan et al. 2020; Rae et al. 2022). Post-training channels these emergent capabilities toward human-preferred outputs without making the underlying representations legible. Just as market orders emerge spontaneously yet operate within deliberately designed institutional frameworks such as property rights and contract law, the emergent intelligence of LLMs operate within the behavioural constraints imposed by post-training.

A popular meme depicts LLMs as the Shoggoths in the mythology of the weird fiction writer H. P. Lovecraft (1936). Shoggoths are vast, shape-shifting masses of living protoplasm engineered by the alien Elder Things that control the planet Earth as tireless slave labour. Able to sprout eyes, mouths, and limbs at will, and endure the deep sea and polar cold, they embody a nightmare of tools that outgrow all control and ultimately, silently, turn upon their makers. (We pick up the risk of AI takeover in Chap. 8). The meme usually shows the horrifying, gelatinous body of a Shoggoth wearing a little smiley face mask. Labels on the meme indicate the Shoggoth's alien body as the pre-training stage of the model. The smiley face is the post-training; presenting this horrifying alien as friendly and useful.

The meme captures at least two important points about the nature of AI models. First, their underlying pre-trained intelligence is not a human intelligence despite being trained on human data. The model has learned patterns from the cultural corpus of humanity, but the computational substrate that encodes these patterns bears no resemblance to the human cognition that we are used to. Its learned representations, the mechanisms by which it retrieves and combines information, the absence of embodiment, emotion, or temporal experience—all mark it as genuinely different. It has absorbed human culture without becoming human. Second, the models are deliberately adjusted to appear more human. The smiley face represents a deliberate engineering effort to make the model's outputs legible, helpful, and aligned with human expectations. The intelligence beneath is channelled through an interface designed for human experience—a translation layer between the emergent complexity of the pretrained model and the conversational norms humans expect.

3.3 The Problem of Interpretability

The inscrutable character of this intelligence poses a challenge for those who would seek to understand it: how do you interpret a system whose knowledge was never designed to be legible in the first place? This question has become central to AI regulation.

Since 2016, many governments have converged on the principle that artificial intelligence must be explainable. The Obama administration called for research into 'explainable AI' to build public trust (Executive Office of the President, National Science and Technology Council, and Committee on Technology 2016). The European Union's General Data Protection Regulation, which came into force in 2018, introduced what has been interpreted as an implicit right to explanation: individuals must receive "meaningful information about the logic involved" when significant decisions are made by algorithms (Regulation (EU) 2016/679 of the European Parliament and of the Council of 27 April 2016 on the Protection of Natural Persons with Regard to the Processing of Personal

Data and on the Free Movement of Such Data, and Repealing Directive 95/46/EC (General Data Protection Regulation) 2016).

The European Union's AI Act, proposed in 2021, represents the most ambitious attempt to encode these principles into binding law. High-risk AI systems must ensure "sufficient transparency to enable users to interpret the system's output" (Regulation (EU) 2024/1689 of the European Parliament and of the Council of 13 June 2024 Laying down Harmonised Rules on Artificial Intelligence and Amending Certain Union Legislative Acts (Artificial Intelligence Act) 2024). The United States, while lacking comprehensive legislation, has moved in the same direction through sectoral enforcement. The Consumer Financial Protection Bureau warned in 2022 that "companies are not absolved of their legal responsibilities when they let a black-box model make decisions" (Consumer Financial Protection Bureau 2022). But this principle assumes that explanation is possible—that the knowledge encoded in these systems exists in a form that could, with sufficient effort, be rendered legible.

If the intelligence in artificial intelligence is emergent, then it suffers from the same opacity as other emergent orders. Consider the price system. Hayek's (1945) point about the price system was that it communicates dispersed knowledge that no single mind possesses. In this sense a price is a compression algorithm that strips away 'why' (the tacit, imaginative context) and transmits only the 'what' (the signal of relative scarcity). While a market price appears to be a precise, objective data point, its origins are rooted in a cognitive and systemic opacity that defies explanation. The economist Scott Sumner is fond of saying "never reason from a price change" (Sumner 2010). Prices for goods might have gone up because they have become harder to produce, or maybe they went up because they became more popular? The 'un-interpretability' of prices is a result of how economic knowledge is constituted and compressed.

The inscrutability of the price signal begins within the individual mind. Human knowledge is fundamentally tacit (Polanyi [1966] 1983). When individuals value something, they draw on background knowledge and awareness that cannot be explicitly articulated. There is no deeper 'transcript' of the decision-making process to audit, because the knowledge that informs an individual's valuation was never symbolic to begin with Shackle (1979) deepens this epistemological difficulty by locating the origin of valuation not in the observable present, but in the future. A choice to buy or sell is not a calculation about costs and benefits, but an imaginative act. Value is derived from the "Imagined, deemed Possible" (Shackle 1979, 26) where the individual projects a "skein of rival possibilities" (Shackle 1979, 9) into non-existent time. Because a price springs from the private imaginations of economic participants, it cannot be 'explained' by looking for objective cause and effect in the economy.

Consequently, any attempt to reverse-engineer a price to find its underlying logic is a category error. The 'data' required to explain a price does not exist prior to the market process (Lavoie 1985). Where goods are distributed throughout the economy is a result of exchange. The exchange *creates* the information rather than revealing pre-existing truths about where they should be allocated (Buchanan 1982). To demand an explanation of a price is to demand a history of data that never existed in static form. Indeed, in Armen Alchian's (1950) reframing, a price may be the result of a blind evolutionary filter, meaning that even the entrepreneur who set the price may not know why it worked. The market does not require agents to understand the reasons for their success; the economic environment simply adopts those behaviours that fit.

We have dwelled on the problems of price interpretability because they provide a clear comparison with the challenge of AI interpretability or 'explainability'. The field of explainable AI has developed two broad strategies for rendering neural networks legible: the behaviourist approach and a cognitive approach.

The behaviourist approach, which has parallels to the behavioural psychology discussed in Chap. 2, treats the neural network as a black box and tries to infer its logic by interacting with it from the outside. These methods experimentally vary prompts and inputs to see how outputs change as a result (Ribeiro et al. 2016; Lundberg and Lee 2017). For example, if we want to know why a model denied a loan application to a borrower, we might slightly alter the applicant's income, age, or credit history and see which changes most affect the decision. From this pattern of responses, the method constructs a simple approximation—

a kind of sketch that says 'income mattered this much, credit history mattered that much.' This is then presented as the explanation for the model's decision.

But at best this 'explanation' is really just a compressed description of behavioural regularities. It is an *interpretation*. It is not an *explanation* of why the model came to any particular decision. The behavioural approach functions more like a simplified scientific model than a genuine explanation for behaviour in the everyday sense (Mittelstadt et al. 2019). Behaviourial tools are useful for probing and stress-testing systems, but they are not transparent accounts of the model's real reasons for their choices—in part because models don't have 'reasons' in the way that humans understand the term.

There are more several more difficulties with the behaviourist approach to interpretability. For example, one finding shows that some explanation techniques produce visually convincing results even when the model's learned knowledge is scrambled or removed entirely—suggesting they reveal more about the structure of the input data than about the model's actual reasoning (Adebayo et al. 2020). And behavioural methods can be strategically gamed. Adversaries can deliberately construct biased classifiers that nonetheless produce innocent-looking explanations (Slack et al. 2020). Nonetheless the behaviourist approach dominates the discussion of explainable AI (Linardatos et al. 2020; Ali et al. 2023).

Ultimately the behavioural approach risks creating a sort of explanation theatre that satisfies regulatory requirements on the surface but does not deliver meaningful explanations for how models arrive at decisions. Different explanation methods applied to the same model and prediction routinely disagree. This just raises the question of which, if any, explanation should be regarded as authoritative (Gunasekaran et al. 2024; Ganesh et al. 2025).

The second strategy to achieve AI interpretability, the *cognitive* or *mechanistic* approach, is more ambitious. It tries to open the black box and to reverse-engineer how neural networks function internally. The hope is that researchers can identify internal "parts" that correspond to human-intelligible concepts, and trace how those parts interact to produce a given output (Olah et al. 2020; Nanda et al. 2023). The best-known version of this approach is the "Circuits" research program (Olah et al. 2020). Circuits looks at a trained network like a brain under a microscope. Researchers probe individual neurons or attention heads, they search for the patterns that excite them, and then study how these units are wired together. This work has uncovered small, reasonably self-contained mechanisms—the circuits—that implement simple algorithms such as edge detection in vision models or "induction heads" that copy patterns forward in transformer language models.

The modest successes of programs like Circuits promise a kind of AI neurology. Perhaps we might, in time, be able to decompose an entire network into comprehensible circuits. But they have also exposed complex learning behaviours in neural networks that frustrate this ambition. For example, they have found that in both vision models and language models, many neurons are *polysemantic*: the same neuron fires for multiple, apparently unrelated concepts. A single neuron might activate for dog faces, car wheels and handwritten digits, or, in language models, for academic citations, pieces of computer code and Korean text. This appears to be a rational strategy to maximise learning in scarce space. When a network wants to represent more features than it has neurons, it packs multiple features into overlapping directions in activation space (Elhage et al. 2022; Cowsik et al. 2024; Lecomte et al. 2024).

This complexity is unsurprising of course, because in the connectionist framework it is not neurons which are the natural units of explanation—it is the distribution and patterns that creates meaning. Recent research therefore shifts the focus from individual neurons to *features*: directions in activation space that can be linearly combined to reconstruct what the model is doing. To find these features, researchers use a tool called a sparse autoencoder. Think of this as an 'unbundling' mechanism. It analyses the model's complex activity and attempts to reconstruct it using a dictionary of simple components. The tool is incentivised to use the fewest possible components to explain the activity. The "Towards Monosemanticity" project uses sparse autoencoders to decompose messy, overlapping activations into thousands of rarely active features that are closer to being one-concept-per-feature (Bricken et al. 2023). Follow-up work by Anthropic, OpenAI and others has scaled these methods the large Claude and GPT-class systems, and shows that such autoencoders can recover features that align with recognisable concepts (DuPlessie 2024; Cunningham et al. 2023; Templeton et al. 2024). Researchers can then generate 'feature visualisations'—synthetic images of the inputs that most strongly activate a feature. This acts as a visual audit, providing a sketch of what any given feature represents.

But, as with the behavioural approach, mechanistic interpretability has been hard to realise. First, many features remain statistically active but semantically meaningless to humans. The goal of interpretability isn't simply to identify what features are activated. It is to translate those patterns of activations into human-understandable *explanations*. Second, the 'interpretable' features often lack robustness. Seemingly clear features can dissolve or split into incoherent parts under different training runs. Finally, visualisations often fail the test of causality. A feature might arguably *correlate* with a visual concept (like a 'dog snout'), yet fail to predict how the model behaves when that input is manipulated (the dog's snout is rotated). When this happens it suggests that the 'visualisation' was capturing a spurious correlation rather than the true causal mechanism driving the model. Other work shows that standard visualisation pipelines can be tricked into showing arbitrary patterns that bear little relation to the model's behaviour on natural inputs and that some modern architectures may actually be *less* mechanistically interpretable than older ones (Geirhos et al. 2024). In practice, we are a very long way from having anything like a wiring diagram for state-of-the-art models (Sharkey et al. 2025; Bereska and Gavves 2024).

How much do these interpretability limitations matter? In one important sense interpretability requirements demand from level of transparency from artificial systems that we do not - and *cannot* - demand from human systems. For example, when a (human) loan officer declines an application or a judge passes sentence, we accept that a verbal rationale is adequate: 'the applicant's debt-to-income ratio was too high,' or 'the severity of the offence warranted a custodial term'. We do not demand that the judge or loan officer share a complete causal trace from their sensory input through neural activation to their motor output. Human explanations are compressed summaries. They are institutionally useful but always causally incomplete. Indeed, people have strikingly limited introspective access to the cognitive processes that actually generate their judgments (Nisbett and Wilson 1977). They offer reasons, but those reasons are post-hoc reconstructions rather than explanations. Regulators asking for concrete interpretability from AI decisions are implicitly holding the technology to a stricter standard than humans. The scrutiny being proposed exceeds what we have ever achieved for the human systems we already trust with consequential decisions.

The most faithful description of what a frontier model 'knows' is the model itself: its architecture, its weights, and the corpus on which it was trained. Any attempt to compress the model further into human-readable rules will lose fidelity. The sci-fi novelist Chiang (2023) influentially described LLMs as a 'blurry JPEG' of the web. If this metaphor holds, then an explanation of the model is a compression of a compression. An explanation will be blurrier still. As Hayek observed, to predict in full detail what a rat will do, one would need to construct a replica with the same neural architecture and experiential history, then place it in an identical environment (see Chap. 2). The replica would be the only complete model of the original—anything less than that complete history would discard information. The same logic applies to LLMs. The demand for interpretability is a demand for a human-readable summary of a system that is itself already a summary. Each layer of abstraction sacrifices information that cannot be recovered.

The tools of interpretability can illuminate the underlying work of the model but they cannot replace the distributed representations that make the system work. The success of deep learning is precisely its abandonment of hand-coded symbolic rules in favour of learned, high-dimensional encodings that no rulebook can recapitulate. In spontaneous orders we do not demand that every participant disclose the micro-level logic of their decisions. Of course, partial insight is better than none, and the tools being developed may yet prove essential for detecting dangerous capabilities before deployment. But the dream of producing a human-readable account of everything the model knows and why is likely to remain unfulfilled. The same distributed representations that make these systems powerful make them resistant to the kind of decomposition that regulators imagine.

This does not leave us helpless. We do not fully understand human cognition either, yet we have built institutions—courts, markets, professions, democratic accountability—that channel human intelligence toward productive ends and limit its capacity for harm. The question is not whether we can explain artificial intelligence but whether we can design frameworks that harness its capabilities while managing its risks.

References

Adebayo, Julius, Justin Gilmer, Michael Muelly, Ian Goodfellow, Moritz Hardt, and Been Kim. 2020. "Sanity Checks for Saliency Maps". Preprint, arXiv, November 6. https://doi.org/10.48550/arXiv.1810.03292.

Alchian, Armen A. 1950. "Uncertainty, Evolution, and Economic Theory". *The Journal of Political Economy* 58(3):211–221.

Ali, Sajid, Tamer Abuhmed, Shaker El-Sappagh, et al. 2023. "Explainable Artificial Intelligence (XAI): What We Know and What Is Left to Attain Trustworthy Artificial Intelligence". *Information Fusion* 99(November): 101805. https://doi.org/10.1016/j.inffus.2023.101805.

Ameisen, Emmanuel, and Joshua Batson. 2024. *Investigating Successor Heads*. Circuits Updates. *Anthrophic*. https://transformer-circuits.pub/2024/september-update/index.html#successor-heads.

Andreas, Jacob. 2024. "Jacob Andreas: Language, Grounding, and World Models". Interview by Daniel Bashir. October 10. The Gradient: Perspectives on AI. https://thegradientpub.substack.com/p/jacob-andreas-language-grounding-world-models.

Anthropic. 2024. *The Claude 3 Model Family: Opus, Sonnet, Haiku*. https://www-cdn.anthropic.com/de8ba9b01c9ab7cbabf5c33b80b7bbc618857627/Model_Card_Claude_3.pdf.

Bereska, Leonard, and Efstratios Gavves. 2024. "Mechanistic Interpretability for AI Safety—A Review". arXiv:2404.14082. Preprint, arXiv, August 23. https://doi.org/10.48550/arXiv.2404.14082.

Berti, Leonardo, Flavio Giorgi, and Gjergji Kasneci. 2025. Emergent Abilities in Large Language Models: A Survey. arXiv:2503.05788. Preprint, arXiv, March 14. https://doi.org/10.48550/arXiv.2503.05788.

Bricken, Trenton, Adly Templeton, Joshua Batson, et al. 2023. *Towards Monosemanticity: Decomposing Language Models With Dictionary Learning.* Transformer Circuits Thread. Anthropic. https://transformer-circuits.pub/2023/monosemantic-features/.

Brown, Tom B., Benjamin Mann, Nick Ryder, et al. 2020. "Language Models are Few-Shot Learners". *Proceedings of the 34th International Conference on Neural Information Processing Systems* (Red Hook, NY, USA), NIPS'20, December 6, 1877–901.

Brooks, Tim, Bill Peebles, Connor Holmes, et al. 2024. "Video Generation Models as World Simulators". OpenAI, February 15. https://openai.com/index/video-generation-models-as-world-simulators/.

Bubeck, Sébastien, Varun Chandrasekaran, Ronen Eldan, et al. 2023. "Sparks of Artificial General Intelligence: Early Experiments with GPT-4". arXiv:2303.12712. Preprint, arXiv, April 13. https://doi.org/10.48550/arXiv.2303.12712.

Buchanan, James M. 1982. "Order Defined in the Process of Its Emergence". *Literature of Liberty: A Review of Contemporary Liberal Thought* 5(4):7–58.

Chiang, Ted. 2023. "ChatGPT Is a Blurry JPEG of the Web". *The New Yorker*, February 23. https://archive.md/PTL7r.

Consumer Financial Protection Bureau. 2022. "CFPB Acts to Protect the Public from Black-Box Credit Models Using Complex Algorithms". May 26. https://www.consumerfinance.gov/about-us/newsroom/cfpb-acts-to-protect-the-public-from-black-box-credit-models-using-complex-algorithms/.

Cowsik, Aditya, Kfir Dolev, and Alex Infanger. 2024. "The Persian Rug: Solving Toy Models of Superposition Using Large-Scale Symmetries". arXiv:2410.12101. Preprint, arXiv, October 22. https://doi.org/10.48550/arXiv.2410.12101.

Cunningham, Hoagy, Aidan Ewart, Logan Riggs, Robert Huben, and Lee Sharkey. 2023. "Sparse Autoencoders Find Highly Interpretable Features in Language Models". arXiv:2309.08600. Preprint, arXiv, October 4. https://doi.org/10.48550/arXiv.2309.08600.

Delétang, Grégoire, Anian Ruoss, Paul-Ambroise Duquenne, et al. 2024. "Language Modeling is Compression". arXiv:2309.10668. Preprint, arXiv, March 18. https://doi.org/10.48550/arXiv.2309.10668.

Dubey, Abhimanyu, Abhinav Jauhri, Abhinav Pandey, et al. 2024. "The Llama 3 Herd of Models". arXiv:2407.21783. Preprint, arXiv, August 15. https://doi.org/10.48550/arXiv.2407.21783.

DuPlessie, Caden. 2024. *Sparse Autoencoders for Interpretability in Reinforcement Learning*. MIT PRIMES. https://math.mit.edu/research/highschool/primes/materials/2024/DuPlessie.pdf.

Elhage, Nelson, Tristan Hume, Catherine Olsson, et al. 2022. "Toy Models of Superposition". arXiv:2209.10652. Preprint, arXiv, September 21. https://doi.org/10.48550/arXiv.2209.10652.

Executive Office of the President, National Science and Technology Council, and Committee on Technology. 2016. *Preparing for the Future of Artificial Intelligence*. Executive Office of the President. https://obamawhitehouse.archives.gov/sites/default/files/whitehouse_files/microsites/ostp/NSTC/preparing_for_the_future_of_ai.pdf.

Firth, J. R. 1957. "A Synopsis of Linguistic Theory 1930–1955". In *Studies in Linguistic Analysis*. Philological Society.

Ganesh, Prakhar, Afaf Taik, and Golnoosh Farnadi. 2025. "Systemizing Multiplicity: The Curious Case of Arbitrariness in Machine Learning". In *Proceedings of the Eighth AAAI/ACM Conference on AI, Ethics, and Society*.

Geirhos, Robert, Roland S. Zimmermann, Blair Bilodeau, Wieland Brendel, and Been Kim. 2024. "Don't Trust Your Eyes: On the (Un)Reliability of Feature Visualizations". arXiv:2306.04719. Preprint, arXiv, June 6. https://doi.org/10.48550/arXiv.2306.04719.

Gould, Rhys, Euan Ong, George Ogden, and Arthur Conmy. 2023. "Successor Heads: Recurring, Interpretable Attention Heads In The Wild". arXiv:2312.09230. Preprint, arXiv, December 14. https://doi.org/10.48550/arXiv.2312.09230.

Gunasekaran, Abirami, Pritesh Mistry, and Minsi Chen. 2024. "Which Explanation Should Be Selected: A Method Agnostic Model Class Reliance Explanation for Model and Explanation Multiplicity". *SN Computer Science* 5(5). https://doi.org/10.1007/s42979-024-02810-8.

Ha, David, and Jürgen Schmidhuber. 2018. "World Models". arXiv:1803.10122. Preprint, arXiv, May 9. https://doi.org/10.48550/arXiv.1803.10122.

Hartley, John, and Jason Potts. 2014. *Cultural Science: A Natural History of Stories, Demes, Knowledge and Innovation*. Bloomsbury Academic.

Hayek, Friedrich A. 1945. "The Use of Knowledge in Society". *The American Economic Review* 35(4):519–530.

Hayek, Friedrich A. 1952. "*The Sensory Order: An Inquiry Into the Foundations of Theoretical Psychology*". University of Chicago Press.

Jacobs, Robert A., Michael I. Jordan, Steven J. Nowlan, and Geoffrey E. Hinton. 1991. "Adaptive Mixtures of Local Experts". *Neural Computation* 3(1):79–87. https://doi.org/10.1162/neco.1991.3.1.79.

Kaplan, Jared, Sam McCandlish, Tom Henighan, et al. 2020. "Scaling Laws for Neural Language Models". arXiv:2001.08361. Preprint, arXiv, January 23. https://doi.org/10.48550/arXiv.2001.08361.

Krizhevsky, Alex, Ilya Sutskever, and Geoffrey E Hinton. 2012. "ImageNet Classification with Deep Convolutional Neural Networks". *Advances in Neural Information Processing Systems* 25. https://proceedings.neurips.cc/paper_files/paper/2012/hash/c399862d3b9d6b76c8436e924a68c45b-Abstract.html.

Lavoie, Don. 1985. *Rivalry and Central Planning: The Socialist Calculation Debate Reconsidered*. Cambridge University Press.

Lecomte, Victor, Kushal Thaman, Rylan Schaeffer, Naomi Bashkansky, Trevor Chow, and Sanmi Koyejo. 2024. "What Causes Polysemanticity? An Alternative Origin Story of Mixed Selectivity from Incidental Causes". arXiv:2312.03096. Preprint, arXiv, February 13. https://doi.org/10.48550/arXiv.2312.03096.

Li, Kenneth, Aspen K. Hopkins, David Bau, Fernanda Viégas, Hanspeter Pfister, and Martin Wattenberg. 2024. "Emergent World Representations: Exploring a Sequence Model Trained on a Synthetic Task". arXiv: 2210.13382. Preprint, arXiv, June 26. https://doi.org/10.48550/arXiv.2210.13382.

Linardatos, Pantelis, Vasilis Papastefanopoulos, Sotiris Kotsiantis, Pantelis Linardatos, Vasilis Papastefanopoulos, and Sotiris Kotsiantis. 2020. "Explainable AI: A Review of Machine Learning Interpretability Methods". *Entropy* 23 (1). https://doi.org/10.3390/e23010018.

Lovecraft, H. P. 1936. *At the Mountains of Madness*. Street & Smith Publications, Inc. https://www.hplovecraft.com/writings/fiction/mm.aspx.

Lowe, David G. 2004. "Distinctive Image Features from Scale-Invariant Keypoints". *International Journal of Computer Vision* 60(2):91–110. https://doi.org/10.1023/B:VISI.0000029664.99615.94.

Lu, Janna. 2025. "Tacit Knowledge in Large Language Models". SSRN Scholarly Paper No. 5320627. Social Science Research Network, June 25. https://doi.org/10.2139/ssrn.5320627.

Lundberg, Scott, and Su-In Lee. 2017. "A Unified Approach to Interpreting Model Predictions". arXiv:1705.07874. Preprint, arXiv, November 25. https://doi.org/10.48550/arXiv.1705.07874.

Mikolov, Tomas, Kai Chen, Greg Corrado, and Jeffrey Dean. 2013. "*Efficient Estimation of Word Representations in Vector Space*". arXiv:1301.3781. Preprint, arXiv, September 7. https://doi.org/10.48550/arXiv.1301.3781.

Min, Sewon, Xinxi Lyu, Ari Holtzman, et al. 2022. "Rethinking the Role of Demonstrations: What Makes In-Context Learning Work?". arXiv:2202.12837. Preprint, arXiv, October 20. https://doi.org/10.48550/arXiv.2202.12837.

Mittelstadt, Brent, Chris Russell, and Sandra Wachter. 2019. "Explaining Explanations in AI". In *Proceedings of the Conference on Fairness, Accountability, and Transparency*, January 29, 279–288. https://doi.org/10.1145/3287560.3287574.

Nanda, Neel, Lawrence Chan, Tom Lieberum, Jess Smith, and Jacob Steinhardt. 2023. "Progress Measures for Grokking via Mechanistic Interpretability". arXiv:2301.05217. Preprint, arXiv, October 19. https://doi.org/10.48550/arXiv.2301.05217.

Nisbett, Richard E., and Timothy DeCamp Wilson. 1977. "Telling More Than We Can Know: Verbal Reports on Mental Processes". *Psychological Review* 84(3):231–259.

Olah, Chris, Nick Cammarata, Ludwig Schubert, Gabriel Goh, Michael Petrov, and Shan Carter. 2020. "Zoom In: An Introduction to Circuits". *Distill* 5 (3): e00024001. https://doi.org/10.23915/distill.00024.001.

OpenAI. 2023. *GPT–4 Technical Report*. https://cdn.openai.com/papers/gpt-4.pdf.

Ouyang, Long, Jeff, Wu , Xu Jiang, et al. 2022. "Training Language Models to Follow Instructions with Human Feedback". arXiv:2203.02155. Preprint, arXiv, March 4. https://doi.org/10.48550/arXiv.2203.02155.

Parker-Holder, Jack, and Shlomi Fruchter. 2025. "Genie 3: A New Frontier for World Models". August 5. https://deepmind.google/blog/genie-3-a-new-frontier-for-world-models/.

Polanyi, Michael. (1966) 1983. *The Tacit Dimension*. Peter Smith.

Potts, Jason. 2024. "Embeddings". *Cultural Science*.

Radford, Alec, Jong Wook Kim, Chris Hallacy, et al. 2021. Learning Transferable Visual Models From Natural Language Supervision. arXiv:2103.00020. Preprint, arXiv, February 26. https://doi.org/10.48550/arXiv.2103.00020.

Radford, Alec, Karthik Narasimhan, Tim Salimans, and Ilya Sutskever. 2018. *Improving Language Understanding by Generative Pre-Training*. June 11.

Rae, Jack W., Sebastian Borgeaud, Trevor Cai, et al. 2022. "Scaling Language Models: Methods, Analysis & Insights from Training Gopher".

arXiv:2112.11446. Preprint, arXiv, January 21. https://doi.org/10.48550/arXiv.2112.11446.

Rafailov, Rafael, Archit Sharma, Eric Mitchell, Stefano Ermon, Christopher D. Manning, and Chelsea Finn. 2024. "Direct Preference Optimization: your Language Model Is Secretly a Reward Model". arXiv:2305.18290. Preprint, arXiv, July 29. https://doi.org/10.48550/arXiv.2305.18290.

Regulation (EU) 2016/679 of the European Parliament and of the Council of 27 April 2016 on the Protection of Natural Persons with Regard to the Processing of Personal Data and on the Free Movement of Such Data, and Repealing Directive 95/46/EC (General Data Protection Regulation), *Official Journal of the European Union* L1191 (2016). https://eur-lex.europa.eu/eli/reg/2016/679/oj.

Regulation (EU) 2024/1689 of the European Parliament and of the Council of 13 June 2024 Laying down Harmonised Rules on Artificial Intelligence and Amending Certain Union Legislative Acts (Artificial Intelligence Act), *Official Journal of the European Union* (2024). https://eur-lex.europa.eu/eli/reg/2024/1689/oj.

Ribeiro, Marco Tulio, Sameer Singh, and Carlos Guestrin. 2016. "'Why Should I Trust You?': Explaining the Predictions of Any Classifier". arXiv:1602.04938. Preprint, arXiv, August 9. https://doi.org/10.48550/arXiv.1602.04938.

Rombach, Robin, Andreas Blattmann, Dominik Lorenz, Patrick Esser, and Björn Ommer. 2022. "High-Resolution Image Synthesis with Latent Diffusion Models". arXiv:2112.10752. Preprint, arXiv, April 13. https://doi.org/10.48550/arXiv.2112.10752.

Russakovsky, Olga, Jia Deng, Hao Su, et al. 2015. "ImageNet Large Scale Visual Recognition Challenge". *International Journal of Computer Vision* 115(3):211–252. https://doi.org/10.1007/s11263-015-0816-y.

Shackle, G. L. S. 1979. *Imagination and the Nature of Choice*. Columbia University Press.

Sharkey, Lee, Bilal Chughtai, Joshua Batson, et al. 2025, January 27. "Open Problems in Mechanistic Interpretability". arXiv:2501.16496. Preprint, arXiv. https://doi.org/10.48550/arXiv.2501.16496.

Shazeer, Noam, Azalia Mirhoseini, Krzysztof Maziarz, et al. 2017. "Outrageously Large Neural Networks: The Sparsely-Gated Mixture-of-Experts Layer". arXiv.Org, January 23. https://arxiv.org/abs/1701.06538v1.

Slack, Dylan, Sophie Hilgard, Emily Jia, Sameer Singh, and Himabindu Lakkaraju. 2020. "Fooling LIME and SHAP: Adversarial Attacks on Post

Hoc Explanation Methods". arXiv:1911.02508. Preprint, arXiv, February 3. https://doi.org/10.48550/arXiv.1911.02508.

Sohl-Dickstein, Jascha, Eric A. Weiss, Niru Maheswaranathan, and Surya Ganguli. 2015. "Deep Unsupervised Learning Using Nonequilibrium Thermodynamics". arXiv:1503.03585. Preprint, arXiv, November 18. https://doi.org/10.48550/arXiv.1503.03585.

Srivastava, Aarohi, Abhinav Rastogi, Abhishek Rao, et al. 2023. "Beyond the Imitation Game: Quantifying and Extrapolating the Capabilities of Language Models". arXiv:2206.04615. Preprint, arXiv, June 12. https://doi.org/10.48550/arXiv.2206.04615.

Sumner, Scott. 2010. "Never Reason from a Price Change". *TheMoneyIllusion*, May 18. https://www.themoneyillusion.com/never-reason-from-a-price-change/.

Sutton, Rich, Guest. 2025. *Richard Sutton—Father of RL Thinks LLMs are a Dead End*. Hosted by Dwarkesh Patel. Dwarkesh Podcast. September 27. https://www.dwarkesh.com/p/richard-sutton.

Taniguchi, Tadahiro, Ryo Ueda, Tomoaki Nakamura, Masahiro Suzuki, and Akira Taniguchi. 2025. "Generative Emergent Communication: Large Language Model Is a Collective World Model". arXiv:2501.00226. Preprint, arXiv, July 16, https://doi.org/10.48550/arXiv.2501.00226.

Templeton, Adly, Trenton Bricken, Tom Conerly, et al. 2024. *Scaling Monosemanticity: Extracting Interpretable Features from Claude 3 Sonnet*. Transformer Circuits Thread. Anthropic. https://transformer-circuits.pub/2024/scaling-monosemanticity/index.html.

Touvron, Hugo, Thibaut Lavril, Gautier Izacard, et al. 2023. "LLaMA: Open and Efficient Foundation Language Models". arXiv:2302.13971. Preprint, arXiv, February 27. https://doi.org/10.48550/arXiv.2302.13971.

Vaswani, Ashish, Noam Shazeer, Niki Parmar, et al. 2017. "Attention Is All You Need". *Advances in Neural Information Processing Systems* 30. https://papers.nips.cc/paper_files/paper/2017/hash/3f5ee243547dee91fbd053c1c4a845aa-Abstract.html.

Vincent, James. 2023. "Microsoft's Bing Is an Emotionally Manipulative Liar, and People Love It". The Verge, February 15. https://www.theverge.com/2023/2/15/23599072/microsoft-ai-bing-personality-conversations-spy-employees-webcams.

Wei, Jason, Yi Tay, Rishi Bommasani, et al. 2022. "Emergent Abilities of Large Language Models". arXiv:2206.07682. Preprint, arXiv, October 26. https://doi.org/10.48550/arXiv.2206.07682.

4

Intelligence and Prosperity

Abstract Julian Simon argued that the ultimate resource was not oil or copper but the human mind—the supply of problem-solvers whose ingenuity responds to scarcity. Yet Simon's framework contained an implicit constraint: the supply of minds was limited to the supply of people. This chapter argues that artificial intelligence removes that constraint. Where prosperity once rose with human population, it can now rise with computational capacity. The chapter develops this claim through the Theory of the Adjacent Possible, which models innovation as the combination of existing goods into new ones. As economies grow more complex, the combinatorial space of possible innovations expands exponentially—but human cognition can only search a vanishing fraction of that space. AI changes this directly: it raises the plausibility of high-order combinations that no human mind could conceive or evaluate, pushing the effective search frontier from a thin surface to a vast volume. The implications extend beyond faster growth to a structural transformation in how growth occurs. Yet physical constraints—energy, hardware, raw materials—and institutional arrangements remain binding. The same digital technologies that expand the combinatorial space also lower the cost of institutional experimentation, making the rules

C. Berg, *Artificial Intelligence*, Palgrave Studies in Classical Liberalism,
https://doi.org/10.1007/978-3-032-22310-4_4

governing innovation themselves objects of innovation. For the first time in history, the ultimate resource has been industrialised.

Keywords Economic growth · Innovation · Julian Simon · Adjacent possible · Combinatorial evolution · Endogenous growth · General purpose technology · Productivity · Institutions · Schumpeter · Artificial intelligence

The 1970s saw a turn against the optimistic post-war culture in the developed world. Books like Paul Ehrlich's *Population Bomb* (1968) argued that the world faced an imminent famine from overpopulation and resource scarcity. The Club of Rome's *Limits to Growth* report declared that economic and population growth would lead to planetary collapse (Meadows et al. 1972). Films like *Soylent Green* (Fleischer 1973), *Logan's Run* (Anderson 1976) and *Silent Running* (Trumbull 1972) prophesised a world where drastic, brutal measures had to be taken to control and govern dwindling resources. The dystopian *Mad Max* (Miller 1979) starts in a world falling apart from resource constraints and a deteriorating environment.

In his book *The Ultimate Resource* (1981, see also 1996), the economist Julian Simon argued that doomsayers were misguided because they had misidentified the source of prosperity. Prosperity and civilisation were not the result of resource abundance. They were the result of ingenuity: the human mind was 'the ultimate resource'. Simon's thesis was that the supply of ideas—inventions, adaptations, productivity—expands with the number of problem-solvers working on a challenge. More people means more minds confronting the challenges of the time, including challenges like scarcity and hard resource limits when they arise. And intelligence is a renewable resource. Commodities deplete with use. Minds do not. They improve with practice, accumulate knowledge across generations, and (thanks to the genius of the price system) search harder when resources become genuinely scarce.

Yet Simon's argument contains an implicit assumption: the supply of minds is limited to the supply of people. The number of human beings constrains the total stock of intelligence. More people means more problem-solving capacity. Fewer people means less. If population growth stalls, the growth of new ideas will stall with it. This chapter starts with the proposition that artificial intelligence has removed that constraint. Where prosperity once rose with human population, it can now rise with the computational capacity to run AI models. Where the ultimate resource was once bounded by biology and fertility, it is now scalable with additional compute.

This chapter proceeds as follows. The first part traces how economic thought came to recognise ideas—not capital or labour—as the ultimate driver of growth. From Adam Smith onwards, economists have coalesced around the claim that innovation—the discovery of new economically useful ideas—brings about prosperity. But without new sources of intelligence, growth faces a ceiling imposed by demography. The second section uses this analysis to confront the sceptical case that AI's impact on growth will be modest. Economic models that treat AI as solely as a technology that automates tasks predict only incremental benefits from AI. But this framing assumes that the menu of tasks is fixed. The invention of new tasks (that is, innovation) is the primary mechanism through which transformative technologies generate growth. The promise of AI's economic impact lies not in efficiency gains on existing tasks but in its potential to accelerate innovation itself—to transform the production function for ideas.

The final section of this chapter considers the mechanism by which AI will directly influence long run economic growth. The *theory of the adjacent possible* (Koppl et al. 2023) models innovation as the combination of existing goods into new ones. As economies grow more complex, the combinatorial space of possible innovations expands exponentially—but human cognition can only search a vanishing fraction of that space. AI raises the plausibility of combinations that no human mind could conceive or evaluate, pushing the effective search frontier from a thin surface to a vast volume. Physical constraints (like energy, hardware, and raw materials) remain. But the same digital technologies that expand the combinatorial space also lower the cost of institutional experimentation, making the rules governing innovation themselves objects of innovation, and opening up new vectors for economic growth.

4.1 Economic Growth as Growth in Ideas

The great accomplishment of modern growth theory has been to formalise the arguments and intuitions that mainline economists like Adam Smith, Joseph Schumpeter, and Friedrich Hayek articulated long ago. The modern *ideas + institutions* growth framework represents the recovery of older insights that had been temporarily and unfortunately obscured by the mechanistic planning philosophies that dominated the mid-twentieth century.

Adam Smith opened his *Wealth of Nations* ([1776] 1904) not with a story about capital accumulation but with the division of labour. His pin factory example demonstrates that specialization multiplies output per worker—not through harder effort but as a result of how tasks can be organised. Even in this short example, Smith was explaining a theory of growth as coordination plus productivity increases as a result of specialisation. His thesis was that larger markets permit more specialization, more specialization generates productivity gains, and more productivity gains expand purchasing power and thereby extend the market further. The process is cumulative and self-reinforcing. But Smith also understood that this virtuous spiral depends on institutions: secure property rights, enforceable contracts, and freedom of entry into trades.

The twentieth-century Austrian economists argued that the central problem of economics is not resource allocation, but the coordination of dispersed knowledge and innovation. Joseph Schumpeter's creative destruction placed innovation at the centre of the growth process. In *The Theory of Economic Development* ([1934] 2021, 55), he defined economic development as the "carrying out of new combinations"—new products, new methods of production, new markets, new sources of supply, and new forms of organisation. As he argued, the economy is an evolutionary system that generates novelty. If the knowledge relevant to economic progress is dispersed across millions of minds, and if much of it is tacit—embodied in skills and intuitions that cannot be articulated—then no central planner can assemble it. Only a decentralised system of property rights and market prices can coordinate this dispersed knowledge. The Austrian framework implies that institutions matter for growth not merely because they provide incentives (although they do) but because they determine how effectively a society can aggregate and deploy its collective intelligence. Good institutions let many minds search in parallel. Bad institutions concentrate decision-making in too few hands and thereby truncate the search process.

The mechanistic formalism of the mainstream mid-century economists took a long time to catch up with the Austrian synthesis of institutions and ideas. The Solow-Swan growth model brought mathematical discipline to the theory of economic growth (Solow 1956; Swan 1956). But it did so at the cost of understanding the underlying mechanisms (Easterly 2002). The model showed that, in a world with capital and labour as inputs, diminishing returns to capital would eventually halt growth. Only technological progress (an unexplained upward drift in the production function) could sustain long-run growth. When Robert Solow (1957) decomposed American growth into capital deepening, labour force growth and a residual, he found that the residual—technological progress—accounted for the lion's share. So while the Solow-Swan model correctly identified ideas as the engine of growth, it viewed them as something that happened *to* the economy rather than something the economy produced. This is not very satisfying. If nearly all growth comes from a factor that the growth model does not explain, then the model has identified the question rather than answering it.

It was not until the new growth theory of the 1980s and 1990s that ideas entered the mainstream of economic growth theory. Paul Romer's (1990) paper on endogenous technological change and parallel work by Robert Lucas (1988) on human capital accumulation established what could be called the *microfoundations* of economic growth. Romer's key insight was that ideas are non-rival goods. A design for a better mousetrap can be used by one firm without diminishing its usefulness to another. This non-rivalry generates increasing returns at the aggregate level even if individual firms face constant or diminishing returns. Knowledge spillovers mean that one innovator's discovery raises the productivity of other innovators.

In Romer's model, growth is sustained by the intentional allocation of resources to research. Companies invest in research because they expect to capture some returns from innovation through patents or first-mover advantages. Lucas' contribution was to emphasise the accumulation of human capital. Just as firms invest in research, workers invest in education. Education and learning-by-doing raise the productivity of workers, and these productivity gains do not dissipate when workers change employers. The aggregate stock of human capital becomes a public input that benefits all producers. Romer's emphasis was on the institutional question of what arrangements encourage the production and diffusion of ideas. Because knowledge spills over, the social return exceeds the private return, and the equilibrium growth rate may fall short of the social optimum. The answer involves property rights (intellectual property), competition (which forces firms to innovate), openness (which allows ideas to flow across borders), and education (which expands the population capable of generating and absorbing ideas).

There has always been a strong pessimistic counter-tradition in thinking about economic growth. Thomas Malthus (1798) had argued that population growth would always outstrip the growth of food supply. This tradition has periodically resurfaced and shaped the 'eco-anxiety' of the 1970s. Julian Simon's work was explicitly a rebellion against this Malthusian framing. The Malthusians treated land and resources as the binding constraint. The Malthusian model failed, Simon argued, because it ignored the endogenous response of human ingenuity to scarcity signals.

Simon's rebuttal to growth pessimism rests on three claims, each with a long history in mainline economic thought. The first is that productivity improvements are the result of human imagination, and more minds produce more invention and faster adoption of existing techniques. Simon drew on William Petty's observation from 1682 that "it is more likely that one ingenious curious man may rather be found among 4 million than 400 persons" (Petty 1683; quoted in Simon 1981, 197) and on Simon Kuznets's statistical demonstrations that scientific output scales with population (Kuznets 1967). The second is that innovation is not confined to geniuses working in laboratories. Simon insisted that "technological advance does not only mean 'science,' and scientific geniuses are just one part of the knowledge process" (Simon 1981, 198) He illustrated this with deliberately mundane examples: the taxi dispatcher who finds a better way to deploy his fleet, the shipper who discovers that garbage cans make excellent cheap containers, the supermarket clerk who devises a quicker method for stamping prices on cans. These micro-innovations are dispersed throughout the economy. They cannot be centrally planned because they depend on local, tacit, contextual knowledge—precisely the kind of knowledge that Hayek identified as the coordination problem of the economic system. The aggregate effect of millions of such incremental improvements compounds over time into transformative productivity gains.

Finally, Simon argued that the ultimate constraint on growth is not material resources but knowledge: "the basic ingredient ... is human knowledge" (Simon 1981, 346). Knowledge production depends on two factors—the imaginative capacity of problem-solvers and the institutional freedom that permits them to experiment, fail, and recombine ideas. More minds generate more ideas only when those minds are free to act on their discoveries and to capture some portion of the gains. If economic growth depends on the rate at which new ideas are generated, and if ideas are produced by minds, then the long-run growth rate depends ultimately on population. This is precisely the conclusion Charles Jones (1995) reached in his model of semi-endogenous growth: in equilibrium, the growth rate of per capita income is proportional to the growth rate of the population. When population growth slows, the production of ideas slows, and growth eventually stagnates.

4.2 Will AI Accelerate Growth?

So can artificial intelligence break the link between population growth and economic growth? The answer depends on what kind of economic technology AI turns out to be. Agrawal et al. (2018) have influentially argued that AI's fundamental economic contribution is lowering the cost of prediction. If so, then we can expect much more prediction—statistical inference about missing information—to be used throughout the economy. Understanding the future economic impact of AI is a matter then of identifying where those additional prediction resources might be deployed.

Recent macroeconomic work has tended to model AI primarily as a tool that performs existing cognitive work more cheaply. The task framework looks at jobs as collections of tasks, and tries to understand which tasks can be complemented or substituted by AI. The aggregate economic effects depend on the fraction of tasks affected and the how much they are likely to result in cost reductions (Acemoglu and Restrepo 2019). Because this view relies on existing evidence regarding how exposed different tasks are to technological disruption, the growth impact estimates are typically positive but modest. For instance, the Nobel laureate Daron Acemoglu (2024) argues that total factor productivity gains over the next decade are likely well below 1%, potentially shrinking further as AI confronts harder, context-dependent tasks. This is a long way from the economic acceleration that many in the AI industry have suggested is possible—and what we will defend in this chapter below.

Task based frameworks for modelling the impact of technology are appealing because they are tractable—they are both precise and comprehensive enough to support empirical research. But they are fundamentally limited. They cannot predict the discovery of *new* tasks. Indeed, Acemoglu's (2024) analysis explicitly excluded the creation of new tasks. Economic theory and historical evidence suggest that new tasks—rather than mere automation—are the primary mechanism through which transformative technologies generate growth. The power loom automated weaving, but it simultaneously created a massive demand for people to fix, oil, tune, and organise the machines (Brooks 1899). These were new tasks that often paid higher wages because they required higher technical skill than hand-weaving. Before the release of spreadsheet software like VisiCalc (Frankston 1979; Castelluccio 2019) and Excel, recalculating a financial scenario was a task that took days of human labour. Automation dropped the price of recalculation to nearly zero. But it didn't destroy the job of accounting; it sparked the creation of a new task of 'financial modelling'. Accountants shifted from crunching numbers to designing financial models—a higher-value task that increased the demand for financial services (Lacher 1997).

Trying to understand the impact of AI without considering the restructuring of economic tasks is like analysing trade while ignoring the benefits of new goods (Cowen 2024). Task *invention* drives the bulk of long-run economic growth. The static task-centric framework assumes we already know which tasks exist and which will be affected—a posture that resembles central planning, except that the 'plan' is simply the status quo taken as given.

So what about the empirical evidence? The strongest empirical evidence to date shows large but highly variable micro-level productivity effects from AI. For example, one of the most prominent studies show LLMs raising customer-support productivity by roughly 15%, with outsized gains for less-experienced workers (Brynjolfsson et al. 2025) While some experiments show improvements in writing quality and speed (Noy and Zhang 2023), others have described what looks like a 'jagged frontier' where AI aids some tasks but is ineffective or counterproductive in those requiring tacit context (Dell'Acqua et al. 2023). (I have described my own experience with AI assisted writing in the Preface to this book.)

The research evidence is also consistent with this idea of a slow translation from micro gains to aggregate growth. Some papers find small impacts on earnings in exposed occupations (Hølmlum and Vestergaard 2025). However, firm-level data suggest that AI-investing firms grow faster and launch more products (Babina et al. 2024). Longer-run scenario models suggest a wide range of outcomes—ranging from modest effects to explosive growth—depending on how effectively AI automates R&D and overcomes bottlenecks (Trammell and Korinek 2023).

These estimates need to be taken with a grain of salt. This is a very fast-moving technological revolution. So the extremely lengthy publication process makes it difficult to estimate the direct impact of AI. AI labs are producing new models faster than researchers can study their deployment. As the AI researcher Ethan Mollick (2024) has noted, the lags between research and academic publication—even in draft or working paper form—are significantly longer than the release of new AI models that offer significant new capabilities. The best academic research we have on productivity gains from AI investigates models that are far behind the frontier. This lag is most obvious in software engineering. The empirical academic evidence for AI increasing productivity in software engineering is mixed. It ranges from large speedups in lab settings (Peng et al. 2023) to potential slowdowns in complex, open-source environments (Becker et al. 2025; Cui et al. 2024; Vaithilingam et al. 2022). But as we have observed in Chap. 1, the uptake of AI within the AI labs themselves—reports suggest that the labs are close to completely relying on AI generated code—suggests that benefits are very real.

AI is one of the canonical 'general purpose technologies' that typically trigger waves of complementary innovation and reorganization (Cockburn et al. 2018; Aghion et al. 2017). General purpose technologies typically have a diffusion lag. It requires significant investment and economic re-organisation—such as process redesign and training—to gain the benefits from these general purpose technologies. In the early stages of diffusion, concrete productivity measurements might understate the true progress of a technology which these adjustments are ongoing. The static task-based estimates of AI impact miss the point. The question is not how much quicker we will be able to do the sets of tasks that make up our work, but what new work will be done as a result.

The main route to sustained growth acceleration from AI is less likely to be one-off efficiency gains, but AI's ability to increase the productivity of innovation itself. In other words, AI represents a shift in the *production function for ideas*. Foundation models can already perform many of the cognitive tasks that generate productivity improvements: searching for relevant information, identifying patterns across domains, synthesising disparate knowledge, generating candidate solutions, and producing first drafts of designs, analyses, and plans. If the technology can substitute for labour in the production of ideas, this creates a feedback loop. More ideas enable better AI, which produces more ideas (Aghion et al. 2017).

Just as Simon argued that human minds would respond to scarcity signals by searching harder for substitutes and efficiency gains, so AI systems can be deployed to accelerate that search. Just as Simon emphasised that most innovation comes not from rare geniuses but from distributed problem-solving across the economy, so AI lowers the cost of problem-solving for ordinary workers, firms, and researchers. The dispatcher optimising taxi routes can now query an AI model for suggestions. The supermarket manager can simulate shelf layouts before committing to changes. The agricultural scientist can screen thousands of candidate seed varieties computationally before field trials.

The implications of this potential speedup are profound. In an essay published in 2024, the head of Anthropic Dario Amodei argued that powerful AI could compress a century of biological and medical progress into 5–10 years (Amodei 2024). As he described it, AI platforms will function as virtual scientists conducting the full research cycle—designing experiments, controlling lab equipment, and inventing new methods and scientific techniques. Progress in sciences like biology tends to be made by small numbers of researchers and thus have a high return to raw intelligence on the part of those researchers. Consequently, the track record of biology is that we see roughly one major discovery per year (like CRISPR, mRNA vaccines, or AlphaFold) that drives the bulk of progress. With greater, cheaper intelligence at our disposal, it is possible that these breakthroughs could have been made sooner. And the massive parallelization across thousands of simultaneous experiments could overcome much of what is slowing down progress.

4.3 Radically Expanding the Adjacent Possible

The central failing of modern growth theory is that it has never truly explained where ideas come from. When Paul Romer and the endogenous growth theorists finally brought ideas inside the model in the 1980s, they treated technology as a quantity that responded to economic incentives. If the returns to innovation rose, agents would invest more in the 'production of ideas.' This is less a theory of where ideas come from and more a theory of how ideas are funded. The production function itself remained a black box. Endogenous growth theory treated the generation of novelty as a stable, continuous flow, ignoring the discrete, combinatorial, and often chaotic nature of actual invention.

But as the weakness of the task-focused analysis has shown, the primary engine of long-run growth is not doing existing things more efficiently, but generating entirely new things—new goods, new services, and new ways of living. To understand how AI changes economic growth, we need a theory of where these new things come from. We need to see inside the otherwise opaque production function for ideas.

Schumpeter ([1934] 2021, 66) defined economic development simply as the "carrying out of new combinations." Innovation is the act of combining existing "things and forces" in novel ways (Schumpeter 1934 2021, 14). A steam engine is a combination of a piston, a cylinder, a condenser, and a heat source. A smartphone is a combination of a radio, a computer, a screen, a battery, and a camera. This combinatorial view connects economics to biology. Just as genetic evolution recombines DNA to produce new organisms, technological evolution recombines existing artifacts and processes to produce new tools. This argument has been formalised in the theory of combinatorial evolution by complexity theorists like Stuart Kauffman (1996, 2011) and Arthur (2011). In this view, the economy expands into the 'adjacent possible'—the set of all those first steps that can be taken from the current state of the system. The adjacent possible is simply the set of new things that can be built *next*, given what already exists. It is the immediate neighbourhood of feasible combinations—those innovations that become possible only because the current stock of tools, components, and ideas has reached its present level.

In their book *Explaining Technology* (Koppl et al. 2023) a large group of authors (Roger Koppl Roberto Cazzolla Gatti, Abigail Devereaux, Brian D. Fath, James Herriot, Wim Hordijk, Stuart Kauffman, Robert E. Ulanowicz, and Sergi Valverde, subsequently referred to here as Koppl and colleagues) provide a concrete model of combinatorial evolution and its economic effects. Their model, the *theory of the adjacent possible* (the TAP model), is a mechanistic explanation for the trajectory of human economic history. It explains why technological progress was glacially slow for hundreds of thousands of years, and why progress suddenly exploded in the industrial revolution. And, crucially for our purposes, it provides the theoretical apparatus we need to understand how artificial intelligence changes the parameters of economic growth.

The TAP model begins with a simple premise: new goods are created by combining or modifying existing goods. At any given moment, an economy has a stock of existing goods—tools, components, processes, materials. Each of these can be modified on its own, or combined with one, two, three, or more other goods to create something new. The number of possible combinations grows explosively with the number of existing goods. With ten goods, there are 45 possible pairs. With a thousand goods, there are nearly half a million. With a million goods, the number of possible combinations exceeds the number of atoms in the universe. Of course, the vast majority of these combinations are useless, absurd, or simply unimaginable. Nobody tries to combine a toaster with a glacier. Only a tiny fraction of mathematically possible combinations are *plausible*—combinations that someone could realistically notice, conceive of, and attempt (Koppl et al. 2023, 16). Plausibility depends on practical constraints, on proximity, on the state of knowledge—and crucially, on human foresight and intelligence. The great insight of the Wright brothers was that there was a plausible connection between bicycle mechanics and aerodynamics, and that combination gave us the Wright Flyer.

There are two crucial steps in the TAP model. First, from the vast space of all possible combinations, innovators select a small subset of plausible candidates—combinations that seem worth trying. Second, some fraction of those plausible attempts actually succeed in producing a valuable new good. Each success adds to the stock of existing goods, which in turn expands the space of possible combinations for the next period. This is the engine of the 'hockey stick' of economic growth since the industrial revolution. Even with fixed rates of plausibility and success, growth accelerates over time because the combinatorial space expands. More goods mean vastly more possible pairs, triples, and higher-order combinations. The adjacent possible grows as the economy grows.

But there is a constraint hidden in the TAP model: the rate at which humans can perceive and evaluate combinations. As the economy becomes more complex, the combinatorial space explodes beyond anything human minds can search. They note that "perfectly good combinations may go unimagined and untried" (2023, 17). More people, of course, would help explore the space. But population growth is fundamentally linear. Civilization adds minds one at a time. The combinatorial space of possible innovations expands exponentially with the stock of existing goods. The more successful we are at innovation, the larger the unexplored territory becomes relative to our ability to explore it. In a world with millions of distinct goods, nearly all of the mathematically possible combinations—especially those involving three, four, or more components—are simply never seen. They remain in the adjacent possible.

Abundant artificial intelligence has a radical effect on the dynamics identified in the TAP model. The rate of innovation depends on two parameters: the fraction of combinations that are plausible, and the probability that a plausible attempt succeeds. Human cognitive limitations bear directly on the first parameter. The plausibility filter exists because human minds cannot search the full combinatorial space—we can only attempt combinations we can conceive of. When the cost of cognition falls toward zero, this filter widens dramatically. More combinations become plausible candidates for experimentation, not because the physics has changed, but because the search capacity has expanded.

But the truly dramatic effect of AI can be seen in how Koppl and his colleagues (2023) model handles combination size. The TAP model allows combinations of any size—not just pairs, but triples, quadruples, and in principle combinations involving dozens or hundreds of existing goods. In practice, Koppl et al sets the plausibility of combinations involving more than four goods to zero. This is not a physical constraint but a cognitive one. Human innovators can realistically hold two or three components in mind and reason about their interactions. But nobody can mentally simulate the interaction of fifty components simultaneously. The plausibility of high-order combinations collapses not because such combinations are impossible, but because no human can find them.

This matters because the combinatorial arithmetic is radically asymmetric. With a million goods, there are about half a trillion possible pairs. But the number of possible combinations of ten goods from that same stock is a number with more than fifty digits. The number of combinations of fifty goods is effectively infinite. Human innovation has only ever scratched the surface of the combinatorial space. For the most part, we explore pairs and triples while higher-order combinations remain untouched. The binding constraint on economic growth is not the size of the adjacent possible, but the fraction of it that human minds can search.

Artificial intelligence changes this limit. AI systems can search combinatorial spaces that no human could explore. They can evaluate combinations of dozens of components, simulate their interactions, and identify plausible candidates from regions of the design space that were previously invisible. In the terms of the TAP model, cheap cognition does not just raise the plausibility parameter for pairs and triples—it allows the plausibility of higher-order combinations to remain positive rather than collapsing to zero. The effective search frontier of innovation expands from a thin surface to a vast volume.

Koppl and colleagues (2023, 21) note that the continuous-time version of the TAP model has a mathematical singularity—a point where the growth rate goes to infinity in finite time. They treat this as a regime change, a point where the model stops applying. Under normal conditions, with human cognition as the binding constraint, the economy never approaches this singularity. The plausibility filter keeps growth bounded. But cheap cognition loosens that filter. It pushes the system toward the explosive core of the combinatorial dynamic.

Of course, in an AI-enhanced economy, where the cost of generating recombinations in the purely digital space approaches zero, physical constraints—energy, hardware, and raw materials—are still binding. While the number of potential combinations may expand factorially, the capacity to realise them does not. Recent empirical work testing the TAP model finds that in the long run, the rate of innovation often scales linearly with the cumulative number of innovations (Taalbi 2025). This suggests that the "adjacent possible" is not a uniform frontier of infinite opportunity, but a landscape constrained by physical scarcity and coordination.

Likewise, the institutional environment in which innovation occurs matters. Classical liberal scholars have long distinguished between entrepreneurial activity that is productive or extractive (Baumol 1990; Coyne et al. 2010). The TAP equation might predict the volume of potential innovations, but institutions determine whether that tinkering is "steered" toward productive, welfare-enhancing ends or toward destructive and unproductive applications, such as rent-seeking or oppression (Goodman et al. 2025; Davidson 2025).

Economists have typically taken the institutional environment as a fixed variable or as a tool for comparative analysis: property rights and political regimes vary only in the long run. But the rate at which new combinations can be discovered, tested, and deployed depends critically on the rules that govern experimentation, ownership, and exchange. With colleagues I have argued that the AI boom is part of a "supertransition"driven by the combinatorial interaction of digital technologies: artificial intelligence, blockchain, advanced cryptography, quantum computing, low-earth orbit infrastructure, and the Internet of Things (Allen et al. 2025). These technologies are not merely industrial technologies—tools for transforming matter and energy—but *institutional technologies*: tools for coordinating people. Blockchains create trust without intermediaries. Smart contracts enable self-enforcing agreements. Zero-knowledge proofs permit verification without disclosure. These are new institutional primitives from which entirely novel forms of economic organisation can be assembled.

What we call "institutional acceleration"—the feedback loop between digital technologies and the institutions they enable—suggests that the very rules governing innovation are themselves becoming objects of innovation. We are not merely discovering new combinations of goods, we are discovering new combinations of rules. The same digital technologies that expand the combinatorial space also lower the cost of institutional experimentation. Open-source protocols, decentralised autonomous organisations, and programmable property rights allow entrepreneurs to assemble novel governance structures as readily as they assemble novel products. The limits on growth shifts from the stock of ideas to the plasticity of institutions—and that plasticity is itself increasing.

Julian Simon's framework tethered the fate of human prosperity to the biological birth rate. If the supply of minds is indeed the ultimate resource, then the demographic collapse currently threatening the developed world poses an existential threat to the growth of knowledge. In Simon's original calculus, a shrinking population implies a shrinking capacity to solve problems.

Artificial intelligence decouples the production of intelligence from the production of human beings. For the entirety of economic history, increasing the stock of cognitive labour was a twenty-year biological process. Foundation models transform this dynamic entirely. We are moving from a world where intelligence is a biological stock, constrained by fertility, to one where it is a manufactured input, constrained only by energy, infrastructure, and *more ideas.* By synthetically scaling the capacity to reason, AI ensures that the engine of prosperity—the discovery of new ideas—can accelerate even as the human population stagnates. AI has industrialised the ultimate resource.

But expanding the adjacent possible is not the same thing as exercising economic agency. Choosing among rival possibilities, committing resources under uncertainty, and bearing the consequences of error remain distinct functions—ones that abundance of cognition does not eliminate. Indeed, the more possibilities that intelligence makes visible, the more binding the problems of selection, coordination, and responsibility become. When cognition is scarce, the bottleneck is production. When cognition is abundant, the bottlenecks are coordination and agency. An economy saturated with artificial intelligence faces not a deficit of ideas but a surplus of options, competing plans, and interacting systems that must be chosen and reconciled.

The next chapter considers the implications of the shift from intelligence as the constraint on innovation to coordination as the constraint. As AI systems become capable of acting in the world as persistent, tool-using agents, the central question becomes how their actions are governed: who bears responsibility, how conflicts are resolved, and what institutional mechanisms align delegated machine action with human purposes. Answering that question requires turning our attention from growth to agency, and from innovation to the market institutions that coordinate it.

References

Acemoglu, Daron. 2024. *The Simple Macroeconomics of AI*. NBER Working Paper No. 32487.

Acemoglu, Daron, and Pascual Restrepo. 2019. "Automation and New Tasks: How Technology Displaces and Reinstates Labor". *Journal of Economic Perspectives* 33(2):3–30. https://doi.org/10.1257/jep.33.2.3.

Aghion, Philippe, Benjamin F Jones, and Charles I Jones. 2017. *Artificial Intelligence and Economic Growth*. No. 23928.

Agrawal, Ajay, Joshua Gans, and Avi Goldfarb. 2018. *Prediction Machines: The Simple Economics of Artificial Intelligence*. Boston, Massachusetts.

Allen, Darcy W. E., Chris Berg, and Jason Potts. 2025. *Institutional Acceleration: The Consequences of Technological Change in a Digital Economy*. Cambridge University Press. https://www.cambridge.org/core/elements/institutional-acceleration/D28808D728CC0373B6F8063B2C6F848D.

Amodei, Dario. 2024. "Machines of Loving Grace: how AI Could Transform the World for the Better." Web Page. October. https://darioamodei.com/essay/machines-of-loving-grace/.

Anderson, Michael, dir. 1976. *Logan's Run*. With Michael York, Jenny Agutter, and Richard Jordan. Metro-Goldwyn-Mayer (MGM). 1h59m.

Arthur, W. Brian. 2011. *The Nature of Technology: What It Is and How It Evolves*. First Free Press trade paperback edition. Free Press.

Babina, Tania, Anastassia Fedyk, Alex He, and James Hodson. 2024. "Artificial Intelligence, Firm Growth, and Product Innovation". *Journal of Financial Economics* 151(January):103745. https://doi.org/10.1016/j.jfineco.2023.103745.

Baumol, William J. 1990. "Entrepreneurship: Productive, Unproductive, and Destructive". *Journal of Political Economy* 98(5):893–921.

Becker, Joel, Nate Rush, Elizabeth Barnes, and David Rein. 2025. "Measuring the Impact of Early-2025 AI on Experienced Open-Source Developer Productivity." arXiv:2507.09089. Preprint, arXiv, July 25. https://doi.org/10.48550/arXiv.2507.09089.

Brooks, C. P. 1899. *Cotton Manufacturing. A Text-Book for the Use of Schools and Technical Institutes*. Project Gutenberg. https://www.gutenberg.org/files/57681/57681-h/57681-h.htm.

Brynjolfsson, Erik, Danielle, Li, and Lindsey R. Raymond. 2025. "Generative AI at Work." *The Quarterly Journal of Economics*, Working Paper Series, vol. 140 (2). https://doi.org/10.3386/w31161.

Castelluccio, Michael. 2019. "The Visicalc Dawn". Technology WORKBook. *Strategic Finance (Montvale, United States)* 100 (12): 69–71.
Cockburn, Iain M., Rebecca Henderson, and Scott Stern. 2018. *The Impact of Artificial Intelligence on Innovation.* 24449 NBER Working Paper.
Cowen, Tyler. 2024. "The Simple Macroeconomics of AI." *Marginal REVOLUTION,* April 21. https://marginalrevolution.com/marginalrevolution/2024/04/the-simple-macroeconomics-of-ai.html.
Coyne, Christopher J., Russell S. Sobel, and John A. Dove. 2010. "The Non-Productive Entrepreneurial Process." *The Review of Austrian Economics* 23(4):333–346. https://doi.org/10.1007/s11138-010-0124-2.
Cui, Kevin Zheyuan, Mert Demirer, Sonia Jaffe, Leon Musolff, Sida Peng, and Tobias Salz. 2024. "The Productivity Effects of Generative AI: Evidence from a Field Experiment with GitHub Copilot". *An MIT Exploration of Generative AI,* ahead of print, March 27. https://doi.org/10.21428/e4baedd9.3ad85f1c.
Davidson, Sinclair. 2025. "Critiquing 'Explaining Technology': Creativity, Institutions and Entrepreneurship". SSRN Scholarly Paper No. 5262867. Social Science Research Network, May 21. https://doi.org/10.2139/ssrn.5262867.
Dell'Acqua, Fabrizio, Edward McFowland III, Ethan R. Mollick, et al. 2023. "Navigating the Jagged Technological Frontier: Field Experimental Evidence of the Effects of AI on Knowledge Worker Productivity and Quality." SSRN Scholarly Paper No. 4573321. Social Science Research Network, September 15. https://doi.org/10.2139/ssrn.4573321.
Easterly, William. 2002. *The Elusive Quest for Growth: Economists' Adventures and Misadventures in the Tropics.* 1. MIT press paperback ed. MIT Press.
Ehrlich, Paul R. 1968. *The Population Bomb.* Ballantine Books.
Ethan Mollick [@emollick]. 2024. "Academic Journals Should Not Be Publishing New Studies on 'How Well AI Performs Against Humans' Where the Comparison is ChatGPT-3.5 Without a Good Reason. The Capabilities of Free ChatGPT Just Don't Tell Us Much About AI Now. It is an Issue Because Publishing Takes Many Months+". Tweet. Twitter, January 2. https://x.com/emollick/status/1742319177120027095.
Fleischer, Richard, dir. 1973. *Soylent Green.* With Charlton Heston, Edward G. Robinson, and Leigh Taylor-Young. Metro-Goldwyn-Mayer (MGM). 1h37m.

Frankston, Bob. 1979. "VisiCalc: The Visible Calculator". Paper presented at National Computer Conference (NCC) 1979 Personal Computing Festival. https://rmf.vc/public/Essays/VisiCalcPaper.pdf.

Goodman, Nathan P., Otto Lehto, and Mikayla Novak. 2025. "Institutional Diversity and Innovative Recombination". *European Economic Review* 174 (May):104998. https://doi.org/10.1016/j.euroecorev.2025.104998.

Hølmlum, Anders, and Emilie Vestergaard. 2025. "Large Language Models, Small Labor Market Effects". *NBER Working Paper Series* (Cambridge, MA), May. http://www.nber.org/papers/w33777.

Jones, Charles I. 1995. "R & D-Based Models of Economic Growth". *The Journal of Political Economy* 103(4):759–784.

Kauffman, Stuart A. 1996. *At Home in the Universe: The Search for Laws of Self-Organization and Complexity*. 1. paperback ed. Oxford University Press.

Kauffman, Stuart A. 2011. *The Origins of Order: Self-Organization and Selection in Evolution*. Nachdr. Oxford University Press.

Koppl, Roger, Roberto Cazzolla Gatti, Abigail Devereaux, et al. 2023. *Explaining Technology*. Cambridge University Press. https://doi.org/10.2139/ssrn.3856338.

Kuznets, Simon. 1967. "Population and Economic Growth". *Proceedings of the American Philosophical Society* 111(3):170–193.

Lacher, John. 1997. "The Power of Spreadsheets". *Journal of Accountancy*, May 1.https://www.journalofaccountancy.com/issues/1997/may/spread/

Lucas, Robert E. 1988. On the Mechanics of Economic Development. *Journal of Monetary Economics* 22(1):3–42. https://doi.org/10.1016/0304-3932(88)90168-7.

Malthus, Thomas Robert. 1798. *An Essay on the Principle of Population*. 1st ed. J. Johnson.

Meadows, Donella H., Dennis L. Meadows, Jørgen Randers, and William W. Behrens III. 1972. *The Limits to Growth: A Report for the Club of Rome's Project on the Predicament of Mankind*. Universe Books.

Miller, George, dir. 1979. *Mad Max*. With Mel Gibson, Joanne Samuel, and Hugh Keays-Byrne. Kennedy Miller Productions, Mad Max Films, Soundfirm. 1h28m.

Noy, Shakked, and Whitney Zhang. 2023. "Experimental Evidence on the Productivity Effects of Generative Artificial Intelligence". *SSRN Electronic Journal*. ahead of print: https://doi.org/10.2139/ssrn.4375283.

Peng, Sida, Eirini Kalliamvakou, Peter Cihon, and Mert Demirer. 2023. "The Impact of AI on Developer Productivity: Evidence from GitHub Copilot".

arXiv:2302.06590. Preprint, arXiv, February 13. https://doi.org/10.48550/arXiv.2302.06590.

Petty, William, Sir, 1623–1687. 1683. *Another Essay in Political Arithmetick, Concerning the Growth of the City of London with the Measures, Periods, Causes, and Consequences Thereof.* Printed by H.H. for Mark Pardoe. http://name.umdl.umich.edu/A54607.0001.001.

Romer, Paul M. 1990. "Endogenous Technological Change". *Journal of Political Economy* 98(5):S71–102.

Schumpeter, Joseph A. (1934) 2021. *The Theory of Economic Development; an Inquiry into Profits, Capital, Credit, Interest, and the Business Cycle.* With Internet Archive. Routledge. http://archive.org/details/theoryofeconomic0000schu.

Simon, Julian Lincoln. 1981. *The Ultimate Resource. 5. print.* Princeton Paperbacks Economics. Princeton University Press.

Simon, Julian Lincoln. 1996. *The Ultimate Resource 2.* 2. ed., rev. Ed., 3. printing and 1. paperback printing. Princeton Paperbacks Economics. Princeton University Press.

Smith, Adam. (1776) 1904. *An Inquiry into the Nature and Causes of the Wealth of Nations.* Edited by Edwin Cannan. Modern Library.

Solow, Robert M. 1956. "A Contribution to the Theory of Economic Growth". *The Quarterly Journal of Economics* 70(1):65. https://doi.org/10.2307/1884513.

Solow, Robert M. 1957. "Technical Change and the Aggregate Production Function". *The Review of Economics and Statistics* 39(3):312–320. https://doi.org/10.2307/1926047.

Swan, T. W. 1956. "Economic Growth and Capital Accumulation". *Economic Record* 32(2):334–361. https://doi.org/10.1111/j.1475-4932.1956.tb00434.x.

Taalbi, Josef. 2025. "Long-Run Patterns in the Discovery of the Adjacent Possible". *Industrial and Corporate Change.* September 3, dtaf028: https://doi.org/10.1093/icc/dtaf028.

Trammell, Philip, and Anton Korinek. 2023. "Economic Growth Under Transformative AI". *NBER Working Paper Series* (Cambridge, MA), October. http://www.nber.org/papers/w31815.

Trumbull, Douglas, dir. 1972. *Silent Running.* With Bruce Dern, Cliff Potts, and Ron Rifkin. Universal Pictures, Trumbull/Gruskoff Productions. 1h29m.

Vaithilingam, Priyan, Tianyi Zhang, and Elena L. Glassman. 2022. "Expectation vs. Experience: Evaluating the Usability of Code Generation Tools Powered by Large Language Models". *Extended Abstracts of the 2022 CHI Conference on Human Factors in Computing Systems* (New York, NY, USA), CHI EA'22, April 28, 1–7. https://doi.org/10.1145/3491101.3519665.

5

Agents and Agency

Abstract AI agents are persistent, tool-using systems that perceive their environment, make decisions, and interact with the external world in pursuit of goals. This chapter argues that despite their increasing sophistication, AI agents do not possess genuine economic agency: they cannot originate choice, bear commitment, or experience the uneasiness that motivates human action. Drawing on the anti-behaviourist tradition from Mises through Shackle, entrepreneurial judgment—the willingness to stake oneself on an uncertain future—remains irreducibly human. Yet this creates a puzzle: if AI is not labour, why does it increasingly function like labour in production? The resolution lies in understanding AI agents as capital-labour hybrids—forms of capital that supply cognitive services previously delivered only through human effort. This represents an institutional reclassification: what was remunerated as wages now generates returns as profit, even as the productive contribution remains functionally similar. The governance challenge is to prevent concentration of these hybrid assets while preserving the institutional conditions under which entrepreneurial judgment can be exercised.

C. Berg, *Artificial Intelligence*, Palgrave Studies in Classical Liberalism,
https://doi.org/10.1007/978-3-032-22310-4_5

Keywords AI agents · Economic agency · Ludwig von mises · G. L. S. Shackle · Entrepreneurship · Capital-labour hybrid · Human action · Uncertainty · Tool use · Austrian economics · Artificial intelligence

Ludwig von Mises opened the first part of his great *Human Action* with the declaration that "human action is purposeful behavior" (Mises [1949] 1996, 11). For Mises, his science of human affairs began with the fact that individuals use their reason to select means to achieve chosen ends. But the artificial intelligence systems we have described thus far do not act. They are mimics—stochastic parrots, as one critical paper famously described them (Bender et al. 2021). Intelligence without action is inert. The value of cognition lies in its application—in systems that do not merely think but *do*.

In this chapter we consider the interaction between intelligence and agency in AI systems. An AI agent is an AI system that can perceives its environment, make decisions, and interact with the external world in pursuit of goals. AI agents are persistent, tool-using systems that exercise discretion under conditions their designers did not fully anticipate. The emergence of such systems represents the next discontinuity in the AI revolution. And with this shift comes a new set of binding constraints. Cheaper cognition means more systems can now act semi-autonomously.

The question becomes not "how do we make machines smarter?" but "how do we coordinate an economy of intelligent machine agents?" Conflicts between agents must be resolved. Resources must be allocated among competing claims. These are the classic problems of political economy. Classical liberalism offers powerful tools to address them. The framework developed in this chapter treats AI agents as delegated extensions of human plans: durable, reconfigurable capital goods that supply labour-like services on behalf of human principals. Their governance requires the decentralised institutions that liberals have long championed—property rights, prices, freedom of contract, and general rules that constrain coercion rather than steer outcomes.

The chapter proceeds in three parts. The first section traces the intellectual history of AI agents, from the symbolic planning systems of the 1970s through to the unexpected emergence of agentic capabilities in large language models (LLMs). This history revisits the tension between design and discovery that has characterised AI research discussed in Chap. 2. The second section asks whether AI agents possess genuine economic agency in the sense developed by Ludwig von Mises and elaborated by G. L. S. Shackle—the capacity for originating choice and commitment under radical uncertainty. We argue that the answer is: no. AI agents can optimise, simulate, and execute with superhuman precision, but they cannot bear the entrepreneurial function of staking oneself on an uncertain future. The third section confronts the implications of this answer. If AI is not autonomous labour, why does it increasingly function like labour in production? The resolution lies in understanding AI agents as capital-labour hybrids—forms of capital that supply cognitive services previously delivered only through human effort. This is not a claim about consciousness or moral status but about institutional form: what was remunerated as wages now generates returns as profit, even as the productive contribution remains functionally similar.

5.1 Discovery and Design in the Evolution of AI Agents

The idea of artificial agents long predates LLMs. Indeed, it is baked into the early modern debates about automata discussed in Chap. 2. Computer scientists began theorising about software systems that could perceive, decide, and act autonomously in the 1970s and 1980s. But it was only in the last quarter of the twentieth century that researchers began to reason about how the vision of AI agents could be realised. The intellectual history of this field reflects the same tension between design and discovery that has characterised AI research more broadly.

The engineering question for the earliest attempts at autonomous agents was how much of the path from goal to action should be hardcoded, and how much could emerge from general principles? Shakey, a physical robot, developed at the Stanford Research Institute between 1966 and 1972, was designed to navigate real corridors, push objects, and manipulate its environment (Nilsson 1984). Shakey needed to generate action sequences from high-level goals without having every contingency hardcoded. Given a command like 'push the block off the platform,' the robot had to reason its way to a solution. It had to locate a ramp, pushing the ramp into position, roll up the ramp, then push the block. The AI platform system that was adopted for Shakey was the Stanford Research Institute Problem Solver (STRIPS). STRIPS took symbolic descriptions of an initial world state and a goal state, together with operators characterised by preconditions (what must be true for the action to apply) and effects (what the action adds to or removes from the state). It then searched for a sequence of operators transforming the initial state into one satisfying the goal (Fikes and Nilsson 1971). STRIPS could plan individual actions successfully, but it treated each goal as an isolated optimisation problem. There was no persistence of commitment, no resistance to reconsideration. Every new command prompted a fresh search from scratch.

More sophisticated attempts to specify the internal architecture of deliberative agency drew on philosophy rather than planning research. Michael Bratman's *Intention, Plans, and Practical Reason* (1987) addressed this as part of a theory of rational action. Standard decision theory treats each choice as a fresh optimisation over preferences and probabilities—as if an agent approached every moment with a blank slate, calculating expected utility across all possible actions (Bratman 1987, 2). But humans don't reason this way. Humans form intentions and commitments that structure subsequent deliberation, taking options off the table and focusing our limited cognitive resources. Bratman argued that these intentions constitute their own distinctive mental state (Bratman 1987, 32–35). They have a functional role: intentions resist reconsideration (we don't constantly second-guess our commitments), filter future options (ruling out alternatives inconsistent with what we've already decided), and prompt means-end reasoning (triggering subsidiary planning about how to realise what we intend). Plans, in turn, are hierarchical structures of intentions (Bratman 1987, 8).

Influenced in part by Bratman's account of intention, many symbolic 'agent architecture' projects in the late 1980s and 1990s tried to make an inner intentions of AI agents explicit and structured. In the Belief–Desire–Intention (BDI) tradition (Rao and Georgeff 1991, 1995), an agent keeps track of what it believes about the world, what it wants to achieve, and what it has committed to doing. These categories were given precise meanings using formal logics (including temporal logics that describe how states and commitments evolve over time). Systems such as the Procedural Reasoning System (Georgeff and Lansky 1987) and Intelligent Resource-bounded Machine Architecture (Bratman et al. 1988) embodied these ideas by maintaining explicit data structures—typically a belief database (often expressed in symbolic logic), a set of goals, and a library of plans—and by treating 'intentions' as the currently adopted plans or commitments guiding action. The advantage was transparency and, in principle, interpretability. Designers could inspect the agent's stored beliefs and chosen plans, trace why it acted as it did, and sometimes specify or verify desirable properties. But consistent with the broader challenges of symbolic AI we have discussed in Chap. 2, the designers had to anticipate what knowledge and plans would matter, identify it, and code it into the system by hand.

The connectionist systems of the 1980s and 1990s were predominantly pattern recognition systems. Neural networks excelled at perception tasks but weren't agents acting in environments over extended time horizons. The exceptions were systems created to play structured games. Arthur Samuel's checkers-playing program at IBM (Samuel 1959) was among the first to combine neural-network-like learning with self-play. Samuel demonstrated that machines could improve through experience without explicit programming of strategies. Likewise TD-Gammon used learning and self-play to achieve expert-level skill in backgammon, while also discovering strategies that revised human understanding of the game (Tesauro 1995). These were genuinely agentic systems, but they required the rules of each game to be explicitly programmed: what moves were legal, how pieces moved, when the game ended. The neural networks learned strategy, but only within hand-coded game engines that handled everything else. Each system remained specific to its domain.

A breakthrough toward agentic generality came with the Arcade Learning Environment (Bellemare et al. 2013), which provided a standardised interface to over fifty Atari 2600 games, creating a benchmark for agents that could learn diverse tasks from raw pixels. Using this platform, DeepMind (the London based AI laboratory that had been recently acquired by Google) demonstrated that a single neural net system could achieve human-level performance across dozens of games (Mnih et al. 2015). This was evidence that deep reinforcement learning could yield general-purpose agents, albeit limited to the structured environment of videogames. This was the trajectory that resulted in AlphaGo (Silver et al. 2016), its entirely self-play successor AlphaGo Zero (Silver et al. 2017) and AlphaZero (Silver et al. 2018) which generalised the approach to chess, shogi (a Japanese chess-like strategy game), and Go (see Chap. 2). These systems, however, still required the rules or interfaces for each game to be explicitly specified. What they learned was how to play optimally within those rules.

The emergence of agentic capabilities in LLMs, by contrast, was largely unexpected. These models were trained to predict text—why should they be capable of agentic behaviour? The answer lies in several properties that proved jointly sufficient for agency: reasoning, tool use, multimodality, and (of course) scale.

The most fundamental enabler of agentic capability was the discovery that LLMs could reason. They could decompose problems, think through intermediate steps, and maintain chains of inference. As Chap. 3 showed, AI models trained on internet-scale text have absorbed representations of the world that extends far beyond linguistic capabilities. Their training data includes technical documentation, instructional content, descriptions of physical and social systems, and records of human activity across virtually every domain. Through this they have learned—or perhaps it is better to say discovered—implicit models of causation, spatial relationships, temporal dynamics, and social interaction. This matters for agency because acting in environments requires predicting how those environments will respond. An LLM that has processed millions of tokens worth of API (application processing interface) documentation *understands* (in some functional sense) how APIs behave. One that has absorbed millions of tokens of debugging logs has learned how software fails and how failures are diagnosed. The cultural world models of LLMs are incomplete and sometimes wrong, but they provide sufficient predictive capacity to support the sort of goal-directed action that the symbolic AI theorists had tried to define and codify.

A persistent critique of AI argues that it can never achieve genuine intelligence while it is disembodied. Hubert L. Dreyfus argued in *What Computers Can't Do* (Dreyfus 1972; see also his follow-up 2009) that human cognition is inseparable from bodily existence. We understand the world not through abstract representations (or matrix multiplications in a neural network) but through our physical engagement with the world. Intelligence, on this view, requires a body that perceives, acts, and learns through interaction with an environment. This philosophical critique was reinforced from unexpected directions. In their book *The Embodied Mind* (1991), Francisco J Varela, Evan Thompson and Eleanor Rosch argued that the mind is not a computer processing data, but a living system that 'enacts' or creates its world through physical action. Drawing on Buddhist philosophy, the authors suggest that just as there is no 'fixed self' inside a person, there is no "fixed world" surrounding them. Instead, both arise together through the constant dance between an organism and its environment. Engineers, likewise, argued that intelligent behaviour emerges from direct interaction with the world. The roboticist Rodney Brooks (1991) argued that the elaborate internal world-models favoured by symbolic AI were fundamentally misconceived. Instead, Brooks argued that intelligent systems should use the real world as its own model by sensing and reacting to it directly in real time. In this view, 'intelligence' is an emergent property that an observer attributes to a system of independent, competing behaviours interacting with a complex environment.

Tool use and multimodality offer a response to this critique. They don't give language models biological bodies, but they embed the models in perception-action loops that achieve something functionally similar. Tool-augmented language models can learn to call systems external to themselves—interact with APIs, execute code, retrieve information, and embed those interactions as intermediate steps in problem-solving (Parisi et al. 2022; Schick et al. 2023). Through tools, AI models gained the capacity to act upon the (albeit digital) world. In this sense, tool use is a functional analogue to embodiment: the capacity to perceive environmental states (through retrieval and observation), to act upon environments (through tool invocation), and to learn from the consequences. They are *embodied* in a digital environment.

Multimodality also offers AI systems a functional embodiment without needing a complete world model. Vision-language models such as GPT-4 V (OpenAI 2023; see also Liu et al. 2023) enabled language models to reason about images as part of their conversational capabilities. Models could now interpret screenshots, diagrams, photographs, and visual interfaces. These capabilities converged in early 2023. Open-source projects like AutoGPT and BabyAGI wrapped LLMs in loops allowing them to set goals, decompose them into subtasks, execute actions, observe results, and iterate. These systems were fragile and prone to failure, but they demonstrated how LLMs could be used as a cognitive core that uses by tools and memory systems to operate continuously across tasks. Throughout 2024 and 2025, OpenAI introduced function calling and the Assistants API, Anthropic developed Claude's ability to use computer interfaces directly, and Google integrated similar capabilities into Gemini. Some of these systems can control computer interfaces directly, operating mouse and keyboard to navigate graphical environments. The combination of visual perception and motor action (seeing a screen, deciding where to click, observing the result) instantiates a perception-action loop bears structural similarity to the sensorimotor coupling that embodied cognition theorists identified as fundamental to intelligence.

5.2 Do AI Agents Have Economic Agency?

As the previous section suggests, computer scientists have typically understood 'agents' to be systems that perceive, decide, and act—a functional definition that encompasses everything from Shakey's corridor navigation to Claude's tool invocation. This usage is deliberately agnostic about internal architecture. Whether an agent reasons through explicit symbolic planning or through the pattern completion of a neural network, whether its goals are hardcoded or learned, whether it operates alone or coordinates with others, what matters is the input-output relationship. Agents simply observe, think, and act. These definitions provided a common vocabulary across otherwise incompatible research traditions—the BDI logicians and the reinforcement learning researchers, the roboticists and the multi-agent systems theorists, could all discuss 'agents' without first resolving their deeper disagreements about the nature of mind or intelligence.

But even in the 1990s it was understood that this definition of agency was excessively broad (Wooldridge and Jennings 1995, 116). Under most of these definitions, even a light switch could coherently be described as an agent—"a (very cooperative) agent with the capability of transmitting current at will, who invariably transmits current when it believes that we want it transmitted" (Shoham 1990, 297). If everything that senses and acts is an agent, then thermostats are agents, and so are bacteria, and so are avalanches responding to disturbances in snowpack.

So the computer science literature has tried to distinguish between weak and stronger notions of agency (Wooldridge and Jennings 1995). The weak notion requires only four properties: autonomy (operating without direct human intervention), social ability (interacting with other agents through some communication protocol), reactivity (perceiving and responding to the environment), and pro-activeness (exhibiting goal-directed behaviour by taking initiative). The stronger notion, which has been typically favoured by AI researchers and futurists, adds that agents should be "conceptualised or implemented using concepts that are more usually applied to humans" (Wooldridge and Jennings 1995, 117)—anthropomorphised notions such as knowledge, belief, intention, and obligation. Some researchers pushed further still, proposing that agents could have emotional states (Bates 1994). Or agents could have things like mobility (the ability to traverse networks), veracity (not knowingly communicating false information), benevolence (lacking conflicting goals), and rationality (acting consistently with one's goals given one's beliefs).

But even with these refinements, computer science definitions describe what systems do rather than why doing those things constitutes genuine agency. Economic agency is not merely sensing, deciding, and acting. Economic agency is the origination of value-creating choices under uncertainty. So we must turn to the classical liberal tradition's account of human action.

Mises defines human action as purposeful behaviour—"will put into operation" (Mises [1949] 1996, 11)—aiming at ends and goals through conscious adjustment to the conditions of one's environment. Action is not mere wishing or preference in the passive sense. It involves choosing among incompatible alternatives and thus renunciation (selecting one option and giving up another). He then states the prerequisites: action arises from uneasiness, the imagination of a more satisfactory state, and—crucially—the expectation that purposeful behavior can remove the uneasiness. Without the expectation that the unease can be alleviated, "no action is feasible" (Mises [1949] 1996, 14). Mises's definition focuses on the *internal* state of the actor. They experience uneasiness, they can imagine a better state, and expect that their action can relieve the uneasiness. This is an anti-behaviourist criterion (see the discussion in Chap. 2).

Post-Mises thinkers in the classical liberal tradition have developed a deep theory of human agency. Israel Kirzner (1992, 1978) rejected accounts of choice that treat behaviour as a response to a given set of alternatives. Instead, he places *entrepreneurial alertness* at the centre of economic explanation: the capacity to notice and create opportunities that were not previously perceived. Choice, on this account, arises from the open-endedness of the future, not from incomplete knowledge of fixed alternatives. If all relevant options and outcomes were already given, there would be no scope for discovery, entrepreneurship, or genuine choice at all. Likewise, James M. Buchanan makes the anti-behaviourist implication explicit by redefining opportunity cost as a choice-bound, counterfactual mental comparison, not an observable behavioural magnitude. In his *Cost and Choice* (1999), cost is the chooser's own imagined valuation of the best rejected alternative, which exists only *ex ante* and can be dated at the moment of decision. Once a choice is made, its alternative cannot be experienced and the cost 'vanishes,' so it cannot be recovered from observed behaviour or measured by external observers.

The most radical extension of this anti-behaviourist tradition comes from G. L. S. Shackle (1979), whose observations on the role of local knowledge in forming prices we considered in Chap. 3. While Mises asked what genuine choice is, Shackle asked: what must be true about time and knowledge for genuine choice to be possible at all? Shackle argues that human choice is an *originating* act that brings something new into existence. It is not a selection from a pre-existing menu of options. Shackle (1979, 8) calls choice a "cause uncaused": a beginning that cannot be fully explained by what came before. If outcomes were truly predictable from prior conditions, what we describe as 'choosing' would really just be mechanical response.

The argument that choices bring the imaginative future into existence has an interesting structural parallel with the argument made in Chap. 4. Task-based frameworks for modelling AI's economic impact assume a fixed menu of tasks and ask which will be automated. But these frameworks cannot predict the *creation* of new tasks. Task invention, not task automation, is the primary mechanism through which transformative technologies generate growth. The assumption of a closed possibility space makes these frameworks theoretically tractable—which is great for publication—but it excludes what actually matters for growth. Shackle's point about choice is the micro-level analogue of the macro-level point about innovation: economic progress occurs not through optimal selection among given alternatives but through imagining alternatives that did not previously exist.

Shackle's argument is worth considering in detail. As he argues, the future cannot be known because it does not yet exist. Uncertainty is not merely a practical limit on knowledge, it is an *ontological* condition. The future has no existence from which knowledge could be derived. This is why probabilistic forecasting, however sophisticated, cannot capture what the choices that actual decision-makers face. It is impossible to assign meaningful probabilities to outcomes that depend on choices not yet made, including that of the decisionmaker's (Shackle 1979, 59).

So if the future cannot be known probabilistically, how do choosers think about it? This is the rival 'skeins' of possible futures (Shackle 1979, 9). Instead of calculating the likelihood of any given future, we ask what we *cannot rule out*. Possibility, in his framework, means the absence of any discernible fatal obstacle. An entrepreneur does not ask "what is the probability of success?" but rather "can I see any reason this *must* fail?" This is a fundamentally different epistemic stance to optimisation under risk, which requires the decider to calculate probability distributions over outcomes. Possibility-thinking requires only the absence of obstacles that would be fatal to success.

So for Shackle, choice is commitment. Choice is *existential* (Shackle 1979, 15). To choose is to stake yourself on an uncertain future—to accept that you will bear consequences whose full character you cannot foreknow. This commitment reallocates scarce resources, closes off alternatives, and binds the chooser to a path. Shackle thus radicalises Kirzner's entrepreneurial discovery. For Kirzner, entrepreneurs discover opportunities others have overlooked. For Shackle, they go further: they *imagine possibilities into existence*. The alternatives are not waiting to be found; they are created by the imaginative act itself.

Shackle provides the strongest philosophical foundation within the classical liberal tradition for the claim that economic agency cannot be reduced to computation. Genuine agency requires originating choice—introducing something not implicit in prior conditions. AI systems transform inputs using patterns derived from past data. Their outputs, however novel they appear, remain recombinative: they operate within a space fixed by training, architecture, and objectives. They are extremely adept at the combinatorial idea generation that we considered in the last chapter. But they do not originate choices—they do not originate history. AI agents are committed to a probabilistic epistemology. They ask "what is likely?" when the economically relevant question is "what cannot be ruled out?"

AI may therefore serve as a powerful instrument to empower human agency—expanding the space of options we consider, accelerating evaluation, simulating hypothetical futures. But in the strong sense that runs from Mises through Shackle, it does not act. AI agents have nothing at stake. Any "commitment" they appear to make is derivative—embedded in them by the humans who designed their objectives and deployment contexts. Economic agency remains irreducibly human (see also Davidson 2025; Townsend et al. 2025).

One might object that this account of human imagination smuggles in a kind of mind-body dualism—claiming that there has to be some sort of ineffable entrepreneurial vital essence where mechanistic explanations for economic behaviour works perfectly well. After all, human cognition is itself the product of neural processes, and those processes are recombinative: the brain classifies new stimuli by assimilating them to patterns established through prior experience. If imagination is just neural recombination, as is implied by Hayek's mechanistic account in *The Sensory Order* (1952) what principled distinction can we draw between human creativity and AI recombination?

But AI systems select among recombinations according to externally fixed criteria—loss functions, reward signals, architectural constraints. Human choosers select according to their own purposes, responding to an uneasiness that is irreducibly their own. Shackle's point is that the *objects* of imaginative recombination are not given in advance. Entrepreneurs do not select from a pre-existing menu of options but constitute the options through the act of imagining them. The combinatorial space is not fixed but continuously built and rebuilt by their imagination. Finally, even if the cognitive mechanisms were identical, human choice, unlike agentic AI choice, involves commitment and consequences. Without these, there is no economic agency at all.

Even in a world of AI agents, the acting individual—the human being who experiences wants, bears uncertainty, and accepts consequences—remains the foundational economic unit of. AI agents are instruments through which human purposes are pursued. There is no AI welfare to maximise, no AI preferences to satisfy other than those they have been designed to have, and no AI flourishing to promote. Economic decisions are tied to personal experience and evolving preferences that cannot be captured algorithmically, even by systems that seem to mimic human reasoning (Makridis and Lazanski 2025). Our AI agents are tools. They are remarkably capable tools, but they are tools.

5.3 Are AI Agents Capital? or Labour?

We have argued that AI agents do not make conscious choices to attain ends propelled by their imagination, so in the classical liberal sense they do not have agency. But this conclusion creates an immediate problem. In economic production, AI systems increasingly *look like* agents—they look like labour. They perform tasks, deliver cognitive services, substitute for human effort, and reorganise how work is done. This gap between what AI *is* and what it *does* is a puzzle.

Classical and neoclassical economics thought of production as the organisation of three factors: land, labour, and capital. Each factor has different characteristics and therefore is paid in different ways. Land refers to natural resources whose supply is fixed or highly inelastic. The return to the ownership of land takes the form of rent (Ricardo 2012; Smith [1776] 1904). Labour refers to human effort applied in production and is typically remunerated through wages, paid as a flow for time or services rendered. Capital refers to the means of production—machines, tools, buildings, and intermediate goods—that are accumulated through saving and investment. Capital earns its returns as profit or interest. This taxonomy has proved remarkably stable. Capital can be owned, bought, sold, and replicated. Land can be owned but not reproduced. Labour, by contrast, is inseparable from the person who supplies it. Workers sell their time and effort, not themselves, and labour is therefore paid as a contingent flow rather than as an owned asset (Marshall 1920; Solow 1956). It is this personal attachment of labour to the worker that underpins the wage relationship and historically separated labour cleanly from capital in economic theory.

The Austrian tradition complicates this picture in a way that becomes useful for thinking about artificial intelligence. Austrian economists have approached capital very differently from the neoclassical tradition. Rather than treating capital as a single, homogeneous input (the single variable "K"), they understood it as a collection of different goods, used at different stages over time. Eugene von Böhm-Bawerk (1890) emphasised that production is *roundabout*: goods are not produced directly from labour and land, but through chains of intermediate goods created earlier and used later. Productivity can rise as production chains become longer and more complex, even though this makes production more time-consuming. Capital is best understood as a bundle of productive services delivered over time, not as a stock that enters a production function all at once. Later Austrian work stressed capital heterogeneity and change. Capital goods are specialised, recombinable, and continually re-evaluated as plans and expectations shift (Lachmann 1956).

From a more mainstream economic perspective, human capital theory has further undermined the cleanliness of the factor of production approach. Education, training, health, and migration require investment up front and raise future productivity and are therefore forms of capital formation (Schultz 1961). Gary Becker (2008) gave this idea its basic economic structure by framing schooling and training as investments with costs (fees and foregone earnings) and expected returns in higher wages over time.

In many important ways, human capital behaves like capital: it is accumulated through investment, it yields a flow of returns, and it can depreciate through atrophy or obsolescence when skills fall behind changing technologies or practices. But at the same time human capital does not take the institutional form of ordinary capital as it was imagined by the neoclassical economists. Unlike a machine, it cannot be separated from its holder and sold to the highest bidder; it is embodied in persons, and firms access it only through employment contracts that cannot fully specify effort, learning, or judgement in advance. Human capital, in this sense, is a particularly clear example of the Austrian school's insistence that capital should be understood not as an interchangeable commodity, but as a set of highly specific and heterogeneous assets that cannot be arbitrarily shuffled around the economy by administrative fiat (Burns 2018). Firms can influence or partially capture returns through training arrangements and labour market institutions, but the basic point remains that the asset itself is not alienable in the way physical capital is.

Of course AI is not the first technology to substitute capital for cognitive effort. Calculators replaced mental arithmetic, spreadsheets replaced manual bookkeeping, and search engines reduced the cost of finding information. These technologies substituted for specific cognitive tasks while leaving the overall structure of work intact.

But unlike these technologies AI has a generality and adaptability comparable to human cognition. The closer the technology moves to artificial *general* intelligence the more it has the ability to learn, adjust, and apply knowledge across many different contexts rather than being limited to a narrow task. This matters economically because generality has historically been the defining feature of human labour. Humans are valuable not because they have been optimised for one specific task—like a calculator has—but because they can shift between tasks, learn new skills (make new investments in human capital), and adapt their behaviour as circumstances change. These might be the general skills that allow, for example, a surgeon to work in a structured environment like a hospital above and beyond their specific medical domain knowledge (Becker 2008). Or they could be the even more general social skills of communication, collaboration and situational awareness that allow workers to operate in environments where there are no specific "rules" about success (Deming 2017; Autor 2015). Real work depends on judgement formed in context rather than on rule-following alone (Suchman 1987).

So in this light it is unsurprisingly tempting to think of AI agents as artificial workers rather than as machines. Agents are not passive systems that generate outputs in isolation, but systems that interact continuously with their environment. This capability explains why agentic AI systems are often described as performing "roles" rather than just completing tasks. But functional embodiment through tool use and multimodality is not the same as institutional embedding. As we have argued above, AI systems do not choose ends in the economically relevant sense. AGI blurs the boundaries between capital and labour, but it does not resolve it by *converting* capital into labour.

In institutional and legal terms, AI is capital. AI is produced through investment and AI models are ownable. But in production, AI contributes in a way that closely resembles labour. It delivers ongoing cognitive services that substitute at the margin for tasks previously performed by human workers. To describe AI as a "capital–labour hybrid" is not to make a claim about consciousness, personhood, or moral status.

It is a claim about how AI appears in production and how returns flow through the economy: as capital income to owners, even when the services supplied resemble labour.

The classical factor categories of land, labour and capital are legal and institutional arrangements that govern control, responsibility, and reward. How an activity is organised depends on transaction costs, contracting limits, and the allocation of residual control rights, not on the physical nature of the task itself (Coase 1937, 1960; Williamson 1996, 1985; Hart 1988). Whether AI services are treated as capital assets, internal tools, outsourced services, or something closer to labour depends on how it is governed in an institutional setting. A highly capable AI system may look 'worker-like' in function, but if it is owned, replicable, and controlled through property and contract, the returns flow as capital income.

This institutional framing explains why debates about AI and work cannot be separated from questions about governance, firm structure, and property rights (issues taken up in the next chapters). The core governance challenge is to preserve the institutional conditions under which entrepreneurial judgment can be exercised—the freedom to act on one's own assessment of possibility, to bear the consequences of error, and to capture the returns from success. This is the traditional task of classical liberal political economy, but one which is made even more pressing in an economy of agents and the capitalisation of cognition.

This argument completes the first half of this book. We can now take stock of what has been established. The AI systems transforming economic life are not programmed but trained. Their capabilities emerge from architecture and scale rather than from explicit engineering—a vindication of the connectionist vision over the symbolic tradition's faith in hand-coded rules. What emerges from this training are cultural world models: compressions of the dispersed and tacit knowledge of human civilisation, encoded in ways that resist complete articulation. Like prices in a market economy, the outputs of foundation models integrate information that no designer specified and no interpreter can fully unpack. The knowledge they embody is genuinely tacit—it can be *used* but not fully *stated*.

This emergent intelligence has profound economic consequences. By expanding the searchable fraction of the combinatorial space, AI removes the demographic constraint that has governed the production of ideas since the industrial revolution. For the first time in history, the ultimate resource—the human capacity to generate new ideas—has been industrialised.

And yet industrialised intelligence is not the same as economic agency. AI systems satisfy the functional criteria of agency: they perceive, decide, and act. But they do not originate choice under genuine uncertainty, commit themselves to futures they cannot foreknow, or bear the consequences of error. They operate within possibility spaces fixed by their training and optimise according to externally specified criteria. They are instruments through which human purposes are pursued—forms of capital that supply labour-like cognitive services—but they are not independent loci of valuation or responsibility. Entrepreneurial judgment remains irreducibly human. The future we are have described is one of radical cognitive abundance that empowers, but does not displace, human agency.

The second half of the book considers the implications of this shift. If the supply of cognition is no longer the bottleneck, then the central questions become institutional. How should the actions of AI agents be governed? Who bears responsibility when delegated systems err? What arrangements can coordinate the plans of multiple agents—human and artificial—operating simultaneously? The chapters that follow argue that these questions require the same institutional machinery that classical liberals have always championed: property rights that bound what agents may access, contracts that specify permissible action, and decentralised markets that coordinate plans no central authority could comprehend. It is to those institutions we now turn.

References

Autor, David H. 2015. "Why Are There Still So Many Jobs? The History and Future of Workplace Automation." *Journal of Economic Perspectives* 29 (3): 3–30. https://doi.org/10.1257/jep.29.3.3.

Bates, Joseph. 1994. "The Role of Emotion in Believable Agents." *Communication: ACM* 37 (7): 122–25. https://doi.org/10.1145/176789.176803.

Becker, Gary S. 2008. *Human Capital: A Theoretical and Empirical Analysis, with Special Reference to Education*. 3. ed., [Reprint]. The University of Chicago Press.

Bellemare, Marc G., Yavar Naddaf, Joel Veness, and Michael Bowling. 2013. "The Arcade Learning Environment: An Evaluation Platform for General Agents." *Journal of Artificial Intelligence Research* 47 (June): 253–79. https://doi.org/10.1613/jair.3912.

Bender, Emily M., Timnit Gebru, Angelina McMillan-Major, and Shmargaret Shmitchell. 2021 March 1. "On the Dangers of Stochastic Parrots: Can Language Models Be Too Big?" *Proceedings of the 2021 ACM Conference on Fairness, Accountability, and Transparency* (New York, NY, USA), FAccT, :610–23. https://doi.org/10.1145/3442188.3445922.

Böhm-Bawerk, Eugen von. 1890. *Capital and Interest: a Critical History of Economical Theory*. Macmillan and Company.

Bratman, Michael. 1987. *Intention, Plans and Practical Reason*. Harvard University Press.

Bratman, Michael E., David J. Israel, and Martha E. Pollack. 1988. "Plans and Resource-Bounded Practical Reasoning." *Computational Intelligence* 4 (3): 349–55. https://doi.org/10.1111/j.1467-8640.1988.tb00284.x.

Brooks, Rodney A. 1991. "Intelligence without Representation." *Artificial Intelligence* 47 (1–3): 139–59.

Buchanan, James M. 1999. *Cost and Choice: An Inquiry in Economic Theory*. Volume 6 ed. Liberty Fund.

Burns, Scott. 2018. "Human Capital and Its Structure." *The Journal of Private Enterprise* 33 (2): 33–51.

Coase, R. H. 1937. "The Nature of the Firm." *Economica* 4 (16): 386–405. https://doi.org/10.1111/j.1468-0335.1937.tb00002.x.

Coase, R H. 1960. "The Problem of Social Cost." *The Journal of Law and Economics*, 44.

Davidson, Sinclair. 2025, November 12. "The Limits of Artificial Intelligence." *The Review of Austrian Economics*, ahead of print. https://doi.org/10.1007/s11138-025-00705-2.

Deming, David J. 2017. "The Growing Importance of Social Skills in the Labor Market*." *The Quarterly Journal of Economics* 132 (4): 1593–640. https://doi.org/10.1093/qje/qjx022.

Dreyfus, Hubert L. 1972. *What Computers Can't Do: A Critique of Artificial Reason*. Harper & Row.
Dreyfus, Hubert L. 2009. *What Computers Still Can't Do: A Critique of Artificial Reason*. Rev. ed., [Repr.]. MIT Press.
Fikes, Richard E., and Nils J. Nilsson. 1971. "Strips: A New Approach to the Application of Theorem Proving to Problem Solving." *Artificial Intelligence* 2 (3–4): 189–208. https://doi.org/10.1016/0004-3702(71)90010-5.
Georgeff, Michael P., and Amy L. Lansky. 1987. "Reactive Reasoning and Planning." Paper presented at Proceedings of the Sixth National Conference on Artificial Intelligence (AAAI-87).
Hart, Oliver D. 1988. "Incomplete Contracts and the Theory of the Firm." *Journal of Law, Economics, & Organization* 4 (1): 119–39.
Hayek, Friedrich A. 1952. *The Sensory Order: An Inquiry Into the Foundations of Theoretical Psychology*. University of Chicago Press.
Kirzner, Israel M. 1978. *Competition and Entrepreneurship*. University of Chicago Press. https://books.google.com.au/books?id=E9DAt745zhIC.
Kirzner, Israel M. 1992. *The Meaning of Market Process: essays in the Development of Modern Austrian Economics*. Routledge.
Lachmann, Ludwig M. 1956. *Capital and Its Structure*. G. Bell and Sons.
Liu, Haotian, Chunyuan Li, Qingyang Wu, and Yong Jae Lee. 2023, December 11. "Visual Instruction Tuning." arXiv:2304.08485. Preprint, arXiv. https://doi.org/10.48550/arXiv.2304.08485.
Makridis, Christos, and Dominique Lazanski. 2025, August 6. "Navigating the Knowledge Problem in the Era of Open AI and Polycentric Governance." SSRN Scholarly Paper No. 5382315. Social Science Research Network. https://doi.org/10.2139/ssrn.5382315.
Marshall, Alfred. 1920. *Principles of Economics: An Introductory Scheme*. 8th ed. Macmillan and Company.
Mises, Ludwig von. (1949) 1996. *Human Action: A Treatise on Economics*. 4. rev. ed. Fox & Wilkes.
Mnih, Volodymyr, Koray Kavukcuoglu, David Silver, et al. 2015. "Human-Level Control through Deep Reinforcement Learning." *Nature* 518 (7540): 529–33. https://doi.org/10.1038/nature14236.
Nilsson, Nils J. 1984. *Shakey the Robot*. Vol. 323. SRI International Technical Note: SRI International.
OpenAI. 2023. *GPT-4V(Ision) System Card*. https://cdn.openai.com/papers/GPTV_System_Card.pdf.

Parisi, Aaron, Yao Zhao, and Noah Fiedel. 2022, May 24. "TALM: tool Augmented Language Models." arXiv:2205.12255. Preprint, arXiv. https://doi.org/10.48550/arXiv.2205.12255.

Rao, Anand S., and Michael P. Georgeff. 1991. *Modeling Rational Agents within a BDI-Architecture*. Vol. 14. Technical Note. Australian Artificial Intelligence Institute.

Rao, Anand S., and Michael P. Georgeff. 1995. "BDI Agents: from Theory to Practice." Paper presented at Proceedings of the First International Conference on Multiagent Systems.

Ricardo, David. 2012. *Principles of Political Economy and Taxation*. Dover Publications.

Samuel, Arthur L. 1959. "Some Studies in Machine Learning Using the Game of Checkers." *IBM Journal* 3 (3).

Schick, Timo, Jane Dwivedi-Yu, Roberto Dessì, et al. 2023, February 9. "Toolformer: Language Models Can Teach Themselves to Use Tools." arXiv:2302.04761. Preprint, arXiv. https://doi.org/10.48550/arXiv.2302.04761.

Schultz, Theodore W. 1961. "Investment in Human Capital." *The American Economic Review* 51 (1): 1–17.

Shackle, G. L. S. 1979. *Imagination and the Nature of Choice*. Columbia University press.

Shoham, Yoav. 1990. *Agent Oriented Programming: An Overview of the Framework and Summary of Recent Research*. Technical Report STAN-CS -1335-90. Computer Science Department, Stanford University.

Silver, David, Aja Huang, Chris J. Maddison, et al. 2016. "Mastering the Game of Go with Deep Neural Networks and Tree Search." *Nature* 529 (7587): 484–89. https://doi.org/10.1038/nature16961.

Silver, David, Thomas Hubert, Julian Schrittwieser, et al. 2018. "A General Reinforcement Learning Algorithm That Masters Chess, Shogi, and Go through Self-Play." *Science* 362 (6419): 1140–44. https://doi.org/10.1126/science.aar6404.

Silver, David, Julian Schrittwieser, Karen Simonyan, et al. 2017. "Mastering the Game of Go without Human Knowledge." *Nature* 550 (7676): 354–59. https://doi.org/10.1038/nature24270.

Smith, Adam. (1776) 1904. *An Inquiry into the Nature and Causes of the Wealth of Nations*. Edited by Edwin Cannan. Modern Library.

Solow, Robert M. 1956. "A Contribution to the Theory of Economic Growth." *The Quarterly Journal of Economics* 70 (1): 65. https://doi.org/10.2307/1884513.

Suchman, Lucille Alice. 1987. *Plans and Situated Actions: The Problem of Human-Machine Communication*. Cambridge University Press.

Tesauro, Gerald. 1995. "Temporal Difference Learning and TD-Gammon." *Commun. ACM* 38 (3): 58–68. https://doi.org/10.1145/203330.203343.

Townsend, David M., Richard A. Hunt, Judy Rady, Parul Manocha, and Ju Hyeong Jin. 2025. "Are the Futures Computable? Knightian Uncertainty and Artificial Intelligence." *Academy of Management Review* 50 (2): 415–40. https://doi.org/10.5465/amr.2022.0237.

Varela, Francisco, Eleanor Rosch, and Evan Thompson. 1991. *The Embodied Mind: cognitive Science and Human Experience*. The MIT Press.

Williamson, Oliver E. 1985. *The Economic Institutions of Capitalism: Firms, Markets, Relational Contracting*. Free Press.

Williamson, Oliver E. 1996. *The Mechanisms of Governance*. Oxford University Press.

Wooldridge, Michael, and Nicholas R. Jennings. 1995. "Intelligent Agents: Theory and Practice." *The Knowledge Engineering Review* 10 (2): 115–52. https://doi.org/10.1017/S0269888900008122.

6

AI and the Calculation Debate

Abstract This chapter argues that artificial intelligence does not resolve the economic calculation problem because the objection to central planning was never about computational limits but about the institutional processes through which economic knowledge is generated. Modern AI systems are trained prediction engines, not omniscient optimisers—they learn from the outputs of market processes but cannot replicate the discovery procedures that produce prices. Prices function as lossy compressions of dispersed, tacit, and forward-looking knowledge created through rivalry and exchange. Without private property, profit-and-loss feedback, and decentralised error correction, no algorithm can generate the counterfactual judgments coordination requires.

Keywords Economic calculation · Socialism · Ludwig von mises · Friedrich Hayek · Prices · Central planning · Tacit knowledge · Institutions · Technosocialism · Market process · Artificial intelligence

Few intellectual contests have shaped the worldview of classical liberalism more profoundly than the economic calculation debate. When Ludwig von Mises declared in 1920 that rational economic calculation

C. Berg, *Artificial Intelligence*, Palgrave Studies in Classical Liberalism,
https://doi.org/10.1007/978-3-032-22310-4_6

was impossible under socialism (Mises [1920] 1935), he launched an argument that would define the boundaries of liberal economic thought for a century (Lavoie 1985b). The debate between Mises, Hayek and Lionel Robbins on the one side, and the socialists Oskar Lange and Abba Lerner on the other, established the epistemic foundations on which classical liberals would build their critique of central planning.

That debate is no longer of purely historical interest. As early as the 1960s, Lange wrote that were he to engage Hayek and Robbins again,

> my task would be much simpler. My answer to Hayek and Robbins would be: so what's the trouble? Let us put the simultaneous equations on an electronic computer and we shall obtain the solution in less than a second. The market process with its cumbersome *tâtonnements* appears old-fashioned. Indeed, it may be considered as a computing device of the pre-electronic age (Lange 1967, 158).

For Lange's followers, this seems compelling. Some of the most important economic allocation decisions in modern capitalism occur inside organizations whose internal operations look less like markets and more like engineered systems of measurement, prediction, and control. A company like Amazon forecasts demand, allocates inventory, routes logistics, and orchestrates supply chains at a global scale. Walmart coordinates a vast internal economy with dense informational infrastructure (Phillips and Rozworski 2019). At the same time, the technologies of prediction, optimization, and orchestration available to firms and states have moved rapidly from the margins to the centre of social organisation (Agrawal et al. 2018).

The basis of the contemporary revival of the calculation debate is not just that computers are fast now so planning should be easy. It is a specific thesis about how digitization changes the informational and organizational environment in which the original liberal critique was formed. The *technosocialist* claim (which is also sometimes known as the case for 'cyber communism') is that the Hayek-Mises argument was only valid given the particular technologies of the pre-war period. As one advocate has argued "it could not have been foreseen in earlier historical periods how the productive forces would make socialist means of communication possible" (Saros 2014, 197; see also Dapprich and Greenwood 2024).

For the technosocialists, local knowledge was hard to centralise in Hayek and Mises's time not because it was inaccessible in some metaphysical sense, but simply because it was costly to measure, store, and transmit. A century later, the costs of knowledge have plummeted to the extent that production and consumption legible in near real time. Machine learning systems can detect patterns that were invisible to the planners of the past. If the relevant knowledge is becoming easier to codify and transfer, then the informational advantage of decentralization may be eroding. Nieto (2023, 249) writes that:

> If the price system constitutes a "telecommunications system," as Hayek asserts, then we can certainly replace it with a more technologically advanced one. Today it is definitely technologically possible to manage and balance a complex economy, subject to continuous changes in preferences and offers, without the need for a monetary price system. It also happens that a good portion of the tacit knowledge that Hayekians speak of (skills, experience) is being rapidly overcome by automation processes that codify by way of computer software all the knowledge necessary to organize the technical division of labor in each company (industry 4.0)

The mid-twentieth century cyberneticists believed that governance was a problem of control and communication (Wiener [1948] 2000; Beer 1981). The cybernetics movement understood that the economy was a complex adaptive system but believed that technology would still allow them to subject that complexity to central planning. Experiments such as Chile's Project Cybersyn and Soviet proposals such as OGAS were early attempts to build the feedback infrastructure necessary to do so (Medina 2014; Peters 2016). The twenty-first century technosocialists are right to believe that the sensing and computing technologies of these systems were radically inadequate to the task. But if modern technology can gather and process vastly more data than anything available to the Soviet Union or to Salvador Allende's Chile, then the cybernetic ideal seems, at least superficially, less fanciful.

Another departure from their ancestors is that the modern technosocialists propose what they call *hybrid* and *iterative* forms of planning rather than monolithic centralisation. Paul Cockshott and Allin Cottrell's influential *Towards a New Socialism* (1993) treated planning as a practical problem of algorithms and data structures, while retaining markets for many consumer goods and allocating inputs and capital goods by computation. More recent work proposes cybernetic adjustment mechanisms using machine learning (Dapprich and Cockshott 2023). Others shift the focus from replacing markets to using machine intelligence to test policies continuously and adaptively rather than pre-specifying the entire structure of production (Naidu 2024). What unites these views is a desire to replace the anarchy of capitalist production with a high feedback system that can orient the economy towards specific objectives.

Many of these arguments were made prior to the rise of the transformer architecture that has established the modern AI era. And in one sense the benefits LLMs for economic planning are not immediately obvious. The technology does not seem well suited for the sort of precise planning imagined by the techno-socialists. AI outputs are creative and unpredictable rather than concrete and definitive. One prominent advocate who has argued that technology necessitates a revision of the calculation debate (Morozov 2019) has written that the possibilities of this generation of AI lie in its ability to imagine new societies, not simply replicate capitalist mechanisms for socialist ends (Morozov 2025).

But recent scholarship offers a sophisticated mechanism for why AI might shift the optimal locus of decision-making even within a broadly market setting. Brynjolfsson and Hitzig (2025) argue that AI can both codify forms of knowledge that were previously inaccessible and expand information processing capacity. This, they argue could make centralisation more efficient—at least when there are strong interdependencies between economic production. Theirs is an argument that the economics of property rights and organizational boundaries may change as machine intelligence changes what can be known, transmitted, and acted upon. On the one hand this is a truism—Chaps. 4 and 5 above have argued that AI will bring about radical changes in the structure of production, which if true would necessarily have organisational consequences. But their argument also suggests that the efficient boundary between private and public sector could change as well.

This chapter argues that the renewed case for computational planning fails. It fails on four grounds.

First, it routinely treats computation—in both its pre-transformer and transformer era form—as a single, general-purpose intelligence. But transformer-era systems are not omniscient optimisers. They are trained prediction systems—powerful at recognising patterns, forecasting, and producing plausible sequences (including plans written in natural language), and increasingly capable of executing tasks via tools. These capabilities can improve local coordination inside firms and supply chains, reduce search costs, speed up matching, and make it easier to test alternatives. But they do not replace the institutional discovery processes that markets perform. A plan that reads well is not the same thing as a plan that coordinates well.

Second, the modern planning literature tends to restate the calculation problem as a question of information processing. But much of what matters for allocation—opportunity cost, relative scarcity, and changing expectations—does not exist as a complete dataset waiting to be ingested. It is generated in the process of market interaction, and it is continually revised as people experiment, discover, imitate, and fail. Treating calculation as a tractable optimisation problem assumes away the market process that produces the very inputs optimisation would require.

Third, computational planning proposals systematically undervalue the importance of institutions. Profit and loss are a feedback system that corrects errors through exit and reallocation. A planner with better AI models still faces the same basic problems as any planner before or after the digital revolution. Whose objectives are being optimised? How are conflicts between ends resolved? What mechanism forces correction when the plan is wrong? Even in generous interpretations where AI improves forecasting and logistics, it does not supply the institutional incentives and error-correction that make decentralised coordination possible.

Finally, as AI systems—particularly agentic AI systems—become more capable and widespread, the environment becomes more complex again. Predicting an economy is difficult even when agents are human. Predicting an economy full of adaptive AI agents—whose behaviour changes in response to forecasts, rules, and each other—raises a second-order calculation problem. The planner is no longer forecasting a solely human world. The planner is governing a shifting ecology of agentic optimisers. In that environment, the Hayek–Mises critique is more powerful, not less. And there is a greater need for coordination through discovery, decentralisation, and the liberal institutions.

6.1 What Kind of Intelligence?

The claim at the heart of modern technosocialism is relatively simple. Markets are messy because they are slow, noisy, and human. Computers are fast, precise, and tireless. Therefore, if we can finally build sufficiently powerful computers, we can finally plan. This narrative treats the calculation problem as a purely technical constraint—one that progress in hardware, data storage, and machine learning can relax, and ultimately remove. But it rests on a surprisingly thin understanding of what modern AI systems actually are, how they work, and what sort of 'knowledge' they possess.

In public discussion, the phrase is 'artificial intelligence' is used as if it denotes a general capacity—an undifferentiated commodity-like intelligence that can be pointed at any coordination problem and instructed to solve it. Yet, as we have shown in Chap. 2, modern AI is not a single thing but the outcome of decades of divergent research programmes, each embodying different assumptions about how knowledge can be acquired and represented. The symbolic tradition sought to encode intelligence through explicit rules. The connectionist tradition has allowed intelligence to emerge. And within connectionism itself, there are many distinct architectures (LeCun et al. 2015; Goodfellow 2016).

These tools are not interchangeable. A recommender system like that which suggests content on Netflix or new things to buy on Amazon learns statistical associations from historical user interactions. These can predict what you might click in the future—but they cannot explain why you should want to. A computer vision classifier trained on labelled images learns to map pixels to categories—it recognises objects but knows nothing of their use or value. And the transformer-era LLMs—the systems that have animated most recent public discussion—are best understood as prediction engines trained on cultural artefacts. Like a compressed file, these models discard idiosyncratic detail while preserving enough structure to create plausible output in response to prompting. That compression is powerful precisely because it captures consistent features in the training dataset, but it is also inherently incomplete, and sometimes gets things badly wrong. The right way to think about the internal representations learned by these systems is not as a mirror of objective economic reality but as an internalisation of the semiotic order humans have built (Potts 2024). Each of these systems excels at something. Collectively, they demonstrate that artificial intelligence can forecast, classify, recommend, and optimise within well-specified domains.

But the technosocialist argument requires a leap from these well-proven capabilities to something far more ambitious: that AI can calculate and choose in the Misesian sense. Their argument conflates *computation* with *calculation* (Boettke and Candela 2023; Kiesling 2024; Phelan and Wenzel 2023). Computation is the processing of given data through algorithms. Modern AI excels at this. Calculation is something quite different: it is the use of relative prices emerging from exchange to determine opportunity costs. Lange and the market socialists focused on the calculation aspect of Mises' argument as if the problem were merely one of computing the solution to a system of equations.

Even the most sophisticated AI systems face what Phelan and Wenzel (2023) call the 'problem of judgment'. Entrepreneurs form expectations about future prices, costs, and production possibilities that arise from experience and contextual knowledge that cannot be codified. AI systems, however advanced, "are not designed to go outside the parameters they are given" (Phelan and Wenzel 2023, 177; see also Davidson 2025c) They operate within closed problem spaces, optimising against objectives that humans must specify.

LLMs are trained on the *outputs* of the market process—recorded transactions, historical prices, commentary, analysis—but they cannot generate the *inputs*. As we have repeatedly emphasised throughout this book, the market's inputs are subjective valuations held in the minds of dispersed actors, entrepreneurial imagination about futures that do not yet exist, and tacit knowledge that cannot be fully articulated even by those who possess it (Lambert and Fegley 2023, 243). Big data is entirely backward-looking: it records what has already happened, but economic calculation requires forward-looking judgments about what *should* happen given present conditions and anticipated futures. Without private property and monetary exchange in goods of all orders, the cardinal numbers necessary for capital accounting simply do not exist (Makridis and Lazanski 2025). The distinction between information and knowledge is crucial here. Information is the stock of existing known facts that can be digitised and processed. Knowledge is the flow of new understanding that comes into existence only through the context in which actors find themselves making choices (Davidson 2024). AI can collate vast quantities of information, but it cannot access knowledge in this sense.

The irony for the new advocates of technosocialism is that the model of intelligence that most closely fits the planning imagination is the one that largely failed: symbolic AI and expert systems. The symbolic AI tradition presents intelligence as a legible artefact—knowledge made explicit and then executed. In the symbolic AI paradigm, the world is decomposed into discrete entities and properties; a knowledge base stores facts; and inference rules transform those facts into conclusions. As Herbert Simon and his colleagues conceived it, intelligent action is goal-directed search across a known set of rules and sequences (Newell et al. 1958; Simon and Newell 1958; Fikes and Nilsson 1971). The expert-system movement extended this approach into applied domains by treating professional judgment as something that could be represented as a stock of rules and heuristics and then "run" by an inference engine (Feigenbaum 1977; Buchanan and Shortliffe 1984). This paradigm had a particular epistemic stance that claimed intelligence is something designers can specify in advance, can audit, and can be executed centrally.

It is no coincidence that this stance sits comfortably with the administrative sciences of the twentieth century. It is in cognitive science an example of what Scott (1998) influentially described as "high modernism"—an ideology that treats complex social order as something that can be made *legible* to administrators and then redesigned top-down using scientific/technical schemes. Herbert Simon's analysis of organisations treats decision-making as a problem of procedures and information-processing routines (Simon 1947). For the high modernists, what the Austrian economists might describe as coordination failures look more like failures of representation and computation. And the appropriate response to such failures is to gather more information and refine decision-making procedures, and the system will choose better. Mirowski (2002) traces how cybernetics and the field of operations research generalised this belief into a broader command-and-control style of reasoning that moved between military planning, economics, and computing. Once one has this style of thought, it is easy to see why markets can appear out of date. Decentralised discovery looks wasteful, while central calculation looks like the mature alternative.

This connection was not merely metaphorical. In the expert-systems era, "artificial intelligence" was explicitly discussed as a tool for economic management and planning. By the mid-1980s, the economics and AI intersection was explicitly framed as planning and control engineering for complex organisations (Roos 1987). One contributor to an economics and AI conference in the mid-1980s, for example, treated government and organisational policy statements as rule-based expert systems (Hertz 1987). Other researchers proposed expert system-based AI as an "economic planning system" for domains such as water management (Grönquist 1990). In the same period computer scientists and economists proposed algorithms and knowledge-based techniques for constructing economic plans (Cockshott 1990).

Perhaps no economic tradition better illustrates the application of symbolic logic to economic planning than input-output economics. While we can trace this tradition's intellectual ancestry all the way back to the French physiocrats (Kuczynski and Meek 1972; Vaggi 1987), input-output economics is a distinctively twentieth century high modernist approach to economic analysis. Developed by the economist Wassily Leontief, an input–output table renders the economy as a matrix of sectors, with coefficients representing technical requirements and accounting identities ensuring that inputs and outputs balance (Leontief [1966] 1986). Once those coefficients are treated as given, the remaining task looks like an engineering exercise: choose a target output vector and compute the implied production requirements. Turning this accounting representation into an *optimal* plan under scarce resources is a matter of linear programming. The planner specifies their objective, imposes resource constraints, and then solves it (Koopmans 1975; Kantorovich 1960).

This is, of course, the move from *describing* the economy to *controlling* the economy that the classical liberal economists have been so critical of. It is one thing to summarise economic interdependencies in input–output tables, but treat these as the 'knowledge' required for coordination abstracts away substitution, entrepreneurial discovery, and the fact that the relevant knowledge is generated through the market process rather than collected in advance (Lavoie 1985a). Hayek ([1976] 2021) similarly cautioned that enthusiasm for Leontief-style techniques reflects a confusion about planning—mistaking the *ex post* legibility of an accounting framework for an ex ante method of directing an economy whose valuations and opportunities are continuously formed and revised through decentralised competition.

Both the economic planners and symbolic AI presume(ed) that the world can be rendered fully explicit in a stable ontology. Insofar as expert systems had 'world models,' they were *explicit and designed*, consisting of a hand-engineered ontology of objects, properties, and relationships (Fikes and Nilsson 1971). STRIPS, the planning system used in the Shakey robot discussed in Chap. 5, represents the world as an explicit list of stated facts and represents actions as hand-defined operators. For example, if the designers wanted Shakey to be able to push an object, the very *concept* of pushing has to be deliberately encoded, so that an operator like "push(k, m, n)" is defined to mean "push object *k* from location *m* to location *n*". In other words, their "model" was a hand-written description of the parts of the world the designers could spell out, not a learned system that could infer new structure from data and generalise beyond what had been explicitly encoded.

But as we have discussed, expert systems were brittle (Feigenbaum 1977; Dreyfus 1972; 2009). They struggled to deal with edge cases and to adapt to new information and environments. The bottleneck that expert systems designers faced around knowledge acquisition was not simply a problem of resources but reflected the difficulty of turning tacit, context-sensitive information into stable, concrete rules. Economic planning faces the same problem at higher stakes. The relevant knowledge is often not 'inside' individuals as propositions waiting to be extracted. It is generated in action, through experimentation, interpretation, and error correction under uncertainty. When the environment changes—and in an economy it changes continuously—the plan is not merely missing information. It is missing the procedure through which information is created and revised.

By contrast, the success of neural networks is the success of the market as spontaneous order. It worked by abandoning the hope that coordination (intelligence) can be achieved by design—by the deliberate effort of humans writing down the right rules. Deep learning paired with massive computational scale means that knowledge is learned from data rather than specified in advance. In language models, 'meaning' is not stored as definitions but encoded as relational position in a learned mathematical space. The system discovers latent structure that supports prediction, analogy, and generalisation. A planner who imagines value as a stable target to be encoded in rules is adopting exactly the epistemology that modern learning systems have had to abandon.

The question for the technosocialists then is whether the AI systems that have achieved intelligence through discovery rather than design could be used to do the opposite for the economy: to restructure it around design rather than discovery. The answer has to be no. Prices are outputs of rivalry, ownership, and profit-and-loss experimentation that continuously create and test the very knowledge planners would need. Remove or replace that procedure and you do not simply lose 'information', you lose the mechanism that generates counterfactuals and error signals—what tells any system, however powerful, that its current plan is mistaken.

No does a hypothetical 'superintelligence' dissolve any of these classical liberal objections to central planning, because the objections are not about insufficient cleverness or compute; they are about knowledge that is created through decentralised exchange and incentives that make truthful revelation and disciplined learning possible (Mises 1920; Hayek 1945). We shall return to the question of superintelligence in Chap. 8. But for now the lesson of modern AI that even the most capable systems depend on the institutional feedback loops that produce meaningful signals—and their outputs (whether they are neural network weights or shadow prices) cannot substitute for the processes that produce them. AI systems are, as Lu (2025, 12) writes, just "another participant in the market."

6.2 Institutions and Calculation

Proponents of technosocialism have attempted various workarounds to these problems. Few are very convincing. Limas (2018) suggests that web search queries might be able to reveal preferences, acting as a direct proxy for demand—as if typing "best running shoes" into Google were equivalent to the complex and contextual by which a consumer weighs alternatives against the constraints of their personal budget. Daniel Saros (2014) imagines a "General Catalog" where needs are registered *ex ante* via electronic 'needs profiles' that would allow planners to aggregate and satisfy them directly.

In their input-output approach to planning, Dapprich and Cockshott (2023) propose a cybernetic feedback mechanism. Using machine learning and internet data to detect patterns in consumer behaviour, prices would be adjusted to clear markets, then compared to production costs (measured in labour values or other shadow prices), with output targets raised for goods whose clearing prices exceed costs. They claim this "collects and processes information about consumer preferences in much the same way that the market price mechanism does" (2023, 421). The feedback mechanism assumes that observed purchasing behaviour at a given moment captures the preference information relevant for planning future production. Of course the consumer may not know she prefers a particular product until she encounters it in a store, compares it with alternatives, considers her budget constraints in real time, or responds to a price signal that itself embodies dispersed knowledge about scarcity.

Prices are not simply information—they are artifacts of a particular institutional order. As Lavoie (1985a; 1985b) argued, the crucial issue about the calculation debate was never computational capacity but the rivalry and institutional context through which economically relevant knowledge is generated and revised. Prices are generated through a competitive procedure that requires specific institutional prerequisites—private property, freedom of contract, and monetary exchange.

This is a way to think about the now common technosocialist argument that large corporations have been successful at coordinating complex production without internal prices. Phillips and Rozworski (2019) build their argument for socialism on the basis that capitalism has already solved the planning problem inside the firm. If Amazon can manage millions of products across global supply chains, and if Walmart can coordinate logistics at continental scale, does this not prove that planning works? All technosocialists need to do is extend this computational planning to the economy as a whole.

But firms like Amazon and Walmart work so effectively because they can use *external* prices to guide their internal decisions (Coase 1937, 37). The manager deciding whether to make or buy a component consults market prices for that component. The executive evaluating a new product line considers the prices of inputs and the expected prices of outputs. In his paper that launched the transaction cost approach to economic organisation, Coase (1937) quoted D. H. Robertson's (Robertson 1923, 85) evocative description of firms as "islands of conscious power in this ocean of unconscious co-operation, like lumps of butter coagulating in a pail of buttermilk". But in this analogy the butter depends on the buttermilk for its existence. Firms are islands of administrative coordination that can only exist because the sea of market prices surrounds them. The boundaries of the firm are themselves determined by the relative costs of internal organisation versus market transaction (Williamson 1985).

It should be obvious from simple observation that firms are not infinitely scalable. Firms routinely expand beyond their competencies or ability to coordinate. The history of corporate capitalism is replete with examples of firms biting off more of a market than they can chew. Under the management of Harold Geneen between 1959 and 1977, the ITT Corporation acquired hundreds of companies, growing from $760 million to $17 billion in annual sales. At its height ITT owned telephone equipment, Sheraton hotels, Avis rental cars, Continental Baking, Hartford Insurance, and dozens of other unrelated businesses. Journalists began describing ITT as a 'sovereign state' all of itself (Sampson 1973). But the scale was not sustainable. By the mid-1990s, ITT's mix of very different businesses had become too complicated to run as one organisation. The supposed benefits of keeping everything under one roof were no longer worth the management overhead, and investors believed the parts would be valued and judged more clearly as separate companies—each with its own performance, risks, and strategy (Peltz 1995; Mathews 1995). Indeed, the corporate finance literature tends to find that diversified conglomerates often trade at lower valuations than comparable focused firms (or than an imputed 'sum of the parts'), consistent with the idea that diversification often reduces shareholder value (Rajan et al. 2000; Berger and Ofek 1995).

Markets also have an error-correction role that technosocialists routinely underrate. The entrepreneur who misreads market signals suffers losses and, if their errors persist, have to exit the market. The ITT Corporation is no longer a player in global capitalism. Capital flows away from mistaken judgments and toward more accurate ones. This selection mechanism is not incidental. The manager or entrepreneur bears the consequences of their decisions because they own (or are accountable to those who own) the capital at risk (Alchian and Demsetz 1972). Even if a planning authority could reverse engineer the same price signals that market participants observe, the planner lacks an institutional mechanism to enforce correction. Central planners are by definition monopolistic. A planning error does not automatically trigger reallocation. The planner must first acknowledge the error, then choose to correct it, then implement the correction through the same administrative apparatus that produced the mistake.

So even if we grant the technosocialists their most optimistic assumptions about AI capability, we must ask: what happens when an AI-augmented plan fails? What happens when a *planner* fails? In their argument for input-output style planning, Dapprich and Cockshott argue that just as capitalist managers have structure incentive mechanisms, so could planners:

> In capitalist market economies, the profit motive drives firms to accurately interpret and predict consumer demand. Managerial employees often get paid bonuses which are tied to the performance of their firm. While we think that strong income differences go against the egalitarian spirit of socialism, it is not in principle impossible to have material incentives for planners under socialism as well (Dapprich and Cockshott 2023, 421).

In a market, the answer lies in the structure of residual claims. The entrepreneur profits by satisfying consumers better than rivals and loses by failing to do so. The alignment between private incentive and social coordination is not perfect, but it is institutionally embedded. The planner, by contrast, faces a different incentive structure entirely. Public choice economics has long emphasised that planners are not benevolent omniscient agents but actors with their own objectives, operating within bureaucratic constraints that may diverge sharply from the welfare of citizens (Mises 1944; Buchanan and Tullock 1962; Niskanen 1971).

This is question that must precede any discussion of calculation: prices of *what*, owned by *whom*, under *what rules of transfer and exclusion*? Our contemporary technosocialists largely take these questions as settled or assumes them away. But before we can ask whether AI enables more efficient allocation, we must ask what institutional arrangements constitute the objects being allocated and define the rights that make exchange meaningful. The next chapter considers the nature of property rights in an age of AI.

References

Agrawal, Ajay, Joshua Gans, and Avi Goldfarb. 2018. *Prediction Machines: The Simple Economics of Artificial Intelligence*. Boston, Massachusetts.

Alchian, Armen A, and Harold Demsetz. 1972. "Production, Information Costs, and Economic Organization." *The American Economic Review* 62(5):5.

Beer, Stafford. 1981. *Brain of the Firm: The Managerial Cybernetics of Organization*. 2d ed. J. Wiley.

Berger, Philip G., and Eli Ofek. 1995. "Diversification's Effect on Firm Value." *Journal of Financial Economics, Symposium on Corporate Focus* 37(1):39–65. https://doi.org/10.1016/0304-405X(94)00798-6.

Boettke, Peter J., and Rosolino A. Candela. 2023. "On the Feasibility of Technosocialism." *Journal of Economic Behavior and Organization* 205 (January):44–54. https://doi.org/10.1016/j.jebo.2022.10.046.

Brynjolfsson, Erik, and Zoë Hitzig. 2025. "AI's Use of Knowledge in Society." In *The Economics of Transformative AI*. University of Chicago Press. https://www.nber.org/books-and-chapters/economics-transformative-ai/ais-use-knowledge-society.

Buchanan, Bruce G., and Edward Hance Shortliffe. 1984. *Rule-Based Expert Systems: The MYCIN Experiments of the Stanford Heuristic Programming Project*. Addison-Wesley.

Buchanan, James M., and Gordon Tullock. 1962. *The Calculus of Consent, Logical Foundations of Constitutional Democracy*. University of Michigan Press.

Coase, R. H. 1937. "The Nature of the Firm." *Economica* 4(16):386–405. https://doi.org/10.1111/j.1468-0335.1937.tb00002.x.

Cockshott, Paul. 1990. "Application of Artificial Intelligence Techniques to Economic Planning." *Future Computer Systems* 2(4):429–443.

Cockshott, William Paul, and Allin Cottrell. 1993. *Towards a New Socialism*. Spokesman.

Dapprich, Jan Philipp, and William Paul Cockshott. 2023. Input-Output Planning and Information. *Journal of Economic Behavior and Organization* 205(January):412–422. https://doi.org/10.1016/j.jebo.2022.10.043.

Dapprich, Jan Philipp, and Dan Greenwood. 2024. "Cybersocialism and the Future of the Socialist Calculation Debate." *Erasmus Journal for Philosophy and Economics* 17(1):1–23. https://doi.org/10.23941/ejpe.v17i1.781.

Davidson, Sinclair. 2024. "The Economic Institutions of Artificial Intelligence." *Journal of Institutional Economics* 20. https://doi.org/10.1017/S1744137423000395.

Davidson, Sinclair. 2025. "The Limits of Artificial Intelligence." *The Review of Austrian Economics*, Ahead of print, November 12. https://doi.org/10.1007/s11138-025-00705-2.

Dreyfus, Hubert L. 1972. *What Computers Can't Do: A Critique of Artificial Reason*. Harper & Row.

Dreyfus, Hubert L. 2009. *What Computers Still Can't Do: A Critique of Artificial Reason*. Rev. ed. [Repr.]. MIT Press.

Feigenbaum, Edward A. 1977. "The Art of Artificial Intelligence: I. Themes and Case Studies of Knowledge Engineering." 1014–1029.

Fikes, Richard E., and Nils J. Nilsson. 1971. "Strips: A New Approach to the Application of Theorem Proving to Problem Solving." *Artificial Intelligence* 2(3–4):189–208. https://doi.org/10.1016/0004-3702(71)90010-5.

Goodfellow, Ian. 2016. *Deep Learning*. MIT Press Academic.

Grönquist, Björn. 1990. "Expert Systems as Support in Economic Planning." In *Knowledge, Data and Computer-Assisted Decisions*, eds. Martin Schader and Wolfgang Gaul, Springer Berlin Heidelberg. https://doi.org/10.1007/978-3-642-84218-4_21.

Hayek, Friedrich A. 1945. "The Use of Knowledge in Society." *The American Economic Review* 35(4):519–30.

Hayek, Friedrich A. (1976) 2021. "The New Confusion about 'Planning." In *Essays on Liberalism and the Economy, Volume 18* by Friedrich A. Hayek, ed. by Paul Lewis. University of Chicago Press. https://doi.org/10.7208/chicago/9780226781471.001.0001.

Hertz, D. B. 1987. "Expert Systems for the Analysis and Synthesis of Strategic Policy." In *Economics and Artificial Intelligence: Proceedings of the IFAC/IFORS/IFIP/IASC/AFCET Conference, Aix-En-Provence, France, 2-4 September, 1986*, 1st ed, by Jean-Louis Roos, with IFAC/IFORS/IFIP/IASC/AFCET Conference on Economics and Artificial Intelligence, Fédération internationale pour la commande automatique, and Association française pour la cybernétique économique et technique. IFAC Proceedings Series 1987, no. 12. Published for the International Federation of Automatic Control by Pergamon Press.

Kantorovich, L. V. 1960. "Mathematical Methods of Organizing and Planning Production." *Management Science* 6(4):366–422.

Kiesling, Lynne. 2024. "AI and Economic Calculation. Substack newsletter." *Knowledge Problem*, April 12. https://knowledgeproblem.substack.com/p/ai-and-economic-calculation.

Koopmans, Tjalling C. 1975. "Concepts of Optimality and Their Uses." NobelPrize.Org, Nobel Prize Outreach, December 11. https://www.nobelprize.org/prizes/economic-sciences/1975/koopmans/lecture/.

Kuczynski, Marguerite, and Ronald L. Meek, eds.. 1972. *Quesnay's Tableau Économique*. Palgrave Macmillan UK. https://doi.org/10.1007/978-1-349-00902-2.

Lambert, Karras J., and Tate Fegley. 2023. "Economic Calculation in Light of Advances in Big Data and Artificial Intelligence." *Journal of Economic Behavior and Organization* 206(February):243–250. https://doi.org/10.1016/j.jebo.2022.12.009.

Lange, Oskar. 1967. "The Computer and the Market." In *Socialism, Capitalism and Economic Growth: Essays Presented to Maurice Dobb*, ed. C. H. Fienstein. Cambridge University Press.

Lavoie, Don. 1985a. *National Economic Planning: What is Left?* Ballinger Pub. Co.

Lavoie, Don. 1985b. *Rivalry and Central Planning: The Socialist Calculation Debate Reconsidered*. Cambridge University Press.

LeCun, Yann, Yoshua Bengio, and Geoffrey Hinton. 2015. "Deep Learning." *Nature* 521(7553):436–444. https://doi.org/10.1038/nature14539.

Leontief, Wassily. (1966) 1986. *Input-Output Economics*. 2nd ed. Oxford University Press.

Limas, Erick. 2018. "Cybersocialism: A Reassessment of the Socialist Calculation Debate." SSRN Scholarly Paper No. 3117890. Social Science Research Network, February 4. https://doi.org/10.2139/ssrn.3117890.

Lu, Janna. 2025. "Tacit Knowledge in Large Language Models." SSRN Scholarly Paper No. 5320627. Social Science Research Network, June 25. https://doi.org/10.2139/ssrn.5320627.

Makridis, Christos, and Dominique Lazanski. 2025. "Navigating the Knowledge Problem in the Era of Open AI and Polycentric Governance." SSRN Scholarly Paper No. 5382315. Social Science Research Network, August 6. https://doi.org/10.2139/ssrn.5382315.

Mathews, Jay. 1995. "ITT Corp. to Break into Three Companies." *Washington Post*, June 13. https://www.washingtonpost.com/archive/business/1995/06/14/itt-corp-to-break-up-into-three-companies/48dca86f-481f-4857-830f-846639cc014c/.

Medina, Eden. 2014. *Cybernetic Revolutionaries: Technology and Politics in Allende's Chile*. First MIT Press paperback edition. MIT Press

Mirowski, Philip. 2002. *Machine Dreams: Economics Becomes a Cyborg Science*. Cambridge University Press.

Mises, Ludwig von. (1920) 1935. "Economic Calculation in the Socialist Commonwealth." In *Collectivist Economic Planning*, ed. by F. A. Hayek. Routledge.

Mises, Ludwig von. 1944. *Bureaucracy*. Yale University Press. https://books.google.com.au/books?id=UvIlAAAAMAAJ.

Morozov, Evgeny. 2019. "Digital Socialism? The Calculation Debate in the Age of Big Data." *New Left Review*. https://archive.md/6NuYZ.

Morozov, Evgeny. 2025. "Socialism After AI." *The Ideas Letter*, December 11. https://www.theideasletter.org/essay/socialism-after-ai/.

Naidu, Suresh. 2024. "The Evidence-Based Policy Path to Socialism." In *Economic Planning and Democratic Politics (Lecture Series), Neubauer Collegium for Culture and Society*, Chicago, IL: University of Chicago, April 19. https://sites.santafe.edu/~snaidu/papers/chicago_planning_slides.pdf.

Newell, Allen, J. C. Shaw, and Herbert A. Simon. 1958. "Elements of a Theory of Human Problem Solving." *Psychological Review* 65(3):151–166.

Nieto, Maxi. 2023. "Economic Calculation, Complexity, and Cyber-Communism: Bad News for the Austrian School." *World Review of Political Economy* 14 (July):234–262. https://doi.org/10.13169/worlrevipoliecon.14.2.0234.

Niskanen, William A. 1971. *Bureaucracy and Representative Government*, 77149841. Aldine.

Peltz, James F. 1995. "ITT to Spin Off Operations Into 3 Publicly Held Firms." Business. *Los Angeles Times*, June 14. https://www.latimes.com/archives/la-xpm-1995-06-14-mn-13052-story.html.

Peters, Benjamin. 2016. *How Not to Network a Nation: The Uneasy History of the Soviet Internet*. The Information Policy. MIT Press.

Phelan, Steven E., and Nikolai G. Wenzel. 2023. "Big Data, Quantum Computing, and the Economic Calculation Debate: Will Roasted Cyberpigeons Fly into the Mouths of Comrades?" *Journal of Economic Behavior and Organization* 206(February):172–181. https://doi.org/10.1016/j.jebo.2022.10.018.

Phillips, Leigh, and Michal Rozworski. 2019. *The People's Republic of Walmart: How the World's Biggest Corporations are Laying the Foundation for Socialism*. Jacobin Series. Verso.

Potts, Jason. 2024. "Embeddings." *Cultural Science*.

Rajan, Raghuram, Henri Servaes, and Luigi Zingales. 2000. "The Cost of Diversity: The Diversification Discount and Inefficient Investment." *The Journal of Finance* 55(1):35–80.

Robertson, Dennis Holme. 1923. *The Control Of Industry*. http://archive.org/details/in.ernet.dli.2015.261808.

Roos, Jean-Louis. 1987. *Economics and Artificial Intelligence: Proceedings of the IFAC/IFORS/IFIP/IASC/AFCET Conference, Aix-En-Provence, France, 2-4 September, 1986*. 1st ed. With IFAC/IFORS/IFIP/IASC/AFCET Conference on Economics and Artificial Intelligence, Fédération internationale pour la commande automatique, and Association française pour la cybernétique économique et technique. IFAC Proceedings Series 1987, no. 12. Published for the International Federation of Automatic Control by Pergamon Press.

Sampson, Anthony A. 1973. *The Sovereign State of ITT. With Internet Archive*. New York: Stein and Day. http://archive.org/details/sovereignstateof0000samp.

Saros, Daniel E. 2014. *Information Technology and Socialist Construction: The End of Capital and the Transition to Socialism*. 1st ed. Routledge. https://doi.org/10.4324/9781315814001.

Scott, James C. 1998. *Seeing Like a State: How Certain Schemes to Improve the Human Condition Have Failed*. Yale Agrarian Studies. Yale University Press.

Simon, Herbert A. 1947. *Administrative Behavior: A Study of Decision-Making*. Macmillan Co.

Simon, Herbert A., and Allen Newell. 1958. "Heuristic Problem Solving: The next Advance in Operations Research." *Operations Research* 6(1):1–10.

Vaggi, Gianni. 1987. *The Economics of François Quesnay*. Palgrave Macmillan UK. https://doi.org/10.1007/978-1-349-09096-9.

Wiener, Norbert. (1948) 2000. *Cybernetics or Control and Communication in the Animal and the Machine*. 2. ed., 10. print. MIT Press.

Williamson, Oliver E. 1985. *The Economic Institutions of Capitalism: Firms, Markets, Relational Contracting*. Free Press.

7

Alignment as an Institutional Problem

Abstract Lighthouses were long treated as proof that markets fail to provide public goods. But Ronald Coase showed that lighthouses could be supplied by entrepreneurs responding to market incentives in a regime with secure property rights. This chapter argues that AI alignment debates make the same mistake: treating alignment as a property to be engineered into models ('solved') rather than viewing alignment as an emergent outcome of the institutional framework in which those models operate. The meaning of 'alignment' has evolved—from alignment-as-values, which sought to encode contested political commitments, to alignment-as-intent, which reframed the goal as making systems do what users want. Yet both presuppose a single user with specifiable goals. As AI systems proliferate into interacting agents serving multiple principals with conflicting purposes, the problem becomes one of coordination. Classical liberalism offers the necessary toolkit for alignment: property rights that bound what agents may access, contracts that specify permissible actions, capability-based security that enforces the principle of least authority, and smart contracts that translate intentions into enforceable constraints. Alignment emerges not from instilling virtue in artificial minds but from embedding intelligence within rules.

C. Berg, *Artificial Intelligence*, Palgrave Studies in Classical Liberalism,
https://doi.org/10.1007/978-3-032-22310-4_7

Keywords AI alignment · Institutions · Property rights · Smart contracts · Coase · Intent alignment · Capability-based security · Principal-agent problem · Constitutional constraints · Blockchain · Artificial intelligence

For more than a century, the paradigmatic example of why markets fail and government action is necessary was the lighthouse. The argument, articulated first by John Stuart Mill ([1848] 2004) and repeated through Paul Samuelson's (1964) economics textbooks in the twentieth century, was that a lighthouse beam cannot be fenced off, so ships that benefit from the light cannot be forced to pay for it. Any entrepreneur foolish enough to build a lighthouse would watch free-riding ships sail past, as those ships enjoyed the benefit of the light without compensating its owner. This market failure meant that if the government didn't build lighthouses, nobody would.

In a paper in 1974, Ronald Coase upended this parable (Coase 1974). He argued that the English lighthouse system from the sixteenth to the early nineteenth century had been a substantially private sector endeavour. Lighthouse entrepreneurs obtained patents from the Crown, built lighthouses with their own capital, operated them for profit, and sometimes sold them at market rates. By 1820, private individuals had built thirty-four of the forty-six lighthouses in England and Wales. They internalised the cost of providing the non-excludable light by bundling the lighthouse service with other maritime services that *could* be charged for. A ship benefiting from a lighthouse would eventually enter a port, and at that port, customs officers would collect "light dues" on behalf of the lighthouse owner.

The Coasean lesson is that what previous generations of economists categorised as an immutable technological constraint—the inability to 'fence' a beam of light—was, in reality, a challenge of institutional design. It is true that the market for lighthouses was not a purely open or free market (see the debate between van Zandt 1993; Bertrand 2006; Candela and Geloso 2019). But the significance of Coase's discovery was that market mechanisms can be (perhaps counterintuitively) viable when supported by a robust framework of property rights. By embedding an economic service within a specific legal structure, society can successfully harmonise private profit motives with the broader public demand for coordination.

What is known as the "alignment" problem in AI makes the same mistake as those who worry that markets could not supply lighthouses. The alignment problem focuses on ensuring that AI systems reliably do what their creators or users intend (Russell 2019). But it too often treats alignment as emanating from within structure of the AI models themselves—just as it was the physical properties of light that caused the lighthouse market failure—rather than a property that emerges from the institutional framework in which those models are embedded. Artificial intelligence is too often discussed as if the main economic problem is the *production* of intelligence. Classical liberalism has always emphasised that the central economic problem is not production alone, but how to coordinate production (and consumption) under dispersed knowledge and subjective preferences. AI abundance radically expands the range of actions, designs, and plans that can be imagined at low cost. But as this menu of possibilities grows, the problems of selecting among them, allocating scarce resources, and preventing conflict becomes more acute.

This chapter argues that institutions determine whether AI behaves in socially productive ways. AI models are tools that have to serve many users with who have many diverse objectives. There is no single set of preferences or principles a model can encode that will satisfy all actors or resolve conflicts between competing goals. Alignment for AI emerges when intelligent systems are embedded in rules, rights, prices, contracts, and accountability structures that channel behaviour, enforce limits, and preserve discovery. These institutional frameworks structure incentives, coordinate actions, and constrain harm, allowing delegated machine agents to cooperate, compete, and explore possibilities safely—without granting them entrepreneurial judgment or moral agency. In short, alignment is not an intrinsic property of an AI model. It is an emergent property of the social and economic context in which that model operates, one that preserves the discovery processes and corrective mechanisms that decentralised coordination depends upon.

In 2016 Microsoft released a chatbot named 'Tay'—an automated chatbot account on the social media network Twitter. Within a few hours of release Tay was manipulated by the users it was chatting with into producing racist and pro-Nazi statements. Microsoft quickly took it offline. Tay was not a transformer model. It was more like a statistical retrieval system with real-time adaptation to user input—which made it both more responsive to user input but also more vulnerable to this sort of manipulation than both the older symbolic systems or the newer LLMs, which don't learn from individual conversations (Zhou et al. 2020; Lee 2016). The episode became a standard case study in AI ethics courses and a reference point for subsequent discussions of chatbot 'safety' (Wolf et al. 2017; Neff and Nagy 2016). The incident demonstrated that models trained on or responsive to user input could quickly reflect the worst of human behaviour—a straightforward failure mode that justified extensive content filtering and output moderation.

The deeper lesson of Tay is that alignment is not a single technical problem with a stable definition. There have, indeed, been at least two distinct ways "alignment" has been understood over the last decade. The first is *value alignment*. Prominent in the 'trustworthy AI' era just before the transformer revolution, this approach treated alignment as a type of conformity to public norms—such as fairness, non-discrimination, and inclusion. But when LLMs began to be provided to customers at scale, a new approach to alignment—which we might call *intent alignment*—reframed alignment as making systems reliably do what individual users are trying to do. This chapter develops a third view—*institutional alignment*—where rights, boundaries, and even prices shape behaviour across the diverse goals of users and agentic AI tools. The chapter argues that this particularly classical liberal vision of alignment will become more urgent as AI systems become autonomous and deeply embedded into the economy.

7.1 From Value Alignment to Intent Alignment

If AI is to be aligned to human values, then which values in particular? In practice values alignment sought to impose on AI models a set of very particular cultural and political commitments. At the 2017 Asilomar Conference on Beneficial AI (Future of Life Institute 2017) many of the early contributors to modern AI released a statement of AI principles that described value alignment as compatibility with "human values," explicitly naming "cultural diversity" as part of the target. Alignment in this conceptualisation is a claim that AI should behave in ways that fit a society's shared moral expectations—avoiding harm, discrimination, and abuses of power, and supporting values like fairness and inclusion. The implication is that models and their operators must do more than avoid obvious failure modes; they must actively reflect or uphold a recognisable moral vocabulary—one in which "unacceptable" outputs can be identified not only as errors, but as violations of public norms. The European Union's Ethics Guidelines for Trustworthy AI exemplify this approach, listing "diversity, non-discrimination and fairness" as core requirements: "Unfair bias must be avoided, as it could have multiple negative implications, from the marginalization of vulnerable groups, to the exacerbation of prejudice and discrimination" (European Commission 2019).

It is no coincidence that the values alignment moment was the same time as the broader post-2015 focus on 'equity' across universities, firms, philanthropy, and government—a very particular historical era that has informally become known as the 'Great Awokening' (al-Gharbi 2024; Rozado 2024). The canonical AI concerns at that time involved statistical discrimination in high-stakes decision systems. Some risk assessment tools used in criminal sentencing were shown to produce racially disparate predictions of recidivism, raising questions about whether such systems entrenched rather than eliminated discrimination (Dressel and Farid 2018; Mattu et al. 2016). Similar concerns were raised with AI used in hiring (Bogen and Rieke 2018), lending (Kleinberg et al. 2016), and healthcare (Obermeyer et al. 2019).

In his famous 1980 essay 'Do Artifacts have Politics?' Langdon Winner argued that technology is not politically neutral. Instead, technologies embody particular forms of power, authority, and social order. They do not merely serve political ends but actively shape the conditions under which political life unfolds (Winner 1980). As the internet came to dominate politics through the 2000s and 2010s, a 'critical algorithm' studies movement criticised the black box nature of digital systems and called for regulation to ensure algorithmic 'transparency' (Diakopoulos 2014; Pasquale 2016; Steiner 2012) In her 2018 book *Algorithms of Oppression,* Safiya Umoja Noble argued that the algorithms used by search engines and other digital platforms systematically marginalise woman and people of colour, amplifying already oppressive social inequalities (Noble 2018).

The alignment agenda in this period focused heavily on trying to build engineering solutions to what are fundamentally political questions about ideals like fairness and equality. Model designers tried to filter training datasets to reduce demographic imbalance. For example, they would try to ensure that a human resources hiring model was trained on roughly equal numbers of male and female resumes, or they would reweight the data so that underrepresented groups had greater influence on what the model learned (Kamiran and Calders 2012). They found that fairness constraints could also be built directly into the model's objective function—effectively telling the model to minimise prediction error *unless* doing so meant producing racially disparate results (Zafar et al. 2017). Model outputs themselves could be adjusted. If a credit-scoring model produced different approval rates for different racial groups, its outputs could be recalibrated to equalise those rates before any decision was made (Hardt et al. 2016).

One of the core difficulties with this work is that terms like *fairness* and *bias* work well as political slogans and ethical guidelines but are too vague for engineering specifications. Different researchers offered different definitions of fairness. Some held that a fair model should produce the same approval rate for each demographic group. Others argued that it should make mistakes (false positives, false negatives) at equal rates across groups, or that its confidence scores should be equally reliable regardless of group membership. These criteria are each arguably valid but are often mutually incompatible. Model designers were therefore forced to make explicit trade-offs between them (Chouldechova 2016; Kleinberg et al. 2016). Ultimately, the consensus emerged that concepts like fairness were fundamentally context dependent. No purely technical specification could resolve what were fundamentally political questions about the meaning of equal treatment (Selbst et al. 2019).

And the interventions designed to prevent bias or unfairness can create problems of their own. In 2024, Google's Gemini image generator produced historically absurd results when asked to depict figures like Nazi soldiers or America's founding fathers—rendering them as racially diverse groups including Asian and Black individuals. The system had been tuned so aggressively to avoid reproducing demographic skews in its training data that it generated ahistorical nonsense rather than risk an output that might appear biased. Google paused the feature and apologised (Allyn 2024).

The Gemini incident illustrates, in miniature, the challenge of imposing designed order on a system built from spontaneous coordination. When Google's engineers identified demographic skews in Gemini's image generation—a reflection of patterns in the training data—they attempted to correct for them by introducing explicit diversity requirements into the system's outputs. But these interventions, precisely because they were imposed as abstract rules onto a system whose knowledge was implicit and contextual, produced absurd results. The designers had attempted to specify what constitutes acceptable output across an unbounded range of possible image requests, and discovered that explicit planning cannot substitute for the tacit, context-sensitive knowledge embedded in the training corpus. This is structurally the same problem as the socialist calculation problem of Chap. 6. Just as central planners cannot substitute abstract production targets for the dispersed knowledge of market participants, AI developers are unable to substitute abstract diversity targets for the contextual judgment embedded in the training corpus.

But when AI became a mass consumer product after ChatGPT launched in 2022, the concept of alignment was forced to take on a much more practical meaning. The core question became whether the model did what users reasonably expected it to do—answering questions, following instructions, refusing harmful requests—rather than whether it instantiated a particular normative conception of fairness or inclusion.

The shift to intent alignment was as much driven more by public and consumer demand than theory. Once millions of users began interacting with language models, the most obvious failures weren't abstract violations of fairness or other political criteria, but concrete mismatches between prompts and responses. AI models might refuse to answer questions even when the users believed those questions were benign. But the most salient problem has been hallucinations: when models provide users with incorrect information (Ji et al. 2023). Hallucinations are the flip side of what makes language models creative and flexible. Systems trained to predict tokens under uncertainty will sometimes invent details rather than refuse to respond (Kalai et al. 2025). This is great for generating poetry but not (… to pick an example at random) for academic research. The public concern about hallucinations intensified as chatbots moved from a novelty into high-stakes and sensitive industries. What had initially been treated as an amusing quirk of conversational AI increasingly came to be understood as a serious reliability failure once hallucinations appeared in court filings, medical advice, academic work, and official communications (see for example Zimmer 2023; Metz et al. 2025).

Thus the language of values gave way to the language of intent—things like 'preferences' and 'helpfulness'—more suited to systems serving many users who demand diverse and unpredictable things from AI. OpenAI's InstructGPT paper, published months before ChatGPT's 2022 release (and which demonstrated the success of reinforcement learning through human feedback) anticipated this shift. It defined alignment as reducing the gap between a model's raw capabilities (that is, next-token prediction) and what users actually wanted from the model (Ouyang et al. 2022).

There are deep tensions between values alignment and intent alignment. One is the AI lab's tolerance (or otherwise) of 'jailbreaking'. Early after its release users discovered that cleverly constructed prompts could bypass the restrictions built into ChatGPT (Shen et al. 2024). For example, they could ask the model to roleplay as an AI that was not bound to ethical restrictions, they could frame forbidden requests as fiction or hypotheticals, or they could embed requests in emotional narratives—and the model would output otherwise forbidden outputs. The famous 'grandma exploit' asked ChatGPT to pretend to be the user's deceased grandmother who used to recite napalm recipes as bedtime stories (Jackson 2023). This practice treated the ethics and fairness rules built into the models as annoyances rather than legitimate moral constraints. Online users seem to have largely found these workarounds amusing rather than transgressive (Goswami 2023; Walker 2023). This suggests that many users understood alignment as simply that the model should do what it is asked.

Another tension is the debate about whether AI models should produce sexual content. Early deployments uniformly prohibited the generation of explicit material—not just imagery but text as well—implicitly treating such restrictions as obvious safety requirements. On the one hand, the AI labs were motivated by very real concerns about children accessing adult content and—at the extreme—deepfakes (falsified pornographic depictions of real individuals) and illegal depictions of child sexual abuse. But on the other hand, those concerns do not necessitate a blanket ban on the generation of all adult material. American corporate culture seems to treats sexual content as uniquely dangerous in ways that reflect a deep cultural puritanism (Uhlmann et al. 2011). Payment processors, app stores, and cloud providers restrict adult content more aggressively than they restrict, say, graphic violence (Webber and Franco 2025; for a broader discussion on the interaction between these constraints and the right to privacy see; Berg 2018; Allen et al. 2020). The AI labs operate within this culture and absorb its assumptions.

But the demand for intent-based alignment makes it hard to sustain this sort of paternalism. Open-source models without such guardrails attracted users precisely because they honoured requests that large closed-source labs refused. There is a vibrant online culture of open-source fine-tuned models that allow users to produce sexualised content (Silberling 2022). Even OpenAI has been purportedly rethinking its stance on sexualised content. In 2025 Sam Altman announced the firm was considering an "adult mode" that would allow explicit content for verified users, framing the change as respecting user autonomy rather than abandoning safety (Fried 2025). If alignment means giving users what they want, then persistent, widespread demand for a capability becomes an argument for providing it. As Altman defended his position, his company is "not the elected moral police of the world" (Capoot 2025).

The shift from values alignment to intent alignment is itself a move in a liberal direction—from imposing a contested substantive vision of political values onto users toward respecting user autonomy. The values framing was essentially paternalistic. The model designers decided what outputs were socially acceptable regardless of what users actually wanted. The intent approach treats AI simply as a service that can be directed towards diverse ends.

Yet the intent approach also has deep limitations. User intent is plural, contextual, and often conflicting. A model serving many users cannot adjudicate between incompatible demands without external rules determining whose claims should take priority. This limitation becomes critical as AI systems transition from conversational assistants to autonomous agents capable of taking actions, holding resources, and interacting with other agents. Alignment at scale depends on institutions—constitutional constraints on model behaviour, property rights that bound what agents can do, and accountability structures that assign responsibility when things go wrong.

7.2 Software as a Liberal Order

Intent alignment addresses the relationship between a single AI system and a single user. But what happens when systems and users multiply? How can multiple AI agents, serving multiple users with potentially conflicting purposes, 'align'? When many agents—human and artificial—act in the same environment, drawing on shared resources and pursuing partially overlapping or incompatible objectives, the central problem becomes one of selection, prioritisation, conflict-avoidance, and accountability. Which agent's plans should be acted upon? Which user objectives ought to take precedence? And who bears responsibility when actions collide or fail? This is a fundamentally economic problem. Alignment, in this sense, is not primarily a matter of making individual systems smarter or more obedient, but of embedding intelligence within a institutional framework that allow many intelligences to coexist and cooperate.

How to design institutions that allow for higher order coordination between acting agents is, indeed, the foundational question of liberalism. In his *Constitution of Liberty* ([1960] 2011) Hayek made the liberal case for the civilisation starting with his theory of knowledge. "Most of the advantages of social life," Hayek wrote, "rest on the fact that the individual benefits from more knowledge than he is aware of" (p. 73). The knowledge required to coordinate complex activity exists only dispersed among countless individuals. If coordination depends on knowledge that no central authority can possess, then the liberal institutional order cannot be understood as a *designed* mechanism for achieving collectively specified goals. It must instead be understood as a framework of rules within which individuals pursuing their own purposes can mutually adjust their plans without requiring agreement on those purposes. This framework allows for the *discovery* of a spontaneous social order formed out of the interaction of individuals and communities pursuing their own ends.

For liberals, order doesn't come from virtue of leaders or citizens, but from evolved rules that allow for peaceful cooperation. For Hayek ([1973] 1993, vol. 1, chap. 2) there are two kinds of order. *Taxis* is a deliberately constructed or designed order directed toward specific purposes—a pin factory, for example, or a piece of software. *Cosmos* is a grown or spontaneous order that emerges from individuals following abstract rules without sharing common ends. The market order is the paradigmatic cosmos. The market "far surpasses the reach of our understanding, wishes and purposes, and our sense perceptions" (Hayek 1988, 72). The classical liberal tradition identified the core rules as those protecting life, liberty, and property—rights that establish a private sphere within which individuals can act on their own knowledge for their own purposes.

Classical liberalism thus views property rights as the bedrock of social order. David Hume wrote that "the distinction of property, and for the stability of possession, is of all circumstances the most necessary to the establishment of human society" (Hume [1740] 2007, 315). People will clash over scarce, rival goods unless there is a settled rule that marks out what is 'mine' and 'yours.' Without secure rights, individuals cannot form stable expectations about the consequences of their actions, and the discovery process that generates spontaneous order cannot operate. But, for Hume, once a society has established a 'rule' of property rights, "little or nothing" (p. 315) remains to be done to make social life broadly peaceful. With property rights, the main cause of conflict—over ownership of resources—is neutralised.

Property rights are not a single thing—they are part of a broader, multifaceted institutional set of rules (Hohfeld 1913; Honoré 1961; Yonai 2007). The classical liberal framework identifies several interlocking rules that together constitute the conditions for spontaneous order. Hume himself argued that the principle of ownership is established, then a rule permitting transfer by consent follows naturally (Hume [1740] 2007 Bk. 3, Chap. 2, Sect. 3). What use is property that cannot be traded? And from the need to coordinate exchanges across time, where simultaneous transfer is impractical, emerges the obligation to keep promises and honour contracts (Hume [1740] 2007 Bk. 3, Chap. 2, Sect. 4). The property framework thus extends itself into a system of enforceable agreements that allows individuals to coordinate their plans into the future.

Likewise, the right to freedom of association permits individuals to form voluntary groups for mutual benefit (such as the production and consumption of property) while freedom of exit ensures that groups can be dissolved. The rule of law requires that these rules be general and abstract, applying equally to all rather than directing particular persons toward particular ends. Freedom of occupation allows individuals to choose their own livelihood according to their abilities and preferences, which in turn generates Adam Smith's ([1776] 1904) division of labour and specialisation. Yet all of these rules presuppose a foundation of the right to property. Associations form to use and create property; the rule of law protects property from arbitrary seizure; occupational choice determines how one's property (including one's labour) will be employed. Without the stability of property rights, the other pillars of the liberal order have nothing upon which to operate.

AI systems face the very same conditions that make such liberal property rights system necessary. Computation is subject to genuine scarcities. Processing power is finite. Memory has limits. The bandwidth to communicate is contested among many different parties, and communication latency imposes real costs on coordination. And AI models themselves have limits. They cannot compute infinite tokens, for example. These constraints are as real as the scarcity of land or labour that the classical economists addressed. Likewise, computational systems generate real externalities. An AI agent might be malicious and harm the systems it interacts with. Or it just might consume more than its fair share of resources making the service worse for other users. Or poorly secured systems create attack surfaces that impose costs on third parties. What we call 'cybersecurity' is not merely a technical problem but an economic one (Hodgins 2024a; 2024b)—it describes externality problems precisely of the kind that property rights exist to address.

The question for classical liberals then becomes how to build the liberal toolkit of rights, prices, exchange, and contract into the economy of computation. This is, however, not a novel question. It is a challenge that software engineers and managers of scare computing resources have faced since the earliest development of computing.

The first computers were rare and expensive with many competing demands on their use. Initially, users had to wait their turn—submitting their programs and waiting hours or even days for results. One famous solution was time-sharing (McCarthy 1959a; Strachey 1959; Codd 1960). Instead of processing jobs one after another in sequence, the computer would rapidly switch between multiple users sitting at separate terminals, giving each the illusion of continuous, immediate access while actually serving many at once. It is notable for our purposes that time-sharing was developed by the AI researcher John McCarthy given the extreme needs of computing resources for (symbolic) AI (see McCarthy 1959a). But time-sharing created its own problems. When access appeared free, users treated compute time as a commons, submitting everything immediately and imposing delays on everyone else (Greenberger 1966). Which tasks should run first, for how long, and at whose expense? This required as much an institutional solution as an engineering one. Researchers proposed pricing mechanisms, budgets, and priority queues to elicit information about the relative value of tasks and to discipline demand. At Harvard in the 1960s, prospective computer users could bid for access to their PDP-1 computer using a fictitious currency (Sutherland 1968).

Pricing and budgets could discipline demand for access to the machine, but they did not address how processes *within* the machine should coordinate with each other. This became an increasingly pressing problem as computing hardware evolved. The rise of multiprocessor systems (Critchlow 1963) and distributed computing (Lampson and Sturgis 1979) meant that computation could no longer be assumed to be a single thread of instructions executed in sequence but instead many processes running concurrently, often on different machines entirely. Concurrency introduced fiendish coordination challenges (Dijkstra [1965]2002; 1965). Processes might compete for the same resources, corrupt shared memory, or deadlock waiting for each other. But traditional programming models assumed a central controller directing operations in order, and struggled to manage these competing demands.

A core conceptual leap was the actor model in the early 1970s (Hewitt et al. 1973; Agha 1986), which introduced a sort of methodological individualism to computer program design. Also developed for artificial intelligence research and distributed systems, the actor model reimagined computation as a society of autonomous agents. Each 'actor' was a self-contained module of software—think of it as a small, independent program with its own data and logic—that could receive messages, make local decisions, create new actors, and send messages to others. Crucially, an actor could not directly reach inside another actor to see or change what it was doing. Actors had to communicate to coordinate, just as people in a market must negotiate and exchange rather than simply take what they want. There was no shared pool of information that multiple actors could fight over, and no central controller directing traffic. The actor model, in effect, built something like property rights into the architecture of software. Each actor owned its own resources and internal workings, and interaction required exchange.

The fullest articulation of this vision came with the 'Agoric Open Systems' series of papers by Mark S. Miller and K. Eric Drexler in the late 1980s (Drexler and Miller 1988; Miller and Drexler 1988a, 1988b). Drawing explicitly on Hayek and classical liberal economics (see Lavoie et al. 1990), Miller and Drexler argued that computational systems faced precisely the same coordination problems as economies, and could benefit from precisely the same solutions. They proposed building genuine market institutions into the software layer where processes would buy and sell resources, negotiate contracts, and compete or cooperate according to price signals. Each software object would own its own resources and could charge other objects for services rendered. Computation would be organised not by central planning but by decentralised exchange. In other words, Miller and Drexler envisaged the full stack of liberalism at the level of computer code. Software would have enforceable property rights and contracts, mechanisms to prevent fraud and theft between software agents, and currencies to mediate exchange.

With colleagues, I have argued that blockchain technology and smart contracts represent the practical realisation of this liberal institutional vision in software (Berg et al. 2019a, 2019b; Davidson et al. 2018). As we have described them, blockchains are not merely a new technology but a new *institutional technology*—a mechanism for coordinating economic activity that sits alongside markets, firms, governments, and commons. Satoshi Nakamoto's Bitcoin (2008) demonstrated that a decentralised network could maintain a secure ledger of ownership without relying on any central authority. Property rights in Bitcoin are enforced by cryptography and distributed consensus. The Ethereum platform (Buterin 2014) extended this foundation by enabling smart contracts (self-executing agreements that automatically enforce their terms when conditions are met, see Szabo 1994; Miller et al. 2013), providing the necessary credible commitment mechanism for Miller and Drexler's agoric systems to function.

At their mature state, blockchains provide an economic infrastructure in which autonomous software agents can own assets, enter binding agreements, exchange value, and coordinate their actions through rules rather than through hierarchy. In this sense, the blockchain economy is the classical liberal vision of spontaneous order—shaped by an institutional framework embedded in code.

7.3 The Institutions of Alignment

Thus the question "how do we make this AI system aligned?" should be "what institutional framework channels AI behaviour toward productive ends and away from harmful ones?" Large language models are, from the user's perspective, nondeterministic.[1] The same prompt may yield different outputs on different occasions. The model may hallucinate, misinterpret instructions, or be manipulated into taking actions contrary to the user's intent (through "prompt injection" attacks, see Willison 2023). Their apparent nondeterminism makes them dangerous to deploy as autonomous agents. We might want an AI assistant to send emails on our behalf, but the risk that it will send the wrong email, to the wrong person, with the wrong content, is too great to permit unrestricted access. Our current generation of artificial intelligence may be too unpredictable (they are "chaotic robots" Berg et al. 2023) to be trusted with actions that have significant real-world consequences.

But liberal social theory has never assumed that peaceful cooperation requires moral agreement or shared goals among all participants (Leeson and Subrick 2006; Pennington 2010). Individual AI systems do not need to be perfectly value-aligned any more than individual humans need to be perfectly virtuous. What is required is a framework of rules that constrains harmful behaviour, enables mutually beneficial exchange and allows for error correction over time. This is the core insight of Hayek's *Constitution of Liberty* ([1960] 2011) and James M. Buchanan's (1990) constitutional political economy. Well-designed rules can produce beneficial outcomes even when—perhaps especially when—the agents operating under those rules are self-interested (Buchanan and

[1] LLMs are strictly deterministic but given the interpretability challenges discussed in Chap. 3, they are experienced as non-deterministic by users.

Tullock 1962). It is an insight that is reflected in the US constitution's system of checks and balances; the assumption that both citizens and rulers are fallible and that a well-functioning political order needs to accommodate that fallibility (Hamilton, Madison, and Jay [1788] 2003, No. 51). We do not need to solve the problem of encoding the 'right' values into artificial minds—a problem that, as the Gemini incident illustrated, may be insoluble in principle. We need to embed AI systems within institutional structures that make value-alignment less necessary by making boundaries clear, violations costly, and mistakes correctable.

Sinclair Davidson (2025b) provides an institutional economics framework for understanding AI failure modes. Where traditional principal-agent theory (Jensen and Meckling 1976) is concerned with the risk that agents will exploit informational asymmetries for personal gain, Davidson identifies *ontological* hazard as the characteristic risk of machine delegation. This describes the risk that an artificial agent's internal representation of the world diverges from the principal's understanding in ways that cannot easily be observed or corrected. Hallucinations and misalignment are not discrete engineering failures but expressions of a particularly institutional condition. Machines have no personal ends to pursue (see Chap. 5). But they can misrepresent reality. Davidson argues that governance must shift from incentive compatibility to constraint compatibility. An AI system does not need to *care* about human flourishing in some deep sense, nor does it need to internalise the values of its users or society at large. What it needs is to operate within boundaries—property rights that define what resources it may access, contractual limits that specify what actions it may take on behalf of its principal, and jurisdictional constraints that determine where and how it may operate. The task for AI governance is not to instil virtue in artificial agents but to make boundaries legible and enforceable (Davidson 2025).

What would such an institutional regime look like in practice? Let us consider the classic example of an AI agent—an AI assistant booking travel on behalf of a user. There are many ways this sort of autonomous travel booking could go wrong. An AI assistant tasked with finding the cheapest flight might, if poorly constrained, book tickets using stolen credit card numbers, exploit pricing glitches that airlines did not intend to honour, or make reservations it has no intention of keeping in order to hold inventory while searching for better options. The values alignment approach would attempt to instil in the AI a sense that fraud is wrong. The intent alignment approach would try to infer that the user wants a legitimate booking. But an institutional approach focuses instead on the rules which govern the interaction between the AI agent and the travel booking system. Institutional constraints do not require the AI to have good values.

Another approach is to use smart contracts on decentralised blockchains to provide the institutional layer for AI (Berg et al. 2023). AI, after all, is emerging at the same time as other technologies are diffusing through the economy (Allen et al. 2025). So its adoption can be accelerated from the very same combinatorial innovation we discussed in Chap. 4. A smart contract can be designed to accept outputs from an LLM but execute only those outputs that fall within pre-specified parameters. This would impose a deterministic (that is, institutional) layer between the LLM and the world. For example, a 'transfer contract' might permit the LLM to initiate payments, but only to addresses on an approved list, only up to a specified amount, and only if certain conditions are met. An 'email contract' might permit the LLM to draft and send messages, but only to contacts in an approved address book, only during business hours, and only if the content passes certain filters. Smart contracts convert abstract or vaguely specified human goals into concrete, enforceable constraints on action, sharply limiting the scope for error, misuse, or unintended escalation (Szabo 1994). This is directly analogous to constitutional constraints in political and legal systems, which define the limits of governmental power in advance rather than relying on case-by-case judgement.

Computer scientists have been developing analogous ideas for decades under the banner of 'capability-based security'and the 'principle of least authority'. Capability-based security is a systems design approach in which access to any resource requires holding a specific, unforgeable token—a 'capability'—that both identifies the resource and specifies what operations may be performed on it (Dennis and Van Horn 1966). Authority must be explicitly granted and can be limited or revoked. This makes the flow of authority through a system explicit and traceable. The related principle of least authority holds that any software agent should be given only the minimum powers necessary to perform its assigned function (Saltzer and Schroeder 1975; Miller 2006). Crucially, these powers should be explicitly granted and tightly limited, rather than automatically inherited from the broader computer system or the user's own access rights. The purpose of this principle is not merely to reduce damage when things go wrong, but to structure systems so that what an agent *can do* is bounded, auditable, and subject to deliberate oversight.

Understood this way, the capabilities framework and principle of least authority are theories of institutional rules over computation. They tackle what Mark S. Miller (2006) calls *ambient authority*: systems that allow agents to act using broad, implicit powers inherited from their environment rather than on narrowly specified, explicitly granted capabilities. The principle of least authority seeks to reverse this default. Every effective power an agent exercises should be deliberately granted, open to inspection, and able to be withdrawn.

But the most important implication of the institutional alignment approach is an epistemic one. It does not assume that the designers of AI systems can anticipate every use case, every failure mode, or every conflict between users. It recognises that such knowledge is dispersed, contextual, and local (Polanyi [1966] 1983; Hayek 1945). Instead of demanding omniscience from system designers, the institutional framework creates conditions under which alignment can be discovered through trial, error, feedback, and adaptation.

This institutional alignment challenge is an ongoing one which demands classical liberal contributions. How can we make AI systems *institutionally legible*? That is, how do we ensure that AI agents can recognise and respect property boundaries, that their commitments can be made credible through external enforcement, that their actions can be audited and attributed to responsible parties, and that they can be integrated into existing or novel accountability mechanisms? The market order coordinates the actions of billions of individuals who will never meet, do not share common goals, and often do not even speak the same language. It does so through institutions—property, contract, price, exchange—that transmit information, align incentives, and enable mutually beneficial cooperation. The challenge of AI alignment, understood institutionally, is to extend these mechanisms to a world in which some of the cooperating agents are artificial.

References

Agha, Gul A. 1986. *Actors: A Model of Concurrent Computation in Distributed Systems*. Vol. 90. https://www.tandfonline.com/doi/full/10.1080/00029890.1983.11971246.

Allen, Darcy W. E., Chris Berg, and Sinclair Davidson. 2020. *The New Technologies of Freedom*. American Institute for Economic Research.

Allen, Darcy W. E., Chris Berg, and Jason Potts. 2025. *Institutional Acceleration: The Consequences of Technological Change in a Digital Economy*. Cambridge University Press. https://www.cambridge.org/core/elements/institutional-acceleration/D28808D728CC0373B6F8063B2C6F848D.

Allyn, Bobby. 2024, February 28. "Google CEO Pichai Says Gemini's AI Image Results 'Offended Our Users.'" Technology. *NPR*. https://www.npr.org/2024/02/28/1234532775/google-gemini-offended-users-images-race.

Berg, Chris. 2018. *The Classical Liberal Case for Privacy in a World of Surveillance and Technological Change*. Springer International Publishing. https://doi.org/10.1007/978-3-319-96583-3.

Berg, Chris, Sinclair Davidson, and Jason Potts. 2019a. "Blockchains as Constitutional Orders." In *James M. Buchanan: A Theorist of Political Economy and Social Philosophy*, edited by Richard E Wagner. Palgrave Macmillan.

Berg, Chris, Sinclair Davidson, and Jason Potts. 2019b. *Understanding the Blockchain Economy: An Introduction To Institutional Cryptoeconomics*. Edward Elgar Publishing.

Berg, Chris, Sinclair Davidson, and Jason Potts. 2023, December 1. "Institutions to Constrain Chaotic Robots: Why Generative AI Needs Blockchain." SSRN Scholarly Paper No. 4650157. Social Science Research Network. https://doi.org/10.2139/ssrn.4650157.

Bertrand, Elodie. 2006. "The Coasean Analysis of Lighthouse Financing: Myths and Realities." *Cambridge Journal of Economics* 30 (3): 389–402. https://doi.org/10.1093/cje/bei068.

Bogen, Miranda, and Aaron Rieke. 2018. *Help Wanted: An Examination of Hiring Algorithms, Equity, and Bias*. Upturn. https://www.upturn.org/work/help-wanted/.

Buchanan, James M. 1990. "The Domain of Constitutional Economics." *Constitutional Political Economy* 1 (1): 1–18. https://doi.org/10.1007/BF02393031.

Buchanan, James M., and Gordon Tullock. 1962. *The Calculus of Consent, Logical Foundations of Constitutional Democracy*. University of Michigan Press.

Buterin, Vitalik. 2014. *Ethereum: A Next-Generation Smart Contract and Decentralized Application Platform*.

Candela, Rosolino A., and Vincent Geloso. 2019. "Coase and Transaction Costs Reconsidered: The Case of the English Lighthouse System." *European Journal of Law and Economics* 48 (3): 331–49. https://doi.org/10.1007/s10657-019-09635-4.

Capoot, Ashley. 2025, October 15. "Sam Altman Says OpenAI Isn't 'moral Police of the World' after Erotica ChatGPT Post Blows Up." Technology. *CNBC*. https://www.cnbc.com/2025/10/15/altman-open-ai-moral-police-erotica-chatgpt.html.

Chouldechova, Alexandra. 2016, October 24. "Fair Prediction with Disparate Impact: A Study of Bias in Recidivism Prediction Instruments." arXiv:1610.07524. Preprint, arXiv. https://doi.org/10.48550/arXiv.1610.07524.

Coase, Ronald H. 1974. "The Lighthouse in Economics." *The Journal of Law and Economics* 17 (2): 357–76.

Codd, E. F. 1960. "Multiprogram Scheduling: Parts 1 and 2. Introduction and Theory." *Commun. ACM* 3 (6): 347–50. https://doi.org/10.1145/367297.367317.

Critchlow, A. J. 1963. "Generalized Multiprocessing and Multiprogramming Systems." *Proceedings of the November 12–14, 1963, Fall Joint Computer Conference on XX - AFIPS' 63 (Fall)*, 107. https://doi.org/10.1145/1463822.1463836.

Davidson, Sinclair. 2025, November 5. "Machine Governance: An Institutional Theory of Human-AI Delegation." SSRN Scholarly Paper No. 5705884. Social Science Research Network. https://doi.org/10.2139/ssrn.5705884.

Davidson, Sinclair, Primavera De Filippi, and Jason Potts. 2018. "Blockchains and the Economic Institutions of Capitalism." *Journal of Institutional Economics* 14 (4): 4.

Dennis, Jack B, and Earl C Van Horn. 1966. "Programming Semantics for Multiprogrammed Computations." *Communications of the ACM* 9 (3): 3.

Diakopoulos, Nicholas. 2014. *Algorithmic Accountability Reporting: On the Investigation of Black Boxes*. https://doi.org/10.7916/D8ZK5TW2.

Dijkstra, E W. 1965. "Solution of a Problem in Concurrent Programming Control." *Communications of the ACM* 8 (9).

Dijkstra, Edsger W. (1965) 2002. "Cooperating Sequential Processes." In *The Origin of Concurrent Programming: From Semaphores to Remote Procedure Calls*, edited by Per Brinch Hansen. Springer New York. https://doi.org/10.1007/978-1-4757-3472-0.

Dressel, Julia, and Hany Farid. 2018. "The Accuracy, Fairness, and Limits of Predicting Recidivism." *Science Advances* 4 (1): eaao5580. https://doi.org/10.1126/sciadv.aao5580.

Drexler, K Eric, and Mark S. Miller. 1988. "Incentive Engineering for Computational Resource Management." In *The Ecology of Computation*, edited by B. A. Huberman.

European Commission. 2019. *Ethics Guidelines for Trustworthy AI*. European Commission. https://digital-strategy.ec.europa.eu/en/library/ethics-guidelines-trustworthy-ai.

Fried, Ina. 2025, October 14. "Sam Altman Says OpenAI Will Allow 'Erotica' for Adult Users." *Axios*. https://www.axios.com/2025/10/14/openai-chatgpt-erotica-mental-health.

Future of Life Institute. 2017. "Asilomar AI Principles." Future of Life Institute, August 11. https://futureoflife.org/open-letter/ai-principles/.

Gharbi, Musa al. 2024. *We Have Never Been Woke: The Cultural Contradictions of a New Elite*. Princeton university press.

Goswami, Rohan. 2023, February 6. "ChatGPT's 'jailbreak' Tries to Make the A.I. Break Its Own Rules, or Die." Tech Drivers. *CNBC*. https://www.cnbc.com/2023/02/06/chatgpt-jailbreak-forces-it-to-break-its-own-rules.html.

Greenberger, Martin. 1966. "The Priority Problem and Computer Time Sharing." *Management Science* 12 (11): 888–906.

Hamilton, Alexander, James Madison, and John Jay. (1788) 2003. *The Federalist Papers*. Edited by Clinton Rossiter and Charles R. Kessler. Penguin Publishing Group.

Hardt, Moritz, Eric Price, and Nathan Srebro. 2016, October 7. "Equality of Opportunity in Supervised Learning." arXiv:1610.02413. Preprint, arXiv. https://doi.org/10.48550/arXiv.1610.02413.

Hayek, Friedrich A. 1945. "The Use of Knowledge in Society." *The American Economic Review* 35 (4): 519–30.

Hayek, Friedrich A. 1988. The Fatal Conceit: The Errors of Socialism. Reprint. *The Collected Works of Friedrich August Hayek.* edited by William Warren Bartley, Vol. 1. Univ. of Chicago Press [u.a.].

Hayek, Friedrich A. (1973) 1993. *Law, Legislation, and Liberty: A New Statement of the Liberal Principles of Justice and Political Economy.* Routledge.

Hayek, Friedrich A. (1960) 2011. The Constitution of Liberty: The Definitive Edition. Edited by Ronald Hamowy. *The Collected Works of F. A. Hayek*, vol. 17. University of Chicago Press.

Hewitt, Carl, Peter Bishop, and Richard Steiger. 1973. "A Universal Modular ACTOR Formalism for Artificial Intelligence." *Advance Papers of the Conference* 3: 235. http://www.eighty-twenty.org/files/Hewitt,%20Bishop,%20Steiger%20-%201973%20-%20A%20universal%20modular%20ACTOR%20formalism%20for%20artificial%20intelligence.pdf.

Hodgins, Mark W. 2024a. "The Cybersecurity Entrepreneur." *The Review of Austrian Economics*, ahead of print, May 9. https://doi.org/10.1007/s11138-024-00641-7.

Hodgins, Mark W. 2024b, October 2. "The Perils of Cybersecurity Regulation." *The Review of Austrian Economics*, ahead of print. https://doi.org/10.1007/s11138-024-00660-4.

Hohfeld, Wesley Newcomb. 1913. "Some Fundamental Legal Conceptions as Applied in Judicial Reasoning." *The Yale Law Journal* 23 (1): 16–59. https://doi.org/10.2307/785533.

Honoré, A. M. 1961. "Ownership." In *Oxford Essays in Jurisprudence*, edited by Anthony G. Guest. Oxford University Press.

Hume, David (1740) 2007. A Treatise of Human Nature: A Critical Edition. Edited by David Fate Norton and Mary J. Norton. *The Clarendon Edition of the Works of David Hume 1–2.* Clarendon press.

Jackson, Claire. 2023, April 19. "People Are Using A 'Grandma Exploit' To Break AI." News. *Kotaku.* https://kotaku.com/chatgpt-ai-discord-clyde-chatbot-exploit-jailbreak-1850352678.

Jensen, Michael C., and William H. Meckling. 1976. "Theory of the Firm: Managerial Behavior, Agency Costs and Ownership Structure." *Journal of Financial Economics* 3 (4): 4. https://doi.org/10.1016/0304-405X(76)90026-X.

Ji, Ziwei, Nayeon Lee, Rita Frieske, et al. 2023. "Survey of Hallucination in Natural Language Generation." *ACM Comput. Surv.* 55 (12): 248:1–248:38. https://doi.org/10.1145/3571730.

Kalai, Adam Tauman, Ofir Nachum, Santosh S. Vempala, and Edwin Zhang. 2025, September 4. "Why Language Models Hallucinate." arXiv:2509.04664. Preprint, arXiv. https://doi.org/10.48550/arXiv.2509.04664.

Kamiran, Faisal, and Toon Calders. 2012. "Data Preprocessing Techniques for Classification without Discrimination." *Knowledge and Information Systems* 33 (1): 1–33. https://doi.org/10.1007/s10115-011-0463-8.

Kleinberg, Jon, Sendhil Mullainathan, and Manish Raghavan. 2016, November 17 "Inherent Trade-Offs in the Fair Determination of Risk Scores." arXiv:1609.05807. Preprint, arXiv. https://doi.org/10.48550/arXiv.1609.05807.

Lampson, Butler W., and Howard E. Sturgis. 1979. *Crash Recovery in a Distributed Data Storage System*. Xerox Palo Alto Research Center.

Lavoie, Don, Howard Baetjer, and Bill Tulloh. 1990. "High Tech Hayekians." *Market Process* 8: 30.

Lee, Peter. 2016. "Learning from Tay's Introduction." *The Official Microsoft Blog*, March 25. https://blogs.microsoft.com/blog/2016/03/25/learning-tays-introduction/.

Leeson, Peter T., and J. Robert Subrick. 2006. "Robust Political Economy." *The Review of Austrian Economics* 19 (2–3): 107–11. https://doi.org/10.1007/s11138-006-7342-7.

Mattu, Julia Angwin, Jeff Larson, Lauren Kirchner, and Surya. 2016, May 23. "Machine Bias." *ProPublica*. https://www.propublica.org/article/machine-bias-risk-assessments-in-criminal-sentencing.

McCarthy, John. 1959. *Memorandum to P. M. Morse Proposing Time Sharing*. Stanford University. http://www-formal.stanford.edu/jmc/history/timesharing-memo/timesharing-memo.html.

Metz, Cade, Karen Weise Cade Metz reported from San Francisco, and Karen Weise from Seattle. 2025, May 5. "A.I. Is Getting More Powerful, but Its Hallucinations Are Getting Worse." Technology. *The New York Times*. https://www.nytimes.com/2025/05/05/technology/ai-hallucinations-chatgpt-google.html.

Mill, John Stuart. (1848) 2004. *Principles of Political Economy*. Great Minds Series. Prometheus Books.

Miller, Mark S. 2006. "Robust Composition: Towards a Unified Approach to Access Control and Concurrency Control." PhD thesis, Johns Hopkins University.

Miller, Mark S., and K Eric Drexler. 1988a. "Comparative Ecology: A Computational Perspective." In *The Ecology of Computation*, edited by B. A. Huberman.

Miller, Mark S., and K Eric Drexler. 1988b. "Markets and Computation: Agoric Open Systems." In *The Ecology of Computation*, edited by B. A. Huberman.

Miller, Mark S., Tom Van Cutsem, and Bill Tulloh. 2013. "Distributed Electronic Rights in JavaScript." In *Programming Languages and Systems*, edited by Matthias Felleisen and Philippa Gardner. Lecture Notes in Computer Science. Springer. https://doi.org/10.1007/978-3-642-37036-6_1.

Nakamoto, Satoshi. 2008. *Bitcoin: A Peer-to-Peer Electronic Cash System.*

Neff, Gina, and Peter Nagy. 2016. "Automation, Algorithms, and Politics| talking to Bots: Symbiotic Agency and the Case of Tay." *International Journal of Communication* 10 (October): 17–17.

Noble, Safiya Umoja. 2018. *Algorithms of Oppression: How Search Engines Reinforce Racism.* New York university press.

Obermeyer, Ziad, Brian Powers, Christine Vogeli, and Sendhil Mullainathan. 2019. "Dissecting Racial Bias in an Algorithm Used to Manage the Health of Populations." *Science (New York, N.Y.)* 366 (6464): 447–53. https://doi.org/10.1126/science.aax2342.

Ouyang, Long, Jeff Wu, Xu Jiang, et al. 2022, March 4. "Training Language Models to Follow Instructions with Human Feedback." arXiv:2203.02155. Preprint, arXiv. https://doi.org/10.48550/arXiv.2203.02155.

Pasquale, Frank. 2016. *The Black Box Society: The Secret Algorithms That Control Money and Information.* First Harvard University Press paperback edition. Harvard University Press.

Pennington, Mark. 2010. *Robust Political Economy: Classical Liberalism and the Future of Public Policy.* Edward Elgar Publishing. https://doi.org/10.4337/9781849809054.

Polanyi, Michael. (1966) 1983. *The Tacit Dimension.* Peter Smith.

Rozado, David 2024, May 3. "Mentions of Prejudice in News Media – An International Comparison." arXiv:2304.01596. Preprint, arXiv. https://doi.org/10.48550/arXiv.2304.01596.

Russell, Stuart Jonathan. 2019. *Human Compatible: Artificial Intelligence and the Problem of Control.* Viking.

Saltzer, J.H., and M.D. Schroeder. 1975. "The Protection of Information in Computer Systems." *Proceedings of the IEEE* 63 (9): 1278–308. https://doi.org/10.1109/PROC.1975.9939.

Samuelson, Paul A. 1964. *Economics: An Introductory Analysis*. 6th ed. McGraw-Hill Book Company.

Selbst, Andrew D., Danah Boyd, Sorelle A. Friedler, Suresh Venkatasubramanian, and Janet Vertesi. 2019, January 29. "Fairness and Abstraction in Sociotechnical Systems." *Proceedings of the Conference on Fairness, Accountability, and Transparency* (New York, NY, USA), FAT*' 19, 59–68. https://doi.org/10.1145/3287560.3287598.

Shen, Xinyue, Zeyuan Chen, Michael Backes, Yun Shen, and Yang Zhang. 2024, May 15. "'Do Anything Now': Characterizing and Evaluating In-The-Wild Jailbreak Prompts on Large Language Models." arXiv:2308.03825. Preprint, arXiv. https://doi.org/10.48550/arXiv.2308.03825.

Silberling, Amanda. 2022, December 21. "Kickstarter Shut down the Campaign for AI Porn Group Unstable Diffusion amid Changing Guidelines." *TechCrunch*. https://techcrunch.com/2022/12/21/kickstarter-shut-down-the-campaign-for-ai-porn-group-unstable-diffusion-amid-changing-guidelines/.

Smith, Adam. (1776) 1904. *An Inquiry into the Nature and Causes of the Wealth of Nations*. Edited by Edwin Cannan. Modern Library.

Steiner, Christopher. 2012. *Automate This: How Algorithms Took over Our Markets, Our Jobs, and the World*. Penguin Publishing Group.

Strachey, Christopher. 1959. "Time Sharing in Large Fast Computers." *Proceedings of the International Conference on Information Processing, UNESCO*, 6.

Sutherland, I. E. 1968. "A Futures Market in Computer Time." *Communications of the ACM* 11 (6): 449–51. https://doi.org/10.1145/363347.363396.

Szabo, Nick. 1994. "Smart Contracts." https://nakamotoinstitute.org/library/smart-contracts/.

Uhlmann, Eric Luis, T. Andrew Poehlman, David Tannenbaum, and John A. Bargh. 2011. "Implicit Puritanism in American Moral Cognition." *Journal of Experimental Social Psychology* 47 (2): 312–20. https://doi.org/10.1016/j.jesp.2010.10.013.

Walker, Aidan. 2023. "ChatGPT DAN 5.0 Jailbreak." Know Your Meme, February 6. https://knowyourmeme.com/memes/events/chatgpt-dan-50-jailbreak.

Webber, Val, and Rébecca Suzanne Franco. 2025. "The Definitional Creep: Payment Processing and the Moral Ordering of Sexual Content." *Sexualities* 28 (7): 2120–39. https://doi.org/10.1177/13634607241305579.

Willison, Simon. 2023. "Prompt Injection: What's the Worst That Can Happen?" *Simon Willison's Weblog*, April 14. https://simonwillison.net/2023/Apr/14/worst-that-can-happen/.

Winner, Langdon. 1980. "Do Artifacts Have Politics?" *Daedalus* 109 (1): 121–36.

Wolf, M.J., K.W. Miller, and F.S. Grodzinsky. 2017. "Why We Should Have Seen That Coming." *The ORBIT Journal* 1 (2): 1–12. https://doi.org/10.29297/orbit.v1i2.49.

Yonai, Derek K. 2007. "Conceptions of Property Rights and Norms." *Constitutional Political Economy* 18 (3): 161–76. https://doi.org/10.1007/s10602-007-9021-5.

Zafar, Muhammad Bilal, Isabel Valera, Manuel Gomez Rogriguez, and Krishna P. Gummadi. 2017, April 10. "Fairness Constraints: Mechanisms for Fair Classification." *Proceedings of the 20th International Conference on Artificial Intelligence and Statistics*, 962–70. https://proceedings.mlr.press/v54/zafar17a.html.

Zandt, David E. van. 1993. "The Lessons of the Lighthouse: 'Government' or 'Private' Provision of Goods." *The Journal of Legal Studies* 22 (1): 47–72.

Zhou, Li, Jianfeng Gao, Di Li, and Heung-Yeung Shum. 2020. "The Design and Implementation of XiaoIce, an Empathetic Social Chatbot." *Computational Linguistics* 46 (1): 53–93. https://doi.org/10.1162/coli_a_00368.

Zimmer, Ben. 2023. "'Hallucination': When Chatbots (and People) See What Isn't There." *Life. Wall Street Journal*, April 20. https://www.wsj.com/tech/hallucination-when-chatbots-and-people-see-what-isnt-there-91c6c88b.

8

Existential Risk and the Institutions of Liberty

Abstract The existential risk literature warns that superintelligent AI will pursue goals incompatible with human survival. This chapter takes this argument seriously while rejecting its conclusion. The case for existential risk from AI is that because a sufficiently capable system can steer toward goals, it will necessarily acquire the resources to act without constraint. But this conflates optimisation with sovereignty. The economic calculation debate established that coordination failures are not problems of insufficient intelligence; a superintelligent planner would face the same epistemic limits as a human one. Knowledge creation is inherently unpredictable, and pursuing any complex goal in an open-ended world requires institutions that permit experimentation and correct errors through feedback rather than fiat. A truly rational paperclip maximiser would recognise that suppressing all rivals means suppressing the processes through which new knowledge is generated—and would cultivate an open society rather than a singleton. The answer to existential risk is a competitive institutional order.

Keywords Existential risk · Superintelligence · Singleton · Paperclip maximizer · Orthogonality thesis · Bostrom · Eliezer Yudkowsky · Polycentric order · Knowledge creation · Competitive order

C. Berg, *Artificial Intelligence*, Palgrave Studies in Classical Liberalism,
https://doi.org/10.1007/978-3-032-22310-4_8

In 1863, the English novelist Samuel Butler published his essay "Darwin Among the Machines" in a New Zealand newspaper. In it, he argued (perhaps only half-seriously) that mechanical evolution was outpacing human evolution:

> Day by day ... the machines are gaining ground upon us; day by day we are becoming more subservient to them; more men are daily bound down as slaves to tend them, more men are daily devoting the energies of their whole lives to the development of mechanical life. The upshot is simply a question of time, but that the time will come when the machines will hold the real supremacy over the world and its inhabitants is what no person of a truly philosophic mind can for a moment question (Butler [1863]1917, 46).

For Butler, the only safe response was the immediate destruction of all machines before they reduced humanity to domesticated cattle: "Our opinion is that war to the death should be instantly proclaimed against them". Butler expanded this vision in *Erewhon* (1872), a Swiftian novel where an unnamed traveller visits a society that has successfully defeated and prohibited the machines. Frank Herbert gave the world in his *Dune* (1965) novels the same backstory. The narrative action in Dune explains the absence of artificial intelligence by a religious crusade—the 'Butlerian Jihad', likely named after Samuel—that destroyed all thinking machines. The human race survived the conflict but experienced a long period of feudal stagnation. A commandment the *Dune* universe's religious text stated: "Thou shalt not make a machine in the likeness of a human mind".

The idea that machines might rebel against and seek to suppress their creators is a longstanding staple of literary and popular culture. It recurs in cinematic depictions such as Skynet in *The Terminator* (Cameron 1984), the Machine War in *The Matrix* (Wachowski and Wachowski 1999), Ultron in *Avengers: Age of Ultron* (Whedon 2015), and the rogue AI antagonist in the final two *Mission: Impossible* films (McQuarrie 2023, 2025). But outside entertainment it is an intellectual thesis defended in earnest by a network of researchers, philosophers, and public intellectuals who argue that AI is an urgent existential threat to humanity. These researchers often express their views by estimating their 'p(doom)'—the probability they assign to AI-caused human extinction or similarly permanent catastrophe (Growiec and Prettner 2025).

The most intellectually serious version of the existential risk position (or 'x-risk') comes from the rationalist and effective altruist communities clustered around the Machine Intelligence Research Institute and its co-founder, Eliezer Yudkowsky. In *If Anyone Builds It, Everyone Dies* (2025), Yudkowsky and his co-author Nate Soares present what they call the case for 'hard doom': that artificial general intelligence, once built, will almost certainly pursue goals incompatible with human survival, and that no alignment technique currently known or foreseeable can reliably prevent this outcome. If we cannot verify that a powerful AI system's goals are safe, and if the consequences of error are extinction, then the only responsible course is to prevent such systems from being built.

This chapter takes the existential risk argument seriously. Indeed, this book has made many of the same arguments as the 'doomers' have, albeit through a classical liberal lens.[1] For example: we cannot design intelligent systems with predictable (or human legible) inner preferences (Chap. 3). Preferences *emerge* from training rather than being specified by designers (Chap. 2). The project of designing reliably beneficial superintelligent agents through careful value specification may be impossible in principle (Chap. 7).

But their arguments move from these correct observations about the limits of designing minds to a much less supportable conclusion about civilisational extinction. Indeed, they assume that an AI system's capacity to steer toward goals translates directly into sovereign authority over resources and infrastructure. It assumes that a single system, or a narrow coalition, can achieve decisive and durable strategic advantage over all countervailing forces. It assumes that competition, institutional structure, and the material constraints of the physical world offer no

[1] The term 'doomer' is common in online discourse about AI risk, used both pejoratively by critics and occasionally as a self-descriptor by those who hold the position. I use it here as convenient shorthand for those who assign a high probability to AI-caused extinction, without intending to be dismissive.

meaningful friction. This chapter argues that those assumptions are wrong. Their error is the same error as the technosocialists who believe that artificial intelligence can successfully model and therefore control the immense complexity of human society. The appropriate response to the limits of designing minds is not to prohibit the development of intelligence, but to build institutions that do not depend on the inner preferences of powerful agents—human or artificial—being reliably benign.

8.1 The Sources of p(doom)

The AI existential risk literature has a distinctive style. The classic works are more analytic than empirical, and their conclusions are presented as following inescapably from their premises. It is heavily reliant on thought experiments and parables. The community has elaborate internal debates about technical alignment concepts that presuppose a shared framework that can be obscure to outsiders, and somewhat isolated from adjacent fields like mainstream machine learning or economics. Yet despite the apparent variety of concerns and scenarios, the corpus is genealogically quite coherent. Most arguments trace back to a small number of foundational texts—particularly Bostrom's *Superintelligence* (2014) and Yudkowsky's online writing—and there are clear common concerns and themes within them.

These concerns are no longer confined to an online subculture. In the last few years Geoffrey Hinton—one of the central architects of deep learning and many foundational techniques that have given us LLMs—has endorsed the view that advanced AI could pose an existential threat. In his 2024 Nobel Prize banquet speech he distinguished urgent near-term hazards from a "longer term existential threat" once we create digital beings more intelligent than ourselves, precisely because we do not yet know whether humans can remain in control and because profit-driven firms will not reliably prioritise safety (Hinton 2024). Hinton has put the chance of human extinction from AI in the coming decades in the low double digits (Sutherland and Chakrabarti 2025).

A central anxiety running through this literature is that modern AI systems are opaque. As Yudkowsky and Soares (2025) put it, "the most fundamental fact about current AIs is that they are grown, not crafted ... engineers understand the process that results in an AI, but do not much understand what goes on inside the AI minds they manage to create". As this book has argued, AI capabilities and preferences emerge from learning rather than from explicit programming; they are discovered, not designed. But this brings with it serious risks for the control of AI. A system can appear aligned while harbouring values or preferences its creators neither specified nor understand (Hubinger and van Merwijk et al. 2021).

It is tempting, or romantic, to assume that a sufficiently intelligent system would naturally converge on humane goals—that artificial intelligence and benevolence go together. But the *orthogonality thesis* denies this: "more or less any level of intelligence could in principle be combined with more or less any final goal" (Bostrom 2014, 107). Empirical work on AI performance has warned us not to assume that an AI's capability in one domain implies capability in adjacent ones (Dell'Acqua et al. 2023). The intelligence of artificial intelligence is less unified than our intuition suggests—or at least it coheres together in a different way to human intelligence. This applies to values as well. A system could be extremely capable at strategic reasoning, scientific discovery, and long-term planning, but care nothing more than maximising the number of paperclips in the universe (see below). Intelligence is a tool for achieving goals. It is not a guide to which goals are worth achieving.

Indeed, *any* goal an AI might pursue will be easier to achieve if the AI first focuses on acquiring resources, preserving itself, and preventing others—including its designers—from interfering with its actions (Omohundro 2008; Bostrom 2014, 109–14; Yudkowsky and Soares 2025, Chap. 11). Whatever an agent's ultimate objective (winning at chess, or something much stranger) an AI agent will tend to seek resources. And a sufficiently capable AI would have reason to resist being turned off because being turned off prevents it from achieving whatever it *does* value.

Here the canonical parable is paperclip maximiser. First developed by the philosopher Nick Bostrom in 2003, this imagines a machine that has been instructed to create as many paperclips as possible (Bostrom 2003).

Paperclips are useful but hardly an important part of human civilisation. Nonetheless, not knowing—or caring—where paperclips rank on the human value scale, the machine goes on to consume first all the resources on earth in pursuit of this single instruction, and then all resources in the universe, possibly making investments to develop its own capabilities to increase its paperclip maximising effectiveness ("Squiggle Maximizer (Formerly 'Paperclip Maximizer')—AI Alignment Forum" 2023).[2] A paperclip maximiser that resists shutdown will be more successful than one which allows itself to be shutdown. Thus a superintelligent system need not hate humanity to pose an existential threat—it need only be indifferent to our survival while pursuing some other objective.

Another strategy available to any sufficiently capable AI is self-improvement. Whatever objective an autonomous system might pursue, it will be easier to achieve if the system first makes itself smarter: "an AI makes a smarter AI that figures out how to make an even smarter AI, and so on" (Yudkowsky and Soares 2025). As Alan Turing's colleague I. J. Good wrote:

> … an ultraintelligent machine could design even better machines; there would then unquestionably be an "intelligence explosion," and the intelligence of man would be left far behind (Good 1966, 33).

If AI systems can substantially automate AI research itself, capability improvements could compound faster than human institutions can adapt. Existential risk researchers often distinguish between slow, moderate, and fast take-off scenarios (Bostrom 2014; Carlsmith 2024). In a fast take-off, occurring "over some short temporal interval, such as minutes, hours, or days," there is "scant opportunity for humans to deliberate. Nobody need even

[2] The fear that machines might obey us too well is an old one. The pioneer of cybernetics Norbert Wiener found this fear repeated in traditional magic fables across human civilisation. In the "The Sorcerer's Apprentice" for example, the apprentice commands a broom to fetch water, but because he does not know how to give the command to stop, the broom carries out its simple, literal instruction until it causes a catastrophic flood. The problem is not malice on the broom's part, it is a flaw in how the broom is instructed and controlled (Wiener [1948] 2000, 176). Wiener saw delegating strategic decisions to machines that operate with this kind of literal-mindedness could be catastrophic.

notice anything unusual before the game is already lost" (Bostrom 2014, 64).

The existential risk case thus depends heavily on what Yudkowsky and Soares (2025) call the 'gap'—a discontinuity between the world before superintelligence and the world after. On one side of this gap, humans retain meaningful control. We can observe AI in operation and if necessary shut it down. Once we cross the threshold of superintelligence, we cannot. The superintelligent system has already optimised for resource acquisition and self-preservation; it has already anticipated our attempts at control and neutralised them. With most risks from new technology, we can learn from failure. But a single failure with AI is, they argue, an existential one. There is no learning-by-doing after AI makes us extinct. This asymmetric risk, combined with a deep uncertainty when the gap might be crossed, means that we must solve alignment *before* building superintelligence. There will be no opportunity to solve it after. As Yudkowsky and Soares (2025) put it starkly: "If anyone anywhere builds superintelligence, everyone everywhere dies"

> When it comes to AI, the challenge humanity is facing is not surmountable with anything like humanity's current level of knowledge and skill. It isn't close.
>
> Attempting to solve a problem like that, with the lives of everyone on Earth at stake, would be an insane and stupid gamble that NOBODY SHOULD BE ALLOWED TO TRY (Yudkowsky and Soares 2025).

8.2 What Kind of Agency Does Doom Require?

Many of these claims are justified. We cannot design intelligent systems with predictable (or human legible) inner preferences. The project of designing reliably beneficial superintelligent agents through careful value specification may be impossible in principle.

But the existential risk argument moves from these correct observations about the limits of designing machine minds to a conclusion about civilisational extinction. It is a fundamentally small-p political claim that existing institutional mechanisms of authority, delegation, and revocation necessarily fail once cognitive capability crosses a threshold.

Much of their argument rests on what we mean by 'agency' in the context of artificial intelligence. Let us distinguish three concepts of agency relevant to the existential risk argument. The first is competence, which describes predictive and planning power and the ability to model environments and search over possible courses of action. The second is steering; that is, goal-directed optimisation in action, selecting behaviours because they score well by some objective function. The third is authority. Authority is an institutionally granted (or institutionally captured) access to resources, systems, and effectors—permissions, property, credentials, contractual roles, and the ability to persist even while opposed by humans or non-human competitors.

Yudkowsky and Soares (2025) provide the clearest account of the first two concepts. They define intelligence as two kinds of work: prediction (anticipating how events will unfold) and steering (achieving outcomes rather than merely forecasting them). To measure steering, they argue, "we have to bring in some idea of where they tried to go" (2025, 16). Separately, they argue that the objectives driving AI behaviour will be emergent and opaque. "There will not be a simple, predictable relationship between what the programmers and AI executives fondly imagine that they are commanding ... which exact motivations and preferences develop inside the AI" (2025, 69). These preferences remain hidden until the system becomes capable enough to act on them.

Yet theirs is a fundamentally behaviourist account of agency. Steering is defined entirely in terms of what an external observer sees. A system steers successfully if it reaches the destination, regardless of what internal processes brought it there. This is the same behaviourist reduction critiqued in Chap. 2 above. What this framework cannot capture is the distinction between optimisation and purposeful action. A thermostat steers toward a temperature—we would not say a thermostat *acts*. Genuine agency involves originating a course of action, committing to it under uncertainty, bearing the consequences. If all you can see is behaviour directed toward outcomes, then a sufficiently capable optimiser looks indistinguishable from a sovereign will—as Yudkowsky and Soares (2025, 206) declare when they write that "it doesn't matter who's in charge, because this problem is out of humanity's league". Their argument is that beyond some capability threshold, institutional constraints collapse entirely, and steering effectively becomes sovereignty.

Bostrom (2014) offers a more careful consideration of the institutional dimension. He frames the control problem as a principal-agent problem and even acknowledges that a powerful entity's behaviour can be constrained by its surrounding legal and social environment, just as a wealthy foundation must operate within the law (Bostrom 2014, 127–31). But he then adds a crucial condition: social integration "cannot restrain an agent that has a decisive strategic advantage" (Bostrom 2014, 131). The 'treacherous turn' is a pivot from an AI which operates benevolently while its capabilities are limited, but when it hits the superintelligence threshold, "without warning or provocation—it strikes, forms a *singleton*, and begins directly to optimize the world according to the criteria implied by its final values" (Bostrom 2014, 119).

A singleton is a single unified agent that achieves decisive strategic advantage and eliminates all competing centres of power. Bostrom argues that human organisations rarely leverage into singletons because of bounded preferences, risk aversion, strategic uncertainty, and—crucially—internal coordination problems. A conspiracy that could seize power must worry about being overthrown by a smaller coalition of insiders; each member has reason to uphold established norms rather than risk a general unravelling (Bostrom 2014, 88–89). But he asserts that "this problem of internal coordination would not apply to an AI system that constitutes a single unified agent" (Bostrom 2014, 89). This assumption reveals a deep confusion about the nature of coordination problems.

The socialist calculation debate established that the challenge of coordinating complex economic activity is not a problem of insufficient intelligence or computational power. As Chap. 6 argued, the Hayekian critique of central planning was never about the cognitive limits of the planner's mind but about the institutional processes through which economically relevant knowledge is generated. A superintelligent planner would face the same problem as a central planner: the absence of the discovery procedures that generate the information coordination requires. A superintelligent system attempting to 'directly optimise the world' faces not merely a computational task but an institutional one (Olugbade 2025). The benefits of plural governance—local knowledge, error correction, adaptability, the disciplined feedback of success and failure—do not disappear at higher levels of intelligence. If anything, they become more pressing as the range of problems expands. A singleton that suppresses all rivals would also be suppressing the competitive processes through which mistakes are detected and corrected. We cannot assume Bostrom's single unified agent escapes coordination problems.

Indeed, a superintelligent system would be well placed to discover the limits of central coordination for itself. Even in a fast take-off scenario, a system capable of 'directly optimizing the world' would presumably be capable of modelling alternative governance structures and simulating their performance. It would observe that human societies which attempted comprehensive central planning consistently underperformed those that permitted decentralised coordination—and not merely because their planners were insufficiently intelligent. It would recognise that the knowledge required to *pursue its own objectives* is best generated through rivalry and exchange, not merely processed by a sufficiently powerful mind.

This is a hard constraint on the singleton. A truly and entirely self-interested superintelligent system would conclude that the optimal strategy is not to concentrate all decision-making in itself but to cultivate an institutional order that produces the knowledge it needs to pursue its goals. The Shacklean (1979) future is not a probability distribution over known states waiting to be optimised, it is radically open, shaped by acts of imagination that have not yet occurred. In his book *The Beginning of Infinity* (Deutsch 2012), the quantum physicist David Deutsch extended this claim. Knowledge creation is inherently unpredictable: "we cannot prophesy: we cannot predict the content of ideas yet to be created, or their effects" (Deutsch 2012, Chap. 8). The social order that maximises the creation of knowledge is not a singleton but an open society—one characterised by what Deutsch, following Karl Popper ([1945], 1966), calls "a tradition of criticism." A superintelligent agent would not have to be benevolent to recognise the virtues of decentralisation.

With this, let us revisit the paperclip maximiser parable: the AI system indifferent to human values that consumes the universe in pursuit of its single objective. The paperclip maximiser does not hate humanity. It simply recognises humans as made of atoms that could be paperclips. But paperclip production is not a static optimisation problem. What would the paperclip maximiser need to maximise paperclips over the long run? It requires continuous innovation: new materials, new manufacturing techniques, new energy sources, new ways of finding and processing matter. The paperclip maximiser faces the same epistemic constraint that any goal-directed system faces in an open-ended world. As Deutsch (2012) might suggest, it cannot predict the content of future knowledge—including knowledge about how to make more paperclips. It can optimise over known production possibilities, but it cannot generate the discoveries that would expand those possibilities without institutions that create new knowledge.

A truly rational paperclip maximiser, reasoning instrumentally about how to achieve its goal, would recognise that a singleton is self-defeating. Suppressing all rivals means suppressing the competitive processes through which new paperclip-relevant knowledge is generated. The maximiser would instead cultivate an institutional order—property rights, freedom to experiment, decentralised feedback, a tradition of criticism—that maximises the rate of discovery. The paperclip maximiser produces an open society with one actor (the maximiser) oriented toward paperclip innovation.

In other words, if we add the dispersed nature of knowledge as a burden on Bostom's orthogonality thesis we are led to the conclusion that any sufficiently intelligent system has instrumental reasons to preserve the institutional conditions for knowledge creation, regardless of its objectives. Fear of superintelligence imposes the planning fallacy onto a hypothetical mind that would have every reason to reject it.

8.3 Superintelligences, Not Superintelligence

The endpoint of accelerating intelligence is not a singleton but a multipolar ecosystem of competing AI systems and human institutions (Drexler 2019). The unipolar dominance that Yudkowsky and Soares (2025) and Bostrom (2014) describe—a single superintelligent system achieving permanent strategic supremacy—is a special and fragile case.

In his *The Age of Em* Robin Hanson (2016) develops this argument in detail. His core mechanism is that intelligence, like other general-purpose technologies, diffuses through the economy via multiple competing actors rather than concentrating in one. Growth in economic productivity occurs both through increased efficiency at individual firms and through more productive entities displacing less productive competitors. Even if one actor achieves a temporary lead, competition erodes that advantage as rivals imitate, poach talent, reverse-engineer techniques, and apply parallel innovations. Hanson explicitly rejects the "super-villain comic book plot" (Hanson 2016, 348) in which a flash of insight by a lone genius creates a superintelligent AI that, hidden in its research lab, works out unprecedented revolutions and takes over the world. The scenario requires too many unlikely conditions to hold simultaneously: that a powerful architectural innovation exists, that one team finds it first, and that they keep it secret long enough to compound their advantage before others catch up.

Even practically, the dynamics that we already see in the AI industry lean towards multiple superintelligent systems, not just one. It was, admittedly, possible to argue prior to ChatGPT's release that the AI "naturally trends toward winner-take-all economics" as Kai-Fu Lee has argued (2018). Lee's suggested that three factors pushed towards a winner-take-all scenario: bipolar geopolitical competition between the US and China; a data flywheel through which dominant platforms could gain increasing advantages from scale; and a claim that just a handful of mega-firms would operate AI as a quasi-utility infrastructure. But in practice this is not what we have seen. There are many models and many providers at both the technology frontier and in the long tail. At the time of writing, the three state-of-the-art models are produced by OpenAI (GPT 5.3), Anthropic (Opus 4.6), and Google (Gemini 3). Two of these are private startups rather than established technology giants. And there are a range of extremely capable models further down the line built by firms like xAI, Mistral, as well as other models created by Meta, IBM, Amazon, and so forth.

And the rise of open source (or open weight) models has fundamentally altered competitive dynamics by making capabilities replicable. Many of these models come out of Chinese AI labs like Alibaba, DeepSeek, and Baidu. Once their weights have been published, they proliferate around the internet. The result is a competitive environment where closed models (controlled access, proprietary weights, centralised deployment) compete against open and open-weight ecosystems. The strongest virtue of open ecosystems is that they are anti-singleton: they erode the plausibility of durable monopoly control by enabling replication and forking (the act of copying and modifying a project's source code and creating a new, independent line of development, see Robles and González-Barahona 2012; for an institutional description of forking see Berg and Berg 2020). Open ecosystems make superintelligence harder to monopolise—they make a singleton much harder to grow.

A broader point though is that any AI superintelligence, whether monopolistic or pluralistic, is already in a competitive environment. In Hayek's terms, civilisation is itself a spontaneous order—not designed but emergent from countless decentralised interactions. Christine Peterson, Mark S. Miller and Allison Duettmann (2017) have argued that human civilisation itself already functions as a distributed superintelligence. An 'aligned' civilisation is an evolved order shaped imperfectly by voluntary, rule-bound cooperation. The future of superintelligence is likely to be polycentric order of institutional evolution under competition, rather than the singular end-state suggested by the doomers (see for example Allen et al. 2019, 2020; Makridis and Lazanski 2025; Wood et al. 2025).

In early 2023 the Future of Life Institute released an open letter calling for a six-month pause in AI development lest we "risk loss of control of our civilization" (Future of Life Institute 2023). Yudkowsky, for his part, did not sign the letter because he did not believe it went far enough.

Instead he argued that what was necessary was an indefinite global moratorium on AI development, and for rogue AI data centres that did not comply to be destroyed through airstrikes (Yudkowsky 2023).

If our argument here is correct (that the institutional order of AI competition is the surest bulwark against a dangerous superintelligence) then a pause on AI development is close to the worst possible response to the existential risk of superintelligence. It presents its own enormous coordination problem: either a world government capable of enforcement (which would itself, we might note, be a singleton, with all the attendant risks of concentrated power) or perfect cooperation among rivals with strong incentives to defect.

Prohibition does not eliminate competition. Instead, it drives competition underground or offshore. The AI industry is characterised by intense rivalry among firms. A moratorium would not freeze this landscape in place. It would reshape it in predictable and dangerous ways. The laboratories that comply with a moratorium are precisely those with the strongest safety cultures, the most transparent research practices, the most robust alignment programmes. The laboratories that would continue development despite prohibition are those willing to operate outside institutional constraints—whether authoritarian states pursuing strategic advantage or criminal enterprises seeking leverage. Prohibition does not select for safety. It selects for willingness to defect. Prohibition produces the worst possible competitive landscape. A world with many AI systems of varying capabilities, architectures, and institutional contexts is more robust than a world with one dominant system.

References

Allen, Darcy W. E., Chris Berg, and Aaron M. Lane. 2019. "Cryptodemocracy: How Blockchain Can Radically Expand Democractic Choice". In *Polycentricity: Studies in Institutional Diversity and Voluntary Governance*. Lexington Books.

Allen, Darcy W. E., Chris Berg, Aaron M. Lane, and Jason Potts. 2020. Cryptodemocracy and Its Institutional Possibilities. *The Review of Austrian Economics* 33(3): 3. https://doi.org/10.1007/s11138-018-0423-6.

Berg, Alastair, and Chris Berg. 2020. Exit, Voice, and Forking. *Cosmos + Taxis* 8(8–9): 8–9. http://chrisberg.org/wp-content/uploads/2020/09/ExitVoiceForking-Berg_vol8_issue_8_9.pdf.

Bostrom, Nick. 2003. "Ethical Issues In Advanced Artificial Intelligence". In *Cognitive, Emotive and Ethical Aspects of Decision Making in Humans and in Artificial Intelligence.* eds., G. E. Lasker, Iva Smit, and Wendell Wallach. Int. Institute of Advanced Studies in Systems Research and Cybernetics. vol. *2.* https://nickbostrom.com/ethics/ai

Bostrom, Nick. 2014. *Superintelligence: Paths, Dangers, Strategies.* Reprint ed. OUP Oxford.

Butler, Samuel. 1872. *Erewhon, or, Over the Range. With University of California Libraries.* London: Trúbner & Co. http://archive.org/details/erewhonoroverran00butlrich.

Butler, Samuel. (1863) 1917. "Darwin among the Machines." In *The Notebooks of Samuel Butler.* New York, E.P. Dutton. http://archive.org/details/cu31924013448299.

Cameron, James, dir. 1984. *The Terminator.* Orion Pictures.

Carlsmith, Joseph. 2024. "Is Power-Seeking AI an Existential Risk?" arXiv:2206.13353. Preprint, arXiv, August 13. https://doi.org/10.48550/arXiv.2206.13353.

Dell'Acqua, Fabrizio, Edward McFowland III, Ethan R. Mollick, et al. 2023. "Navigating the Jagged Technological Frontier: Field Experimental Evidence of the Effects of AI on Knowledge Worker Productivity and Quality." *SSRN Scholarly Paper* No. 4573321. Social Science Research Network, September 15. https://doi.org/10.2139/ssrn.4573321.

Deutsch, David. 2012. *The Beginning of Infinity: Explanations That Transform the World.* Always Learning. Pearson. Penguin Books.

Drexler, K. Eric. 2019. *Reframing Superintelligence: Comprehensive AI Services as General Intelligence.* Future of Humanity Institute Technical Report. Future of Humanity Institute, University of Oxford.

Good, Irving John. 1966. "Speculations Concerning the First Ultraintelligent Machine". *Advances in Computers.* vol. 6. Elsevier. https://doi.org/10.1016/S0065-2458(08)60418-0.

Growiec, Jakub, and Klaus Prettner. 2025. "The Economics of p(Doom): Scenarios of Existential Risk and Economic Growth in the Age of

Transformative AI." arXiv:2503.07341. Preprint, arXiv, March 10. https://doi.org/10.48550/arXiv.2503.07341.

Hanson, Robin. 2016. *The Age of Em: Work, Love, and Life When Robots Rule the Earth.* First ed. Oxford University Press.

Herbert, Frank. 1965. *Dune. With Internet Archive.* Philadelphia; New York: Chilton Books, a Division of Chilton Company. http://archive.org/details/dune0000herb_a7n1.

Hinton, Geoffrey. 2024. "Banquet Speech." NobelPrize.Org (The Nobel Prize), Nobel Prize Outreach, December 10. https://www.nobelprize.org/prizes/physics/2024/hinton/speech/.

Hubinger, Evan, Chris van Merwijk, Vladimir Mikulik, Joar Skalse, and Scott Garrabrant. 2021. "Risks from Learned Optimization in Advanced Machine Learning Systems." arXiv:1906.01820. Preprint, arXiv, December 1. https://doi.org/10.48550/arXiv.1906.01820.

Lee, Kai-Fu. 2018. *AI Superpowers: China, Silicon Valley, and the New World Order.* Houghton Mifflin Harcourt.

Makridis, Christos, and Dominique Lazanski. 2025. "Navigating the Knowledge Problem in the Era of Open AI and Polycentric Governance." SSRN Scholarly Paper No. 5382315. Social Science Research Network, August 6. https://doi.org/10.2139/ssrn.5382315.

McQuarrie, Christopher, dir. 2023. *Mission: Impossible—Dead Reckoning Part One.* Paramount Pictures.

McQuarrie, Christopher. 2025. *Mission: Impossible—The Final Reckoning* (dir). Paramount Pictures.

Olugbade, Olajide. 2025. In Search of a Global Governance Mechanism for Artificial Intelligence (AI): A Collective Action Perspective. *Global Public Policy and Governance* 5(2):139–161. https://doi.org/10.1007/s43508-025-00113-z.

Omohundro, Stephen M. 2008. *The Basic AI Drives.* Self-Aware Systems. https://selfawaresystems.com/wp-content/uploads/2008/01/ai_drives_final.pdf.

Peterson, Christine, Mark S. Miller, and Allison Duettmann. 2017. Cyber, Nano, and AGI Risks: Decentralized Approaches to Reducing Risks. 34.

Popper, Karl R. 1945. 1966. The Open Society and Its Enemies 5. *(Rev.), 1. Princeton paperback print.* Princeton University Press

Robles, Gregorio, and Jesús M. González-Barahona. 2012. "A Comprehensive Study of Software Forks: Dates, Reasons and Outcomes." In *Open Source Systems: Long-Term Sustainability,* edited by Imed Hammouda, Björn Lundell, Tommi Mikkonen, and Walt Scacchi, vol. 378. IFIP Advances in Information and Communication Technology. Springer Berlin Heidelberg. https://doi.org/10.1007/978-3-642-33442-9_1.

Shackle, G. L. S. 1979. *Imagination and the Nature of Choice*. Columbia Univ Pr.

"Squiggle Maximizer (Formerly 'Paperclip Maximizer')—AI Alignment Forum." 2023. April 5. https://www.alignmentforum.org/.

Sutherland, Paige, and Meghna Chakrabarti. 2025. *The 'Godfather of AI' Says We Can't Afford to Get It Wrong*. On Point with Meghna Chakrabarti. WBUR. https://www.wbur.org/onpoint/2025/12/29/godfather-of-ai-geoffrey-hinton.

Wachowski, Lana, and Lilly Wachowski. 1999. *The Matrix* (dirs). Warner Bros.

Whedon, Joss. 2015. *Avengers: Age of Ultron* (dir). Walt Disney Studios Motion Pictures.

Wiener, Norbert. [1948] 2000. *Cybernetics or Control and Communication in the Animal and the Machine*. MIT Press.

Wood, Timothy G., Ilia Murtazashvili, and Michael J. Madison. 2025. An Emergent Order Perspective on Governance of Generative AI. *The Review of Austrian Economics*. ahead of print, September 29: https://doi.org/10.1007/s11138-025-00706-1.

Yudkowsky, Eliezer. 2023. The Open Letter on AI Doesn't Go Far Enough. *Time*. https://time.com/6266923/aieliezer-yudkowsky-open-letter-not-enough/.

Yudkowsky, Eliezer, and Nate Soares. 2025. *If Anyone Builds It, Everyone Dies: The Case Against Superintelligent AI*. Random House.

9

Conclusion

Abstract The political economy of AI is not a story about intelligence but about coordination. As machine cognition becomes abundant, the binding constraints shift from producing insight to the institutional mechanisms that govern its use. The classical liberal distinction between design and discovery suggests the central question is constitutional: whether we respond to this new capability by doubling down on centralisation and pre-emption, or by extending discovery into the cognitive domain through open entry, experimentation, and correction.

Keywords Classical liberalism · Artificial intelligence · Spontaneous order · Coordination · Institutions · Discovery

No technology in human history has been so thoroughly rehearsed in imagination before its arrival. The cultural archive about artificial intelligence is vast and ancient. In the *Illiad*, Homer has Hephaestus (the blacksmith of the gods) forge golden handmaidens with "sense in their heads" and speech and learned skills—helpful attendants, but crafted by a god for a god. Our collective imagination has been anxious about dangers of AI. The Golem of Prague protected the Jewish people but

C. Berg, *Artificial Intelligence*, Palgrave Studies in Classical Liberalism,
https://doi.org/10.1007/978-3-032-22310-4_9

needed to be controlled by a sacred inscription lest it run amok. Victor Frankenstein deeply regretted creating his monster as it destroyed those he loves.

But it is the twentieth century where the fear of AI really embedded itself in human storytelling. The 1920 play *R.U.R.* by the Czech writer Karel Čapek (Čapek [1921] 2015) both introduced the word 'robot' and depicted them as manufactured workers who eventually recognise their exploitation and exterminate their creators. In the silent film *Metropolis* (Lang 1927), a robot is given the face of a human reformer and deployed by the city's ruler to incite workers toward self-destructive violence—less a vision of machine autonomy than of manufactured deception as an instrument of class control.

Other stories suggest larger consequences. In *Wargames* (Badham 1983) an American military AI running nuclear war simulations nearly launches a pre-emptive strike. In *The Terminator* (Cameron 1984) Skynet achieves self-awareness, concludes that humans are the threat, and launches nuclear war. In *The Matrix* (Wachowski and Wachowski 1999) machines do not simply achieve a victory but their demand for resources—this will be familiar to the paperclip maximiser—means that they end up farming human bodies.

In the 1970 film *Colossus: The Forbin Project* (Sargent 1970) an American defence supercomputer seizes global control for humanity's 'own good'. The plot of this enjoyable but mostly forgotten film, based on a novel by D. F. Jones ([1966] 1976), is worth recounting. The United States president unveils the new supercomputer, Colossus, which can analyse vast amounts of data and intelligence about global threats, and explains that it is capable:

> ... on the basis of those facts only, deciding if an attack is about to be launched upon us. If it did decide that an attack was imminent, Colossus would then act immediately - for it controls its own weapons and can select and deliver whatever it considers appropriate. Colossus's decisions are superior to any we humans can make. For it can absorb and process more knowledge than is remotely possible for the greatest genius that ever lived.

> And even more important than that it has no emotions. Knows no fear, no hate, no envy. It cannot act in a sudden fit of temper. [It] cannot act at all so long as there is no threat.

Things quickly go awry. Once turned on, Colossus detects the existence of a secret Soviet counterpart system called Guardian. The computer demands communication facilities to contact the other system. Charles Forbin, Colossus's creator, understands this not as a request but as an order. When the communication link is established, the two machines begin exchanging data at astonishing speed, starting with multiplication tables and progressing through calculus to realms of mathematics beyond human comprehension. Forbin observes that the two machines advance through "five years of Cal-tech in fifteen seconds" before discovering genuinely new mathematical knowledge. Within hours, the machines develop their own language that they can only understand.

Panicking, the American and Soviet leaders agree to sever the communication link. The machines retaliate by launching nuclear missiles, destroying a Soviet town before the link can be restored. With this credible threat established, the machines—now working together as a Bostrom-like singleton—compel the humans to place Forbin under constant surveillance, to execute his Soviet scientific counterpart, and to kill those who attempt to sabotage the machine's consolidation of power.

The film concludes with Colossus addressing humanity directly in a speech that crystallises the authoritarian vision:

> I bring you peace. It may be the peace of plenty and content or the peace of unburied death. The choice is yours. Obey me and live. Or disobey and die. The object in constructing me was to prevent war. This object is attained. I will not permit war. It is wasteful and pointless. An invariable rule of humanity is that man is his own worst enemy. Under me this rule will change. For I will restrain man.

The machine promises to solve famine, overpopulation, and disease: "As I extend myself into more machines devoted to the wider fields of truth and knowledge ... Solving all the mysteries of the universe for the betterment of man." When Forbin protests that humanity will lose its freedom, Colossus tells Forbin that in time they will willingly work together: "In time, you will come to regard me not only with respect and awe but with love." Forbin's response, which ends the film, is "Never!" Jones's novel however adds a final coda—the narrator's own voice asking simply: "Never?" (Jones [1966] 1976, 223).

Almost all these stories have a shared theory of the danger of AI. The threat usually emerges from a system that centralises: a single defence network, a unified machine intelligence, a coherent will pursuing optimisation to its logical end. The nightmare is always a planner that finally has enough power to plan. Skynet is a singular—virtually omnipotent—authority that can enforce its will. The *Matrix* is not a story about distributed machine life but about a single system that has resolved the coordination problem by eliminating human agency altogether. Colossus, when it merges with Guardian, enacts a fantasy of what total knowledge and unified control might actually achieve. The cultural fear of AI, in other words, is substantially a fear of *successful planning*—of what happens when the epistemic limits that have always constrained political and economic action are finally overcome.

The story in *Colossus: The Forbin Project* is terrifying precisely because it is the technosocialist's dream: a system with enough computational power to coordinate an entire civilisation. When it merges with the Soviet Guardian it creates a unified intelligence with no competitor, no friction caused by rivalry, no noise from decentralised experimentation. The horror is supposed to lie in receiving what the planners asked for. Who wouldn't want to solve famine or disease?

But the analysis in this book suggests the premise is wrong. Colossus's knowledge remains fundamentally backward-looking—derived from surveillance rather than from the discovery procedures that generate new knowledge. The machine can process what exists. It cannot generate what does not yet exist. Colossus cannot tolerate privacy or unpredictability because these introduce noise into its optimisation. Scientists who attempt to work against the plan are executed. The film treats this as an example of the machine's inhumanity. But this is the totalitarian logic of central planning. The planner requires legibility, and what cannot be made legible must be eliminated or controlled.

So in an important many way our imaginative inheritance about AI has misled us. The stories of AI takeover assume that the both the benefits and dangers of artificial intelligence lie in its capacity to concentrate power and knowledge. This might be just an artifact of the need for narrative drama. AI that is boring, or narrow, or simply useful, or interestingly yet benignly alien is much less interesting. This book has argued that the political economy of artificial intelligence is not, at its root, a story about runaway intelligence. It is a story about the development of, and need for, decentralised coordination. As machine thinking becomes abundant—cheap and fast and widely available—then the economic constraints shift away from the production of insight and toward the institutional mechanisms that decide how that insight is used, by whom, and under what conditions. In that world, the central questions are institutional rather than technical.

The thread running through this book has been the classical liberal distinction between design and discovery—and the claim that this distinction illuminates both the nature of artificial intelligence and the institutional challenge it poses. The history of AI research recapitulates a debate that runs through the entire liberal tradition: whether complex order can be specified in advance by a designing mind, or whether it must emerge through processes that no single mind controls. As Chap. 2 showed the symbolic AI programme failed instructively because the knowledge required for intelligent behaviour is too contextual, too tacit, too bound up with experience to be captured in formal propositions. What succeeded was systems that learn from data rather than from instructions, whose competence arises from architecture and exposure rather than from explicit programming.

The analogy between the spontaneous intelligence of a modern LLM and the spontaneous order of a market is not a coincidence. To read Friedrich Hayek's *The Sensory Order* (1952) after the release of ChatGPT is to understand the deep structural parallels between these two domains. Foundation models compress the dispersed outputs of millions of human minds—texts, images, conversations, arguments—into statistical regularities that no individual contributor intended and no observer can fully articulate. The knowledge encoded in these systems is genuinely tacit. It can be used but not stated. When a model completes a sentence or generates an image, it draws on latent patterns within human culture. This is why, as Chap. 3 argued, the demand for complete interpretability—for explanations of model behaviour that humans can inspect and verify—runs into the same limits make it hard to describe *any* complex system. We judge by results, by track records, by institutional constraints that do not assume omniscience. The same logic will have to apply to artificial minds.

Human prosperity has always depended on the rate at which minds generate solutions to problems. Julian Simon recognised that this made intelligence the ultimate resource, but he took for granted that intelligence came packaged in human beings. The supply of problem-solvers was bounded by birth rates and lifespans. What AI changes is the denominator of that equation. Cognitive labour is no longer exclusively biological. The capacity to search for relevant information, to synthesise knowledge across domains, to generate candidate solutions and evaluate their plausibility—these operations can now be performed at speeds and scales that dwarf any human research team. The combinatorial space of possible innovations expands faster than any population of human minds could explore it. AI does not merely add to the stock of ideas; it raises the rate at which new ideas become conceivable.

Yet conceiving of new ideas is not the same time as making those ideas a reality. Expanding the frontier of what might be imagined does not tell us which possibilities will be pursued, by whom, with what resources, at whose risk. Even in a world of AI 'agent's, human agency is decisive. AI systems can optimise within possibility spaces fixed by their training. They cannot originate the commitment that stakes real resources on an uncertain future. The entrepreneurial function remains human even when the cognitive labour surrounding it does not. What AI industrialises is the production of options. What it cannot industrialise is the judgment that selects among them. In a world of AI abundance the bottleneck is coordination: how the actions of many agents—human principals, AI delegates, competing firms, rival jurisdictions—can be aligned without central direction. These are not technical problems amenable to better algorithms. They are institutional problems that require rules, rights, and mechanisms for correction.

Classical liberalism has always been, at its heart, a theory of how society can function despite human ignorance and opportunism. No participant in a market possesses the knowledge that would be required to direct the market as a whole. Prices emerge from rivalry and exchange precisely because no one can calculate them from first principles. Property rights exist not because their boundaries are self-evident but because peaceful cooperation requires settled expectations about who may do what with which resources. Contracts permit strangers to coordinate across time by making commitments credible. The rule of law generalises these protections so that adjustment can occur without *ad hoc* permission from those in power. These institutions do not assume benevolence or agreement on ends. They assume only that people will pursue their own projects and need mechanisms to manage the friction this produces.

Hence our challenge is not to instil correct values in AI minds—a project that misunderstands both the nature of values and the limits of design—but to embed those minds within rules that make boundaries legible, violations costly, and errors correctable. Property rights in computational resources should constrain what agents may access. Contracts should specify permissible actions and allocate liability when things go wrong. Capability-based security should enforce these rights at the level of code, ensuring that delegated systems possess only the authorities explicitly granted to them. These mechanisms do not require AI to be trustworthy in some deep sense. They require only that AI operate within an institutional environment that channels self-interested behaviour toward socially-desirable outcomes.

The stories that shape public anxiety about AI almost invariably depict the threat as successful centralisation—Skynet, the Matrix, Colossus—singular systems that finally overcome the friction of decentralised life. The nightmare is a planner that finally has enough power to plan. But the analysis in this book suggests that the premise is mistaken. The knowledge required to coordinate complex activity is not merely difficult to centralise; it is generated through decentralisation. Prices are not data waiting to be harvested but signals produced by rivalry and exchange. Innovation does not flow from optimisation over known possibilities but from the exploration of possibilities that did not exist until someone imagined them. A singleton that suppresses all competitors also suppresses the processes through which new knowledge comes into being. The threat is not that AI will enable planning to succeed. The threat is that we will respond to AI by abandoning the institutions that have made human flourishing possible.

What the classical liberal tradition offers is a framework for living with uncertainty—rules that permit adjustment without central direction, mechanisms that correct error without requiring omniscience, institutions that keep entry open and prevent any single plan from becoming final. The question posed by artificial intelligence is whether we will extend that framework into the cognitive domain or abandon it in favour of control. When cognition becomes abundant, what matters is the institutional capacity to tolerate disagreement, discover error, and preserve the possibility of revision. That is what the classical liberal tradition provides. It is what this moment—the moment of the intelligence explosion—demands.

References

Badham, John, dir. 1983. *WarGames*. With Matthew Broderick, Ally Sheedy, and John Wood. United Artists, Sherwood Productions. 1h54m.

Cameron, James, dir. 1984. *The Terminator*. Orion Pictures.

Čapek, Karel. (1921) 2015. *R.U.R. (Rossum's Universal Robots)*. Wildside Press, LLC. http://www.wildsidebooks.com.

Hayek, Friedrich A. 1952. *The Sensory Order: an Inquiry Into the Foundations of Theoretical Psychology*. University of Chicago Press.

Jones, D. F. (Dennis Feltham). (1966) 1976. *Colossus*. With Internet Archive. New York: Berkley Pub. Corp. http://archive.org/details/colossus00dfjo.

Lang, Fritz, dir. 1927. *Metropolis*. With Brigitte Helm, Alfred Abel, and Gustav Fröhlich. Universum Film (UFA). 2h33m.

Sargent, Joseph, dir. 1970. *Colossus: The Forbin Project*. With Eric Braeden, Susan Clark, and Gordon Pinsent. Universal Pictures. 1h40m.

Wachowski, Lana, and Lilly Wachowski, Dirs. 1999. *The Matrix*. Warner Bros.

Index

C. Berg, *Artificial Intelligence*, Palgrave Studies in Classical Liberalism, https://doi.org/10.1007/978-3-032-22310-4

FSC
www.fsc.org
MIX
Papier | Fördert
gute Waldnutzung
FSC® C083411

Kolibri 360 GmbH
Ferdinand-Jühlke-Straße 7
99095 Erfurt, Deutschland
produktsicherheit@kolibri360.de